# CLIMATE CHANGE
# DISASTER MANAGEMENT
# AND
# ENVIRONMENT

*ENV BOOKS SERIES*

# CLIMATE CHANGE DISASTER MANAGEMENT AND ENVIRONMENT


***Editors***

**Dr. Alka Chauhan**

*Department of Environmental Conservation*
*Society for Environment, Health, Awareness of Nutrition & Toxicology (SEHAT)*
*1775, Sohan Ganj, Near Clock Tower*
*Delhi - 110 007 (India)*

**Dr. Pawan Kumar 'Bharti'**

*Vice President*
*Society for Environment, Health, Awareness of Nutrition & Toxicology (SEHAT)*
*1775, Sohan Ganj, Near Clock Tower*
*Delhi - 110 007 (India)*
E-mail: *gurupawanbharti@rediffmail.com*

***Associate Editor***

**Mr. Jaswant Ray**

*Society for Environment, Health, Awareness of Nutrition & Toxicology (SEHAT)*
*Head Office: F/119, Pandav Nagar*
*Meerut - 250 003, (U.P.) (India)*



DPH

**DISCOVERY PUBLISHING HOUSE PVT. LTD.**
**NEW DELHI-110 002**

*Published by:*
**Namit Wasan**
**DISCOVERY PUBLISHING HOUSE PVT. LTD.**
4383/4B, Ansari Road, Darya Ganj
New Delhi-110 002 (India)
*Phone* : +91-11-23279245, 43596064-65
*Fax* : +91-11-23253475
*E-mail* : discoverypublishinghouse@gmail.com
namitwasan9@gmail.com
sales@discoverypublishinggroup.com
*web* : www.discoverypublishinggroup.com

***First Edition:* 2016**

**ISBN: 978-93-5056-784-5**

**Climate Change, Disaster Management and Environment**



*Printed at:*
Infinity Imaging Systems
Delhi

# ENV Books Series, India

Calls lengthy and error free chapters for further volumes of books on various environmental issues. (Send your manuscripts to envbooks@gmail.com)

***Founding Editor (Editor-in-Chief)***

**Dr. Pawan Kumar 'Bharti'**
*Society for Environment, Health, Awareness of Nutrition & Toxicology (SEHAT-India)*
*1775, Sohanganj, Near Clock Tower, Delhi-7, (India)*
E-mail:*gurupawanbharti@rediffmail.com*

**Other Titles by Editor-in-Chief:**

1. **Advances in Biotechnology and Ecological Sciences (2013)**
   Bharti, P.K., Chauhan, A. and Ray, J. (eds.)
   (ISBN: 978-93-5056-358-8).
2. **Advances in Agriculture and Ecology (2013)**
   Bharti, P.K.; Chauhan, A. and Ezeaku Peter Ikemefuna (eds.)
   (ISBN: 978-93-5056-362-5).
3. **Agriculture and Environmental Biotechnology (2014)**
   Bharti, P.K. and Chauhan, A. (eds.)
   (ISBN: 978-93-5056-479-0).
4. **Agriculture Development and Sustainable Environment (2015)**
   Ray, J. and Bharti, P. K. (eds.)
   (ISBN: 978-93-5056-759-3)
5. **Agriculture Ecology and Environment (2014)**
   Bharti, P.K. and Olubukola O. Babalola (eds.)
   (ISBN: 978-93-5056-480-6).
6. **Agriculture, Environment and Nano-science (2015)**
   Bharti, Pawan K. (ed.)
   (ISBN: 978-93-5056-760-5)
7. **Agro-biodiversity Conservation & Sustainable Development (2016)**
   Sharma, Pankaj; Singh, Narayan; and Bharti, P.K. (eds.)
   (ISBN: 978-93-505-782-1)
8. **Agro-forestry and Climate Change (2014)**
   Bharti, Pawan K. and Singh, Narayan (eds.)
   (ISBN: 978-93-5056-514-8).

9. **Aquaculture and Fisheries Environment (2014)**
Gupta, S.K. and Pawan K. Bharti (eds.)
(ISBN: 978-93-5056-408-0).

10. **Aquatic Biodiversity and Pollution (2013)**
Bharti, P.K.; Chauhan, A. and Kaoud, H.A.H. (eds.)
(ISBN: 978-93-5056-359-5).

11. **Aquatic Ecology and Biotechnology (2014)**
Bharti, P.K. and Zaki, M.S.A. (eds.)
(ISBN: 978-93-5056-451-6).

12. **Aquatic Environment and Toxicology (2013)**
Bharti, Pawan K. (ed.)
(ISBN: 978-93-5056-236-9).

13. **Biodiversity, Biotechnology and Environmental Conservation (2015)**
Bharti, P.K. and Bhandari, G. (eds.)
(ISBN: 978-93-5056-750-0).

14. **Biodiversity of Aquatic Ecosystem: *Significance, Threat and Conservation* (2013)**
Bharti, P.K. and Kaoud, H.A.H. (eds.)
(ISBN: 978-93-5056-297-0).

15. **Biological Diversity and Ecology (2016)**
Arya, M.K.; Bharti, P.K. and Ritesh Joshi (eds.)
(ISBN: 978-93-5056-785-2).

16. **Bioremediation and Microbial Biotechnology (2016)**
Gupta, Sandeep; and Bharti, P.K. (eds.)
(ISBN: 978-93-5056-783-8)

17. **Biotechnological Approaches & Water Ecosystem (2016)**
Zaki, M.S.A.; and Bharti, P.K. (eds.)
(ISBN: 978-93-5056-779-1)

18. **Biotechnology, Agro-ecology and Environment (2015)**
Chauhan, Avnish and Bharti, P.K. (eds.)
(ISBN: 978-93-5056-757-9).

19. **Clean Technologies and Environmental Protection (2015)**
Chauhan, A.; Sharma, S. and Bharti, P.K. (eds.)
(ISBN: 978-93-5056-731-9).

20. **Climate Change and Agriculture (2012)**
Bharti, P.K. and Chauhan, Avnish (eds.)
(ISBN: 978-93-5056-148-5).

21. **Climate Change and Biodiversity (2013)**
Bharti, P.K. and Chauhan, Avnish (eds.)
(ISBN: 978-93-5056-360-1).

22. **Conservation and Cultivation of Medicinal Plants (2015)**
Bharti, P.K. and Singh Narayan (eds.)
(ISBN: 978-93-5056-740-1).

23. **Eco-toxicology and Eco-technology (2013)**
Bharti, P.K. and Zaki, M. (eds.)
(ISBN: 978-93-5056-313-7).

24. **Environmental Biotechnology and Application (2013)**
Bharti, P.K. and Chauhan, Avnish (eds.)
(ISBN: 978-93-5056-262-8).

25. **Environmental Conservation and Biotechnology (2014)**
Chauhan, A. and P.K. Bharti (eds.)
(ISBN: 978-93-5056-512-4).

26. **Environmental Health and Problems (2013)**
Bharti, P.K. and Gajananda, Kh. (eds.)
(ISBN: 978-93-5056-263-5).

27. **Environmental Pollution and Biodiversity (2012)**
Bharti, P.K.; Chauhan, Avnish and Kumar, P. (eds.)
(ISBN: 978-93-5056-149-2).

28. **Fisheries and Toxicology (2014)**
Zaki, M.S.A.; Bharti, P.K. and Chauhan, A. (eds.)
(ISBN: 978-93-5056-452-3).

29. **Fish Habitat and Aquaculture (2015)**
Bharti, P.K.; Gupta Kr. Sanjay (eds.)
(ISBN: 978-93-5056-744-9).

30. **Freshwater Ecosystem and Xenobiotics (2013)**
Bharti, P.K.; Zaki, M. and Chauhan, A. (eds.)
(ISBN: 978-93-5056-299-4).

31. **Limnology and Aquatic Science (2015)**
Sharma, S. and Bharti, P.K. (eds.)
(ISBN: 978-93-5056-735-7).

32. **Medicinal Plants:** ***Distribution, Utilization and Significance*** **(2015)**
Sharma, P.; Bharti, P.K. and Narayan Singh (eds.)
(ISBN: 978-93-5056-734-0).

33. **Microbial Applications and Environment (2014)**
Bharti, Pawan K. (ed.)
(ISBN: 978-93-5056-515-5).

34. **Microbial Ecology and Habitat (2014)**
Bharti, Pawan K. (ed.)
(ISBN: 978-93-5056-514-8).

35. **Natural Ecosystem and Climate Change (2015)**
Bharti, P.K., and Kh. Gajananda (ed.)
(ISBN: 978-93-5056-745-6).

36. **Prakriti me Aushadhi (*in Hindi*) (2012)**
Singh, J.R.; Bharti, P.K. and Bharti, B.
(ISBN: 978-93-5056-200-0).

37. **Seed Technology, Plant Growth and Cropping System (2015)**
Tyagi, P.K. and Bharti, P.K. (eds.)
(ISBN: 978-93-5056-738-8).

38. **Soil Characteristics and Agro-ecology (2015)**
Avnish Chauhan and Bharti, P.K. (eds.)
(ISBN: 978-93-5056-758-6)

39. **Soil Contamination and Conservation (2015)**
Ezeaku, P.I. and Bharti, P.K. (eds.)
(ISBN: 978-93-5056-737-1).

40. **Soil Quality and Contamination (2013)**
Bharti, P.K. and Chauhan, Avnish (eds.)
(ISBN: 978-93-5056-361-8).

41. **Waste Disposal and Management (2015)**
Bharti, P.K.; Tabassum, B. and Bajaj, P. (eds.)
(ISBN: 978-93-5056-729-6).

42. **Waste Management and Environmental Health (2016)**
Tabassum, B., Bajaj Priya, and Bharti, P.K. (eds.)
(ISBN: 978-93-5056-777-7).

43. **Water Resources and Agriculture (2014)**
Bharti, P.K. and Ezeaku Peter Ikemefuna (eds.)
(ISBN: 978-93-5056-481-3).

# Preface

Climate change is a change in the statistical distribution of weather patterns when that change lasts for an extended period of time (i.e. decades to millions of years). Climate change may refer to a change in average weather conditions, or in the time variation of weather around longer-term average conditions (i.e., more or fewer extreme weather events). Climate change is caused by factors such as biotic processes, variations in solar radiation received by Earth, plate tectonics, and volcanic eruptions. Certain anthropogenic activities have also been identified as significant causes of recent climate change, often referred to as 'global warming' (IPCC).

The most general definition of climate change is a change in the statistical properties of the climate system when considered over long periods of time, regardless of cause. Accordingly, fluctuations over periods shorter than a few decades, such as El Niño, do not represent climate change. On the broadest scale, the rate at which energy is received from the sun and the rate at which it is lost to space determine the equilibrium temperature and climate of Earth. This energy is distributed around the globe by winds, ocean currents, and other mechanisms to affect the climates of different regions.

Factors that can shape climate are called climate forcings or "forcing mechanisms". These include processes such as variations in solar radiation, variations in the Earth's orbit, variations in the albedo or reflectivity of the continents and oceans, mountain-building and continental drift and changes in greenhouse gas concentrations. There are a variety of climate change feedbacks that can either amplify or diminish the initial forcing. Some parts of the climate system, such as the oceans and ice caps, respond more slowly in reaction to climate forcings, while others respond more quickly. There are also key threshold factors which when exceeded can produce rapid change (wiki).

The term sometimes is used to refer specifically to climate change caused by human activity, as opposed to changes in climate that may have resulted as part of Earth's natural processes. In this sense, especially in the context of environmental policy, the term climate change has become synonymous with anthropogenic global warming. Within scientific journals, global warming refers to surface temperature increases while climate change includes global warming and everything else that increasing greenhouse gas levels will affect (IPCC).

The present book updates the subject matter and issues related to climate change, global warming, earth related processes, environmental changes, whether forecasting, earth ecosystem, environmental pollution. Thanks are due to contributors from various institutions and publisher for their interest in this book. The book will definitely provide a multidisciplinary forum to explore emerging areas in the field of climate change, global warming, earth related processes, environmental changes, whether forecasting, earth ecosystem, environmental pollution.

**–Editors**

(envbooks@gmail.com)

# Contents

Pages: 1-22

CLIMATE CHANGE, DISASTER MANAGEMENT AND ENVIRONMENT

*Edited by:* Dr. Alka Chauhan; Dr. Pawan Kumar 'Bharti'

ISBN: 978-93-5056-784-5

*Edition:* 2016

*Published by:* Discovery Publishing House Pvt. Ltd., New Delhi (India)

# CHAPTER – 1

# Climate Change Perspective Regarding the Hydro-Meteorological Hazards in Himalayan Region

**Sandeep Kumar**[1] and **Santosh**[2]

***ABSTRACT***

Long term significant change in the average weather condition of a specific region or zone over an appropriately significant period of time is generally known as climate change. The fourth assessment report of IPCC, 2007 reported that the average global temperature has increased by 0.6°C over 20$^{th}$ century and projected will be 1.8-4.0°C by 2100s. As per IPCC, 2013, the globally averaged surface temperature is projected to increase by 1.4°C to 5.8°C over the period 1990 to 2100. Various studies shows that the surface temperature in India was increased with considerable regional variations i.e. 0.5 to 0.6°C during 1901-2005 and the projected will be 2-5°C by 2100s. Climate change, whether driven by natural or human activities, can lead to changes in the likelihood of

1 Department of Environment Studies, Punjab University, Chandigarh, India.

2 Department of Environmental Sciences, MDU, Rohtak (Haryana), India.

the occurrence or strength of extreme weather and climatic events. The weather pattern have become more extreme, with more frequent and more intense in rainfall events, subsequent floods and prolonged droughts i.e. the intensity and frequency of hydro-meteorological hazards has increased. Climate change has the potential to impact the hydrological cycle and subsequently the hydro-meteorological disasters. The vulnerability and associated risks in the Himalaya are increasing as over 90% of natural hazards in this region are hydro-meteorological in origin. The manuscript highlights the climate change and its impact on hydro-meteorological hazards in Himalayan region. It also suggest various adaptation and mitigation strategies to cope with impacts of climate change on hydro-meteorological disasters such as capacity building and increasing resiliency among vulnerable communities along with adoption of sustainable lifestyle.

***Keywords:*** Adaptation, Climate change, Himalayan region, Hydro-meteorological hazards, Mitigation, Sustainable, Vulnerability.

## INTRODUCTION

All living organisms, including human beings, interact with each other and also with their environment, over space and time. Humans and environment are mutually related i.e. have influence on each other. Humans have the capacity to change the environment as per their requirements, often with deleterious effects. During pre-industrial era, people knew very well, how to live in harmony with nature and to adapt accordingly. Now, their interference has crossed the limits by intensive over-exploitative activities which successively reverse the environment-organism relationship. Today's environmental problems are the result of cumulative effects of human actions where the boomerang effect of environment is increasing in the form of various natural hazards. Even, the increase in the intensity and frequency of natural calamities resulting out of climate change are indirectly brought by human beings.

Climate change has now been recognised as one of the most important environmental challenges faced by humanity. The scientists, politicians, environmentalists and media are vociferous that the drastic climate change is imminent, with disastrous effects. It is generally defined as the long term significant change in the average weather condition of a specific region or zone over an appropriately significant period of time. Changes in the climate occur as a result of both internal variability within the climatic system and external factors, both natural and anthropogenic. Although, it is difficult to clearly delineate the characteristics of climate change, associated with natural and anthropogenic forcing, due to complex interaction within the climatic system. But during post-industrial revolution i.e. especially after early 20th century, human activities have lead to unprecedented changes in the chemical composition of earth's atmosphere.

There are new and stronger evidences that most of the warming observed over the past 50 years was attributable to human activities (IPCC, 2001a). Meteorological data compiled over the 20th century suggest that earth is warming with significant differences at regional level. Present climate change is mainly caused by anthropogenic emissions of greenhouse gases (GHGs). These gases are released in excess due to unrestricted use of fossil fuels. Though, the presence of these gases in atmosphere is essential for maintaining the global average temperature at 15°C, otherwise it will be -17°C (Houghton *et al.*, 2001). But the increase in concentration has enhanced the global average temperature.

Historically, the responsibility of emission of GHGs lies largely with the industrialised world, though the developing countries are also responsible as important sources. The global atmospheric concentration of carbon dioxide and other green house gases have dramatically increased over the 20th century. During this century, there was increase in $CO_2$ concentration from 280 ppm to more than 385 ppm. The contribution of India to the cumulative global $CO_2$ emissions from 1980 to 2003 was only 3.11% (Sathaye *et al.*, 2006).

According to fourth assessment report of Intergovernmental Panel on Climate Change (IPCC), the global average temperature of the earth was increased by 0.6°C over 20th century. The projected temperature will be 1.8°C to 4.0°C by the end of 21th century. Over the last 50 years, the rise in temperature was 0.1°C per decade and expected will be 0.2°C per decade (IPCC, 2007). The globally averaged surface temperature is projected to increase by 1.4°C to 5.8°C over the period 1990 to 2100 (IPCC, 2013).Such changes may disrupt the earth's heat budget, causing catastrophic consequences. The analysis shows that changes in the earth's mean temperature will be apparent by 2050.

From the various studies, it was found that the surface temperature of India has increased by 0.5°C to 0.6°C during 1901 to 2005, with considerable regional variations. The projected ambient temperature in the Indian sub-continent will be 2°C to 5°C by the end of 21st century. This unprecedented rise in temperature is expected to have severe impacts on the global hydrological cycle and other related phenomena. The hydrological cycle, a fundamental component of climate, is likely to be altered due to change in climatic conditions (Arora *et al.*, 2008).

The hazards are occurring in a wide range of geomorphic settings and climatic zones. Natural hazards are purely natural but changing climatic conditions may exacerbate them. It is expected that the rise in temperature would be confronted with frequent heavy rainfall, warm spells and heat waves. Hence, the high variation in the frequency, intensity and timing of annual and seasonal rainfall should be considered in the context of global warming. Heavy precipitation episodes with subsequent increase in flood peaks can result in catastrophic events. The extreme weather pattern increases the intensity and frequency of hydro-meteorological disasters. Warmer climatic conditions will accelerate hydrological cycle, altering rainfall pattern, magnitude and timing of runoff; increasing the potential of floods due to intense rainfall and retreating of glaciers (Mall *et al.*, 2006).

The climate change induced hydro-meteorological disasters cause more damage than geophysical as they are imminent. These have severe impacts on the developing countries, because of their poor capacity to adapt to climatic variability (Gosain *et al.*, 2006). The losses caused by natural hazards both in terms of life and property are mainly due to unwise human interaction with the geo-environment of the area (Sah and Mazari, 2007). It is now recognised that the manifestation of climatic variability in the occurrence of extreme weather events, particularly on the regional scale, are of paramount importance in assessing the impacts of climate change.

The hydro-meteorological system of Himalayan region is very complex and poorly understood. Most common natural disasters in Himalayan region are water induced. The snow avalanches and glacial lake outburst floods predominate at very high elevations, flash floods in middle elevations and floods in the plains. In these water induced disasters, hundreds of lives, infrastructure and property worth of millions of rupees are lost every year (Joshi, 2006). The mountainous regions are becoming more vulnerable to these disasters where developmental activities over the years have further accentuated the problem by upsetting the natural balance of various physical processes operating in such kind of eco-systems. The fragile ecology of hilly areas coupled with large variations in physio-climatic conditions has rendered it more vulnerable to the vagaries of nature.

The phenomenon of environmental changes have already started showing its significant effect on hydrology and water resources of Himalayan region. These phenomena are expected to increase the frequency and intensity of floods in the region. The region is inherently fragile due to its extreme weak geology, highly rugged topography and heavy monsoonal rainfall. The combination of other factors such as tectonic disturbances, fragile geological characteristics, geomorphology (topography) and lithological structures, slope conditions, loose soil cover, hydrological behaviour, land use/land cover and developmental activities are responsible for creating havoc of natural hazards i.e. converting hazards into disasters. Evidences of global warming in Himalayas are declining snowfall, retreating glaciers, drying up of perennial springs, disruption in rainfall pattern and river flooding. Even the glacial lake outbursts, failure of landslide created dams are directly or indirectly triggered by climate change and its associated phenomena. In regions like the Himalayas, the prevailing climatic conditions and spatio-temporal changes in land use/land cover pattern have major impacts on the occurrence of various hazards. Therefore, it becomes important to study the effect of climate change on hydro-meteorological parameters at regional scale.

In the Himalayan region, a variety of basins exist and broadly, in the terms of source of runoff, these can be categorised into three types (Singh and Bengtsson, 2005):

1. **Rainfed basins:** Runoff is generated exclusively from rainfall. The altitude of such basins varies from 500 to 2000 m.
2. **Snowfed basins:** Runoff is generated from rainfall and snowmelt. The altitude varies from 2000 to about 4000 m. The contribution from snowmelt increases with altitude. The precipitation and temperature patterns in these basins are such that snowfall occurring during the preceding winter is completely melted away during next spring and summer months i.e. basins receive seasonal snow.
3. **Glacierfed basins:** Runoff from such basins is primarily generated from the melting of permanent snow fields and glaciers. Direct rainfall contribution is not significant. These are high altitude basins and cover an elevation range of 4000 to 6000-7000 m.

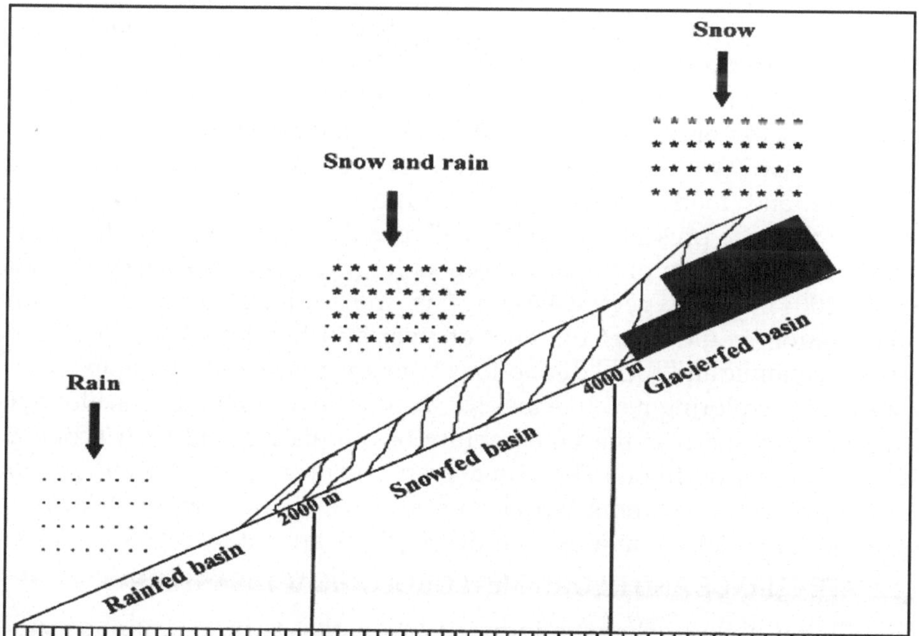


*Fig. 1.1:* **A Schematic Diagram Showing the Form of Precipitation for Different Types of Basins Located at Different Altitudes (*Courtesy*): Singh and Bengtsson, 2005).**

A basin which receives the contribution to streamflow from all types of sources like rainfall, snowmelt and glaciermelt, is defined as a complex basin. It is understood that impact of climate change will be different for different types of basins. The snow cover depends on the terrain and climatic conditions. It can be categorised into temporary, seasonal, permanent snowfields and glaciers. Snow cover that stays for few days and then melts away is termed as temporary snow cover. This usually occurs at lower altitudes during winter and sometimes at higher altitudes during summer. Snow cover that is formed over weeks or months by consecutive snowfalls and melts away gradually during the following summer is termed as seasonal cover. Above certain altitude, some amount of snow is carried over to the next winter season without melting during summer, adding to permanent snowfields and glaciers. Snow cover serves as the vast store house of water for the runoff in the Himalayan Rivers.

In recent decades, hydrological characteristics of the river basins in the Himalayan region seem to have undergone substantial changes as a result of change in land use/land cover, enhanced temporal and spatial variability in rainfall, increase in intensity and frequency of hydro-meteorological disasters. Climate change and its impacts on the hydrological cycle and nature of hydrological extreme events have posed an additional burden to this mountainous region.

It is important to study how the characters of such events could change in response to climate change. Several studies around the globe show that climate change is likely to put significant impact upon the discharge pattern and flood peaks of various river systems. The increased intensity of climate change in last 50 years is in concurrence with increased rate of natural hazards in general and floods in particular. The future climate would be wetter and warmer than the present one which will affect the type, magnitude and the temporal distribution of floods as well as frequency of flood peaks (Loukas *et al.*, 2004). The expected changes in the regional temperature and precipitation would affect the flow of river and flood peak pattern. Flood causes economic and social disruptions to many households living in the risk zone areas. Exploring new avenues for their agricultural practices, along the bank of river, increase the vulnerability of population and their economic activities towards floods.The Himalayan terrain and its climate support numerous river systems which sustain life in the region. Complex physiography and mountains with deep gorges are cut by majestic rivers.

## CLIMATE CHANGE AND HYDRO-METEOROLOGICAL DISASTERS

Global climate changes induced by increases in greenhouse gases concentrations are likely to increase temperatures, change precipitation patterns and probably raise the frequency of extreme events (IPCC, 2001a). It is likely that global climate change will lead to increased climatic variability, thus affecting the frequency and magnitude of extreme events. This would lead to an increased risk of natural disasters (Becker and Bugmann, 1997). A warmer climate, with its increased climatic variability, will increase the risk of both floods and droughts (Wetherald and Manabe, 2002). The changes in the hydrological cycle under conditions of enhanced global warming are likely to be complex and spatially diverse (Beare and Heaney, 2002).

The climate change is expected to cause an intensification of the global water cycle (Cubasch, 2001) with a consequent increase in flood risk (White *et al.*, 2001). This implies higher rates of evaporation, and a greater proportion of liquid to solid precipitation. These physical mechanisms, associated with potential changes in precipitation amount and seasonality, will affect the frequency of flood episodes (Beniston, 2003). One of the most significant potential consequences of changes in climate may be alterations in regional hydrological cycles and subsequent changes in the river quantity and quality regimes (Xu, 2000). The changes in temperature, amount and distribution of precipitation and other climatic parameters are expected to have significant implications on the hydrologic balance and water resources (Loukas *et al.*, 2004). An increase in heavy precipitation might lead to an over-proportional increase in runoff due to non-linear processes (Ashagrie *et al.*, 2006).

In view of climate change, it is necessary to integrate knowledge about catchment characteristics, the prevailing flood regime and the trends of weather patterns in the estimation of extreme events (Petrow *et al.*, 2007). The spatial and temporal variations of snow cover distribution and snowmelt runoff are considered as sensitive indicators for climatic change (Wang *et al.*, 2010). The flash flood hazards are expected to increase in frequency and severity in many areas of world, through the impacts of global change on climate and river discharge conditions (Marchi *et al.*, 2010). Hydrological extremes are expected to become more common in a changing climate (Kundzewicz *et al.*, 2007).

The projected general increase in flood magnitude and frequency is a consequence of projected general increase in the frequency of heavy precipitation events, although the effect of given change in precipitation depends upon the characteristics of catchment area (IPCC, 2001b). Climate change will affect not only changes in the precipitation amount and its proportion of rain and snow but also the spatial distribution of precipitation (Loukas *et al.*, 2002). It was observed that the extent of snow cover decreased by 10% since late 1960s (IPCC, 2001a). Under the warmer climate, the amount of precipitation in the form of snowfall will reduce, resulting in the decrease of snow accumulation (Singh and Bengtsson, 2005).

## CLIMATE CHANGE, PRECIPITATION AND FLOODING PATTERN

Nevertheless, global climate models claim that climate change would drive up extreme precipitation and river discharge (Nijssen *et al.*, 2001). Global warming is expected to significantly affect the runoff regime of mountainous catchments (Huss *et al.*, 2010). Identifying relationships between large-scale climatic circulation, and river basin-scale precipitation and discharge provides insight into understanding the hydro-climatological processes (Kingston *et al.*, 2009). Glacial melt is expected to increase under changed climatic conditions which could lead to increased summer flows in some river systems, for a few decades, followed by a reduction in flow as the glaciers may disappear (IPCC, 2007b).

Floods can be caused by intense and/or long lasting precipitation, snowmelt and landslides built dam break. Floods depend on precipitation intensity, volume, timing, antecedent conditions of rivers and their drainage basins. The frequency of severe floods in large river basins has increased substantially during the 20$^{th}$ century. The emergence of statistically significant positive trends in risk of floods which are consistent with the climate model results and the model suggests that the trend will continue (Milly *et al.*, 2002). Flood magnitude and frequency are likely to increase in most regions (Arnell *et al.*, 2001). The flooded area in Bangladesh is projected to increase at least by 23-29% with a global temperature rise of 2°C (Mirza, 2003). Up to 20% of the world's population lives in river basins that are likely to be affected by increased flood hazard by the 2080s in the course of global warming (Kleinen and Petschel-Held, 2007). The atmospheric warming and changes in land use/land cover may exacerbate future flooding by altering river regimes in the direction of large runoff volumes and shorter low water to flood peak intervals (Mitchell, 2003). The impacts of most extremes are typically felt at a local or regional scale; so regional studies of climate extremes are of the highest priority for Himalayan region to assess the potential climate impacts.

The shifting pattern of precipitation may affect the spatial and temporal distribution of runoff, and may increase the intensity and frequency of hydro-meteorological hazards. The projections indicate that there would be changes in the variability of climate from region to region, and changes in the frequency and intensity of some extreme climatic phenomenon. The flood magnitude and frequency are likely to increase in most regions.There is wide spread concern regarding the weakening of the Indian summer monsoon (Ramesh and Goswami, 2007) and possible increase in the number and intensity of heavy rainfall events in response to global warming (James and Ericksen, 1992; Palmer and Raisanen, 2002). Some studies indicated that there will be decline in monsoon rainfall over the North and central plains of India in the decades ahead because of general weakening of monsoons. This might be due to decrease in land-sea thermal gradient (Lal *et al.*, 2001). Most models project enhanced precipitation during the monsoon season, particularly over the northwestern part of India. As far as the temperature trends are concerned, all the models show positive trends indicating wide spread warming in future.

The different experiments generally indicate that the increase of temperature would be the order of 2-5°C across the country (Rupakumar *et al.*, 2006).

Recent studies have reported increases in precipitation across the Indian sub-continent. These increases have been observed over a range of precipitation intensities, and par-ticularly as heavy and extreme. This has led to extreme hydrological events, par-ticularly floods, may be increasing in frequency and/or magnitude as well. The basis for this is related to climate change, as the increas-ing temperatures will accelerate the hydrologic cycle and increase the occurrence of hydro-meteorological events. One of the anticipated effects of climate change is the possible increase in both frequency and intensity of extreme weather events.In India, on an average, the area actually affected by floods every year is 10 million hectares out of the total area prone to floods i.e. 40 million hectares. Several recent studies suggest an increase in the inter-annual variability of daily precipitation in the Asian summer monsoon with increasing atmospheric concentration of greenhouse gases. The intensity of extreme rainfall events over the Indian sub-continent is likely to be higher in future as a consequence of increased convective activities during the summer monsoon period, thereby suggesting the possibility of more frequent flash floods in parts of India (Chaskar and Verma, 2006).

The increase in rainfall during monsoon, as well as increases in the magnitude of extreme rainfall events, both of which have been projected with climate change, is expected to increase the frequency and intensity of floods (Lal *et al.*, 2001). Climate change is likely to affect the hydrological cycle which will result in more rainfall in lesser time; decrease in number of rainy days; overall increase in precipitation; increased glacial melt runoff initially and then afterwards decrease; increase in flood events particularly of flash floods; increase in drought like situations and increase in landslide events in hilly areas (MoWR, 2008). Damages from weather related disasters are projected to increase, due to a combination of increasing exposure of people and assets, and expected changes in the global climate (Bouwer *et al.*, 2010).

## CLIMATE CHANGE IMPACTS ON HIMALAYAN REGION

The hydro-meteorological disasters are not stranger to the Himalayan region. The region is periodically visited by various weather related disasters. Climate change is now adding significant additional threat to the already volatile risk prone areas by increasing the intensity and frequency of water related natural hazards. The vulnerability and associated risks in the region are increasing especially towards climate change induced hydro-meteorological disasters in space and time. These hazards left adverse impacts on the socio-economic condition of the people and the damage to the physical infrastructure along with deterioration of environmental conditions. Climate change is affecting the temperatures, amount of snow and ice in the region as well as rainfall patterns in the densely populated downstream regions. Causes for climate change over the Himalayas include aerosols with black carbon and dust, deforestation, forest fires, human-induced pollution and many other anthropogenic activities besides the emission of greenhouse gases (UNEP, 2009).

Climate change has impacted the glacial ecosystem tremendously. 67% of the glaciers are retreating at an astonishing rate in the Himalayas and the major causal factor has been identified as climate change (Ageta and Kadota, 1992; Yamada *et al.*, 1992; Fushimi, 2000). Glacial melt will affect the flow of rivers with dramatic adverse effects and possible long-term implication at regional scale. The impact of climate change on river morphology identified a complex series of interactions between the physical processes. Direct climate change impacts are on intensity, duration and frequency of precipitation, leading to change in runoff. The indirect impacts of climate change are through precipitation, temperature and wind affecting land surface cover and erosion (Goudie and Huntington, 1999). Global warming and its impact on the hydrological cycle and nature of hydrological events have posed an additional threat to Himalayan mountain region. Extreme precipitation events have geomorphic significance where they may cause wide spread slope failures (Ives and Messerli, 1989).

The precipitation in the Himalayan region more or less remained trendless during 20$^{th}$ century. The variations in both temperature and rainfall are translated into changes in the hydrological regimes of river basins by way of variability in snow melt runoff, glacier melting and monsoon runoff and increase or decrease average annual and annual peak flood discharges (Bhutiyani *et al.*, 2008). The melting of the Himalayan glaciers as a result of the rise in the earth's temperature will first increase the drainage into the major river systems, followed by reduction in their volumes once the glaciers begin to disappear. It is projected that some of the mightiest Himalayan Rivers might end up as seasonal, monsoon-fed rivers like those in southern India (Pai, 2008).

Numerous studies have been carried out in the Himalayan region to find the linkage between climate change and shrinkage of glaciers. These studies indicate that most of the glaciers are retreating discontinuously with subsequent increase in runoff of Himalayan Rivers. Change in glaciers and snow cover pattern can be considered as the direct indicators of rise in temperature. Various reports suggest that a significant number of Himalayan glaciers are retreating due to climate change. Few studies have been conducted to quantify the snow and glacier contribution to the flow of Himalayan Rivers. The glaciers are considered as the best recorders of climate change. The climatic variability in the glaciated region is best reflected by the depletion in snow cover, volume and snout fluctuation. Shift of snowline towards higher altitude will result in lesser input to glacier mass balance during summer months. With the retreating of glaciers in the higher reaches, considerable changes have occurred in the hydrological system of river.

Many rivers draining glaciated regions are sustained by glacier melt during the summer season (Singh and Kumar, 1997; Mark and Seltzer, 2003; Singh, 2003; Barnett *et al.*, 2005). Higher temperature generates increased flow from glacier melt. As the glaciers retreat due to global warming, river flows are increased in the short term, but the contribution of the glacier melt will gradually decrease over the next few decades.The Himalayan glaciers form the largest body of ice outside the polar caps with nearly 10,000 glaciers. Undoubtedly, the glaciers are retreating due to climate change, but not at a catastrophic rate that disappear in near future (Jain, 2008). Himalayan glaciers have been in a state of retreat since 1850 (Mayewski and Jeschke, 1979) and many confirmed that the rate of retreat is accelerating. But a dramatic increase in the rate seems to have occurred in the last three decades. The immediate responses of dynamic glaciers to weather make them an important indicator of climate change. So it is climate change which seems to be the key factor influencing the glacio-hydrological characteristics of the Himalayan glaciers in the recent years (Kulkarni 2001; Hasnain, 2002). The retreat of glaciers might affect the runoff of the streams originating from these areas (Bahuguna *et al.*, 2004). The fast recession of Himalayan glaciers would lead to ecological imbalance with the threatening of water balance in the region.

Greater melting of glaciers during the coming years could influence water flows in the Himalayan Rivers. The water resources of the Himalayan region may be highly vulnerable to climate change, because more than 50% of the discharge in the various tributaries of the Ganges, Indus and the Brahmaputra river system are highly dependent on snow and glacier melting (Singh *et al.*, 2006). The quantity of surface runoff due to climate change would vary across the river basins. However, there is general reduction in the quantity of the available runoff (Gosain and Rao, 2004). Arora *et al.* (2003) projected an increase in discharge in the Chenab River with increase in rainfall at higher altitudes. The study on the impact of plausible hypothetical scenarios of temperature and rainfall on the melt characteristics and daily runoff of the Chenab river basin shows that the melt is much more sensitive to increase in temperature than to rainfall (Arora *et al.*, 2008).

For the range of climatic scenarios, the changes in runoff of the Himalayan Basin are more sensitive to changes in temperature, compared to rainfall which is likely due to the major contribution of snow and glacier melt water in runoff (Singh *et al.*, 2006). As global warming continues to increase the atmospheric temperature, it will lead to a continuous shift to snow line towards higher altitude of the Himalayas. Thus the glaciated region will receive more rainfall and less solid precipitation in the form of snow. This will lead to rapid retreat of glaciers and downstream flooding in the coming future (Hasnain, 2002). The enhanced rate of retreating of glaciers is attributed to the increased anthropogenic contribution to climate change on account of greenhouse gas emissions.A vast area of the Himalayan river basins is covered by snow during winter (Singh *et al.*, 1997a; Singh and Jain, 2002), making it highly vulnerable to climate change.

The Himalayan glaciers are receding at an accelerating rate, currently at 10-15 meters per year on an average. The rapid melting will first increase the volume of water in rivers, causing widespread floods. But in few decades, this situation will change and the water level in the rivers will decline (WWF, 2005). The global warming has led to receding of most glaciers in the mountainous region such as the Himalayas, substantially during the 20$^{th}$ century. The mapping of Himalayan glaciers with reference to 1962 as bench mark showed that about 67% glaciers have shown retreating trends (Kulkarni *et al.*, 2005). This has influenced the stream runoff of the Himalayan Rivers (Kulkarni *et al.*, 2002).

The shrinking of glaciers is accompanied by the formation of unstable glacial lakes that threaten downstream areas with outburst floods (UNEP, 2007). Glacial Lake Outburst Floods (GLOF) are one of the most immediate and visibly dramatic effects of climate change in the Himalayan region. The frequency of the occurrence of GLOF events has increased in the second half of the 20th century (WWF, 2008). In the Himalayan region, the glacial lakes are increasing in number and volume due to thinning and recession of glaciers (Mool *et al.*, 2001). The glaciers in the Himalayan region are retreating in the face of accelerating global warming which result in formation of lakes and their subsequent breaching due to instability of dam. The impact of these GLOFs in downstream are quite extensive in terms of damage to roads, bridges, trekking trails, villages and agricultural lands along with great loss of human and animals lives (Bajracharya *et al.*, 2006).

The increase in atmospheric average temperature will have the direct impact on retreating of glaciers and formation of glacial lakes in Hindu Kush Himalayan (HKH) region. The glaciers of HKH region are retreating at high pace and as a result, the formation of glacial lakes are increasing in number and size with the potential increase in glacial lake outburst flood events (Bajracharya *et al.*, 2006). In addition more melting is expected to increase the frequency of catastrophic events such as glacier lake outburst floods (GLOF) that have devastating consequences for civil works like bridges, dams and powerhouses, and communities living at downstream. Also, the increase in phenomena such as cloudbursts is widely noted.

Using remote sensing data to investigate glacier thickness changes in the Western Himalaya, Berthier *et al.* (2007) found an annual ice thickness loss of about 0.8 meters water equivalent (m.w.e.) per year between 1999 and 2004, about twice the long-term rate of the period 1977-1999 (UNEP and WGMS 2008). Due to climate change, there is increase in flooding events, resulting from excessive rainfall within a short duration of time and excessive melting of glaciers and consequent high river discharge (Sanyal and Lu, 2004).

High-magnitude rainfall events in the Himalaya are responsible for mass movement on slopes which block the rivers that cause massive floods when failure. Numerous examples of breach floods have been recorded on many Himalayan rivers such as Indus, Satluj, Bhagirathi, Alaknanda etc. (Wohl and Cenderelli, 1998). Scientific projections indicate that the magnitude and frequency of flash floods in the great Himalayan region may increase in the future as a result of change in climate and its variability (Lhasa Declaration, 2006). The frequency of extreme rainfall events in the highly vulnerable and fragile environment of Himalaya is increasing in late monsoon season due to possible climate change which proves to be highly disastrous (Joshi and Kumar, 2006).

In spite of the uncertainties about the precise magnitude of climate change and its possible impacts on the water resources, particularly on regional scales, mitigation and adaptation measures must be taken to anticipate, prevent or minimize the causes and adverse effects of climate change. Risk and associated vulnerability towards flood hazards arise from the inherent variability of geophysical processes and changes in complex socioeconomic factors. Most of these catastrophic events were caused by unusually intense precipitation in mountainous areas (Kaczmarek, 2003).Future flood damages will depend heavily on settlement patterns, land use decisions, the quality of flood forecasting, warning, response systems, the value of structures and other property located in vulnerable areas (Pielke and Downton, 2000). There is a widespread perception that the risk arising from flooding is externally driven by natural disaster; however, the reality is that flood risk is wholly of human origin as people continue to settle in the disaster risk zones (Gahey *et al.*, 2008). The Climate Forecasting System (CFS) component of the Disaster Management Support (DMS) project supports the use of climate and weather forecasts as tools to enhance prediction and early warning of hydro-meteorological events. This will promote better decision making at the local level with scarce natural resources and develop more effective plans to mitigate the adverse effects of these events (Kumar *et al.*, 2006).

In recent years, flood management policy in many countries has shifted from protection towards enhancing society's ability to live with floods (Kundzewicz and Takeuchi 1999). This may include implementing protection measures, but as part of a package including measures such as enhanced flood foresting and warning, regulations, zoning, insurance and relocation. Each measure has advantages and disadvantages, and the choice is site specific: there is no single one-fits-all measures (Kundzewicz *et al.*, 2002).Resilient strategies for flood management, such as allowing rivers to temporarily flood and reducing exposure to flood damage, are preferable to traditional resistance (protection) strategies in the face of uncertainty (Klijn *et al.*, 2004; Oslen, 2006). There are major uncertainties in quantitative projections of changes in hydrological characteristics for a drainage basin. Adaptation procedures need to be developed in the face of these uncertainties regarding the projections of changes in river discharge. It is well established that precipitation variability and future temperature increases due to climate change which affect the snowmelt and runoff in rivers (Kundzewicz *et al.*, 2007).

For the last two decades, the advancement in the field of remote sensing and GIS have greatly facilitated in the preparation of flood hazard maps and risk assessment. It is evident that GIS has a great role to play in natural hazard management because these are multi-dimensional in nature and the spatial component in inherent (Coppock, 1995). With the advancement in RS and GIS analysis techniques, it is easy to delineate flood hazard risk zones in a spatial context. The main advantage of using GIS for flood management is that it not only generates the flood risk maps but also creates potential for further analysis to estimate probable damage due to flood (Clark, 1998).

Based on the outcomes, the following recommendations are suggested which relies on two main approaches: one is mitigation efforts towards controlling climate change and second is adaptation towards the impacts of climate change. Climate change related policies were traditionally focused on mitigation but now there is growing recognition of both mitigation and adaptation strategies. Mitigation refers to anthropogenic interventions to reduce the sources or enhance the sinks of greenhouse gases and 'adaptation' is concerned with addressing the consequences of climate change. There is an urgent need for new and approved mechanisms for strengthening the adaptation and mitigation strategies.

The adaptation strategies are required to reduce the vulnerability of problems arising by climate change and also increasing the resiliency of communities by enhancing the capacity to adapt these strategies. Various adaptation strategies suggested for the Himalayan region are:

1. The analysis of factors such as glacier melt, discharge, tectonic events, spatial-temporal variability in precipitation, geology, geomorphology, land use/land cover, population growth, deforestation etc needs to be carried out in order to better understand the 'cause and effect' relationship between climate change and associated hazards propensity.
2. To establish the short-term and long-term guidelines for the sustainable environmental development of the region as well as their proper implementation. Strict adherence to the environmental concerns should be there as per the government's environmental laws, rules, policies and guidelines.
3. Preparing environmental impact assessment models and sustainable livelihood framework which help in better understanding of link between climate change and Disaster Risk Reduction (DRR) of hydro-meteorological hazards.

4. Preparing the inventory of glacial lakes and building reservoirs to control the excessive runoff from the melting of glaciers and incessant rainfall in the hilly region.
5. Simulation of hydrological condition of various river basins can be analysed under the predicted climatic conditions.
6. The flood discharge during monsoons can be regulated due to construction of dams as the flood peaks in the rivers will get moderated.
7. Establishing cost effective alternative to flow releases i.e. sustainability flows, based on maintenance of minimum flows and periodic flushing flows by the construction of smaller off-stream storages.
8. Determine the vulnerability of region to climate change and identify associated risks and prioritise adaptation responses accordingly.
9. Promoting a holistic approach in integrating risk management by combining various hazards, their vulnerability and risk assessment, especially at local levels.
10. Formulation and consideration of flood hazard mitigation policy during the implementation of hydroelectric projects, expansion of road networks, agricultural and horticultural practices.
11. Community and stakeholder consultations have been considered in environmental management of the basin areas as an integral part of every developmental activity.
12. Increasing the capacity building and resiliency of peoples through awareness programmes, active participation of community in preparedness and response efforts and other decentralised community based approaches.
13. Considerable risks to the fragile mountainous areas can be ameliorated by the execution of catchment treatment plans, integrated river basin and water management schemes which should be cost effective and environmentally efficient.
14. Consideration of socio-economic and environmental aspects along with Disaster Risk Reduction (DRR) as on priority basis before the start of any developmental activity.
15. Development of improved gauge stations, early warning and communication system for providing timely information, keeping in mind the present and future scenarios of climate change and their predicted impacts on hydro-meteorological hazards. The WMO has recommended one rain gauge for every 500 km$^2$ in plain areas and 150-250 km$^2$ in hilly areas.
16. There should be 24x7 weather channels which provide timely and accurate information on weather conditions, climate change, natural hazards and other environmental issues.

17. Preparing the inventory of water induced natural hazards and the area affected with the help of available state of art technologies i.e. remote sensing and GIS.
18. Establishing co-ordination in gathering, storing, sharing and dissemination of hydrological and meteorological data among concerned agencies in the region to improve early warning systems.
19. Explore the possibility of trans-boundary transfer of hydrological information for various river basins of Himalayan region so that advanced warning is issued and catastrophic incidents could be avoided.
20. For the better quantitative assessment of climate change impacts, it is imperative that more accurate ' damages' and ' increasing vulnerability of area' relationship should be established and update periodically.
21. Local people have much knowledge about local-scale variability in climate and its impacts. Therefore, the traditional/indigenous knowledge and its linkage with scientific information will be useful in dealing the consequences of climate change on hydro-meteorological disasters along with feedback mechanism.
22. It is necessary to review the developmental policies and land use regulations in the region, keeping in mind the climate change scenarios and its impacts.
23. Strengthening policies which enable the storage of surplus water during the monsoon, and improving the availability of water during dry season (watershed development, slope stabilisation, afforestation, infrastructure for water storage and hydro-electricity).
24. Human activities such as deforestation, land degradation should be banned as they not only result in huge losses to the environment but also increase the vulnerability of the environment towards disasters. Such activities also alter the resiliency of natural system by reducing its ability to recover effectively after the occurrence of calamity.
25. There should be paradigm shift in disaster management especially under climate change by taking initiatives such as adaptation to change, disaster auditing, legal framework (regulatory authority), cross-sectoral risk analysis, knowledge management, community awareness, training and capacity building, private-public partnership, research and development and the last but not least, rewards for good management practices.

Adaptation will have to be supported by mitigating measures that address the root causes of climate change: the emission of greenhouse gases and other substances that cause global warming. No full proof mechanism is there to combat the impacts of climate change, but suitable and necessary management practices can be adopted as mitigation measures. Various mitigation strategies are:

1. All the countries of world should undertake immediate and rapid action to reduce the emission of greenhouse gases, by ensuring the long-term sustainability of the developmental activities.
2. Adoption of clean development mechanism (CDM) technologies which are benign towards climate and aid to control the phenomenon of climate change.
3. The landmark initiatives should be undertaken for sustainable pathways by shifting to environmental benevolent technologies and their exchange between the countries which can help in controlling climate change.
4. Population control measures, investment in enhancing quality of road and rail networks, energy conservation and efficiency programmes, policies for promoting renewable energy, investment in water conservation practices, resource recycling, land restoration, climate friendly infrastructure, afforestation should be enforced effectively.

The impacts of mitigation will be felt in long run by the future generations while the benefits of adaptation measures are immediate. The proper implementation of these cost-efficient, ecologically effective strategies proves to be useful for management efforts. We know that climate change is a global issue but its consequences are felt at regional level. Available strategies may be effective in reducing negative impacts in short term, up to limited extent, but the necessity is to take steps for stronger mitigation measures and increasing adaptive capacity which requires regional adaptation research, capacity building, developmental priorities and accordingly change in policies. In spite of the uncertainties about the precise magnitude of climate change and its possible impacts particularly of hydro-meteorological events, measures must be taken to anticipate, prevent or minimise the adverse effects. So, it is need of the hour to work at global, national and regional levels to combat the challenges of climate change and its impacts.

## CONCLUSION

The conclusive results make it clear that the problem of climate change is real with many alarming consequences. The impact of projected future climate change may be felt more severely especially on the hydro-meteorological hazards in developing countries, whose economy is largely dependent on agriculture and is already under stress due to high population with their associated demands for energy, water, food etc. As the intensity and frequency of climate change induced floods and runoff increases, the severity of disaster in these highly fragile and sensitive areas of Himalayan region will increase. So, the need of the hour is to identify these areas as precautionary measures. Identification of such zones will help in timely adopting the mitigation and adaptation measures. Preparation of risk zoning maps also helps in regulating indiscriminate and unplanned land use practices in risky areas. In addition to enhancing scientific understanding, it is imperative to generate useful information on the basis of which practical interventions can be crafted for strengthening links between policy makers and practitioners. The 'Gordian Knot' of 'climate change verses development' could be best cut by aligning developmental strategies and regulation of various goals, action plans etc. A comprehensive approach by integrating the social, environmental and economic dimensions is one of the best ways to enhance the plausibility of the solution. From time to time, it is necessary to evaluate the efficacy of various strategies or coping mechanism that may reduce vulnerability towards climate change. There is a need to prepare the communities, institutions and governments of the region to anticipate the consequences of climate change and evolve suitable and cost-effective adaptation responses.

## REFERENCES

Ageta Y. and Kadota T. (1992): Predictions of Changes of Glacier Mass Balance in the Nepal Himalaya and Tibetan Plateau: A Case Study of Air Temperature Increase for Three Glaciers, *Annals of Glaciology*, 16: 89-94.

Arnell N.W., Liu C., Compagnucci R., Da Cunha L., Hanaki K., Howe C., Mailu G., Shiklomanov I. and Stakhiv E. (2001): Hydrology and Water Resources, Climate Change 2001: Impacts, Adaptation and Vulnerability, Contribution of Working Group II to the Third Assessment Report of the Intergovernmental Panel on Climate Change, (eds. McCarthy JJ, Canziani OF, Leary NA, Dokken DJ and White KS), Cambridge University Press. Cambridge, United Kingdom, pp. 191-234.

Arora M., Singh P. and Goel N.K. (2003): Evaluation of Climate Change Impact on Rainfall, Discharge and Temperature for a Himalayan Basin, *Proceedings of the International Conference on Water and Environment*, 15th-18th December, Regional Research Laboratory, Bhopal, Madhya Pradesh, India.

Arora M., Singh P., Goel N.K. and Singh R.D. (2008): Climatic Variability Influences on Hydrological Responses of a Large Himalayan Basin, *Water Resource Management*, 22: 1461-1475.

Ashagrie A.G., de Laat P.J.M., de Wit M.J.M., Tu M. and Uhlenbrook S. (2006): Detecting the Influence of Land Use Changes on Discharges and Floods in the Meuse River Basin – the Predictive Power of a Ninety-year Rainfall-runoff Relation?, *Hydrology and Earth System Sciences*, 10: 691-701.

Bahuguna I.M., Kulkarni A.V. and Nayak S. (2004): Technical Note: DEM from IRS-1C PAN Stereo Coverages Over Himalayan Glaciated Region- Accuracy and its Utility, *International Journal of Remote Sensing*, 25 (19): 4029-4041.

Bajracharya R.S., Mool P.K. and Shrestha B.R. (2006): The Impact of Global Warming on the Glaciers of the Himalayas, *Proceedings of the International Symposium on Geo-disasters, Infrastructure Management and Protection of World Heritage Sites*, 25th-26th November, NEC, ECNSET, Nepal, pp. 231-242.

Barnett T.P., Adam J.C. and Lettenmaier D.P. (2005): Potential Impacts of a Warming Climate on Water Availability in Snow-dominated Regions, *Nature*, 438: 303-309.

Beare S. and Heaney A. (2002): Climate Change and Water Resources in the Murray Darling Basin, Australia: Impacts and Adaptation, *ABARE Conference Paper*, Canberra, Australia, pp. 33.

Becker A. and Bugmann H. (1997): Predicting Global Change Impacts on Mountain Hydrology and Ecology: Integrated Catchment Hydrology/Altitudinal Gradient Studies, *IGBP Report 43*, International Geosphere- Biosphere Programme, A Study of Global Change of the International Council of Scientific Unions (ICSU), Stockholm, Sweden.

Beniston M. (2003): Climatic Change in Mountainous Regions: A Review of Possible Impacts, *Climatic Change*, 59: 5-31.

Berthier E., Arnaud Y., Kumar R., Ahmad S., Wagnon P. and Chevallier P. (2007): Remote Sensing Estimates of Glacier Mass Balances in the Himachal Pradesh (Western Himalaya, India), *Remote Sensing of Environment*, 108(3): 327-338.

Bhutiyani M.R., Kale V.S. and Pawar N.J. (2008): Changing Streamflow Patterns in the Rivers of Northwestern Himalaya: Implications of Global Warming in the 20th Century, *Current Science*, 95 (5): 618-626.

Bouwer L.M., Bubech P. and Aerts J.C.J.H. (2010): Changes in Future Flood Risk due to Climate and Development in a Dutch Polder Area, *Global Environmental Change*, 20: 463-471.

Chaskar D.S. and Verma H.K. (2006): Risk Management of Water Related Disasters, *Proceedings of the First India Disaster Management Congress*, 29th-30th November, National Institute of Disaster Management (NIDM), New Delhi, India.

Clark M.J. (1998): Putting Water in its Place: A Perspective on GIS in Hydrology and Water Management, *Hydrological Processes*, 12: 823-834.

Coppock J.T. (1995): GIS and Natural Hazards: An Overview from a GIS Perspective, In: Geographical Information System in Assessing Natural Hazard, (eds. Carrara A and Guzzetti F), Kluwer Academic, Netherlands, pp. 21-34.

Cubasch U. (2001): In: Climate Change 2001: The Scientific Basis (eds. Houghton JT *et al.*) Chapter 9, Cambridge University Press, Cambridge, United Kingdom.

Fushimi H. (2000): Recent Changes in Glacial Phenomena in the Nepalese Himalayas. In: A Threat to Life: The Impact of Climate Change on Japan's Biodiversity, (eds. Domoto A *et al.*), Tsukiji-Shokan Pub. Co. Ltd., Japan and The World Conservation Union, Gland, Switzerland, pp. 42-45.

Gahey C.M., Samuels P.G., Knight D.W. and OA Hare M.T. (2008): Estimating River Flow Capacity in Practice, *Journal of Flood Risk Management*, 1: 23-33.

Gosain A.K. and Rao S. (2004): Impact of Climate Change on Water Sector In: Climate Change and India: Vulnerability Assessment and Adaptation (eds. Shukla PR *et al.*), Universities Press (India) Pvt. Ltd., Hyderabad, Andhra Pradesh, India, pp. 159-192.

Gosain A.K., Rao S. and Basuray D. (2006): Climate Change Impact Assessment on Hydrology of Indian River Basin, *Current Science*, 90(3): 346-353.

Goudie J. and Huntington S.W. (1999): Implications of Climate Change Predictions for Flood and Costal Defence Research, a Project Report Submitted to Ministry of Agriculture, Fisheries and Food, UK.

Hasnain S.I. (2002): Himalayan Glaciers Meltdown: Impact on South Asian Rivers, *Proceedings of the Fourth International FRIENDS Conference*, International Association of Hydrological Sciences, Cape Town, South Africa, 274: 417-423.

Houghton J., Ding Y., Griggs D., Noguer M., Van Der Linden P., Xiaosu D., Makdell K. and Johnson C. (2001 eds.): Climate Change 2001: The Scientific Basis, Contribution of Working Group I to the Third Assessment Report of the Intergovernmental Panel on Climate Change, Cambridge University Press, Cambridge, United Kingdom, pp. 881.

Huss M., Jouvet G., Farinotti D. and Bauder A. (2010): Future High-mountain Hydrology: A New Parameterization of Glacier Retreat, *Hydrology and Earth System Sciences*, 14: 815-829.

I.P.C.C. (2001a): Climate Change 2001: Synthesis Report, In: (eds. Watson *et al.*), Intergovernmental Panel on Climate Change, Cambridge University Press, Cambridge, UK and New York, USA, pp. 398.

I.P.C.C. (2001b): Report: Climate Change-Impacts, Adaptations and Vulnerability, In: (eds. McCarthy JJ, Canziani OF, Leary NA, Dokken DJ, White KS), Intergovernmental Panel on Climate Change, Cambridge University Press, Cambridge, UK and New York, USA.

I.P.C.C. (2007): Summary for Policymakers, Climate Change 2007: Impacts, Adaptations and Vulnerability, a Report of Working Group II of the Intergovernmental Panel on Climate Change, Cambridge University Press, Cambridge, UK and New York, USA.

I.P.C.C. (2007b): Summary for Policymakers, Climate Change 2007: Mitigation. Contribution of Working Group III to the Fourth Assessment Report of the Intergovernmental Panel on Climate Change, In: (eds. Metz B, Davidson OR, Bosch PR, Dave R, Meyer LA), Cambridge University Press, Cambridge, UK and New York, USA.

I.P.C.C. (2013): Summary for Policymakers, Climate Change 2013: Impacts, Adaptations and Vulnerability, a Report of Working Group II of the Intergovernmental Panel on Climate Change, Cambridge University Press, Cambridge, UK and New York, USA.

Ives J.D. and Messerli B. (1989): The Himalayan Dilemma: Reconciling Development and Conservation, Routledge, London, United Kingdom.

Jain S.K. (2008): Impact of Retreat of Gangotri Glacier on the Flow of Ganga River, *Current Science*, 95 (8): 1012-1014.

James M.K. and Ericksen N. (1992): Effects of Climate Change on Weather Related Disasters, In: Confronting Climate Change: Risks, Implications and Responses (ed. Mintzer I), Cambridge University Press, Cambridge, United Kingdom, 141-152.

Joshi V. (2006): Extreme Rainfall Events (Cloud Bursts) and its Consequences in the Indian Himalayan Region: Needs an in-depth Study, *Proceedings of the First India Disaster Management Congress,* 29th-30th November, National Institute of Disaster Management (NIDM), New Delhi, India.

Joshi V. and Kumar K. (2006): Extreme Rainfall Events and Associated Natural Hazards in Alaknanda Valley, Indian Himalayan Region, *Journal of Mountain Science*, 3(3): 228-236.

Kaczmarek Z. (2003): The Impact of Climate Variability on Flood Risk in Poland, *Risk Analysis*, 23(3): 559-566.

Kingston D.G., Hannah D.M., Lawler D.M. and McGregor G.R. (2009): Climate–river Flow Relationships Across Montane and Lowland Environments in Northern Europe, *Hydrological Processes*, 23: 985-996.

Kleinen T. and Petschel-Held G. (2007): Integrated Assessment of Changes in Flooding Probabilities due to Climate Change, *Climate Change*, 81: 283-312.

Klijn F., Van Buuren M. and Van Rooij S.A.M. (2004): Flood-risk Management Strategies for an Uncertain Future: Living with Rhine River Floods in the Netherlands? *Ambio: A Journal of the Human Environment*, 33: 141-147.

Kulkarni A.V. (2001): Effect of Climatic Variations on the Himalayan Glaciers: A Case Study of Upper Chandra River Basin. In: Remote Sensing Applications (ed. Srinivas MG), Narosa Publishing House, New Delhi, India, pp. 477-486.

Kulkarni A.V., Mathur P., Rathore B.P., Alex S., Thakur N. and Kumar M. (2002): Effects of Global Warming on Snow Ablation Pattern in the Himalayas, *Current Science*, 83: 120-123.

Kulkarni A.V., Rathore B.P., Mahajan S. and Mathur P. (2005): Alarming Retreat of Parbati Glacier, Beas Basin, Himachal Pradesh, *Current Science*, 88 (11): 1844-1850.

Kumar R., Bales J.D., Jubach R., Gyamba P.D., Kane M.D. and Scott A.C. (2006): Flash-flood Warning for the Upper Sutlej River Basin, Northern India, *Proceedings of the First India Disaster Management Congress,* 29-30 November, National Institute of Disaster Management (NIDM), New Delhi, India.

Kundzewicz Z.W. and Takeuchi K. (1999): Flood Protection and Management: Quo Vadimus? *Hydrological Sciences Journal*, 44: 417-432.

Kundzewicz Z.W., Budhakooncharoen S., Bronstert A., Hoff H., Lettenmaier D., Menzel L. and Schulze R. (2002): Coping with Variability and Change: Floods and Drought, *Theoretical and Applied Climatology*, 26: 263-274.

Kundzewicz Z.W., Mata L.J., Arnell N.W., Doll P., Kabat P., JimAenez B.,Miller K.A., Oki T. S9en Z. and Shiklomanov I.A. (2007): Fresh Water Resources and Their Management, Climate Change: Impacts, Adaptation and Vulnerability, Contribution of Working Group II to the Fourth Assessment Report of the Intergovernmental Panel on Climate Change, (eds. Parry ML, Canziani OF, Palutikof JP, Van der Linden PJ and Hanson CE), Cambridge University Press, Cambridge, United Kingdom, pp. 173-210.

Kundzewicz Z.W., Mata L.J., Arnell N.W., Doll P., Kabat P., JimAenez B., Miller K.A., Oki T. S9en Z. and Shiklomanov I.A. (2007): Fresh Water Resources and Their Management, Climate Change: Impacts, Adaptation and Vulnerability, Contribution of Working Group II to the Fourth Assessment Report of the Intergovernmental Panel on Climate Change, (eds. Parry ML, Canziani OF, Palutikof JP, Van der Linden PJ and Hanson CE), Cambridge University Press, Cambridge, United Kingdom, pp. 173-210.

Lal M., Nozawa T., Emori S., Harasawa H., Takahashi K., Kimoto M., Abe-Ouchi A., Nakajima T., Takemura T. and Numaguti A. (2001): Future Climate Change: Implications for Indian Summer Monsoon and its Variability, *Current Science*, 81 (9): 1196-1207.

Lhasa Declaration (2006): A Report on Flash Flood Management and Sustainable Development in the Himalayan Region by Water, Hazards and Environmental Management (WHEM) and International Centre for Integrated Mountain Development (ICIMOD), Kathmandu, Nepal.

Loukas A., Vasiliades L. and Dalezios N.R. (2002): Climatic Impacts on the Runoff Generation Processes in British Columbia, Canada, *Hydrology and Earth System Sciences*, 6(2): 211-227.

Loukas A., Vasiliades L. and Dalezios N.R. (2004): Climate Change Implications on Flood Response of a Mountainous Watershed, *Water, Air and Soil Pollution*, 4: 331-347.

Mall R.K., Gupta A., Singh R., Singh R.S. and Rathore L.S. (2006): Water Resources and Climate Change: An Indian Perspective, *Current Science*, 90 (12): 1610-1626.

Marchi L., Borga M., Preciso E. and Gaume E. (2010): Characterisation of Selected Extreme Flash Floods in Europe and Implications for Flood Risk Management, *Journal of Hydrology*, 394: 118-133.

Mark B.G. and Seltzer G.O. (2003): Tropical Glacier Meltwater Contribution to Stream Discharge: A Case Study in the Cordillera Blanca, Peru, *Climatic Change*, 49: 271-281.

Mayweski P. and Jaschke P.A. (1979): Himalaya and Trans Himalayan Glacier Fluctuation Since 1812 A.D., *Arctic and Alpine Research*, 11(3): 267-287.

Milly P.C.D., Wetherald R.T., Dunne K.A. and Delworth T.L. (2002): Increasing Risk of Great Floods in a Changing Climate, *Nature*, 415: 514-517.

Mirza M.M.Q. (2003): Three Recent Extreme Floods in Bangladesh: A Hydro-meteorological Analysis, *Natural Hazards*, 28: 35-64.

Mitchell J.K. (2003): European River Floods in a Changing World, *Risk Analysis*, 23(3): 567-574.

Mool P.K., Bajracharya S.R., Joshi S.P. (2001): Inventory of Glaciers, Glacial Lakes and Glacial Lake Outburst Floods, Nepal, ICIMOD (International Centre for Integrated Mountain Development), Kathmandu, Nepal.

M,O.W.R. (2008): Priliminary Consolidated Report on Effect of Climate Change on Water Resources, Ministry of Water Resources, Government of India, pp. 35.

Nijssen B., O'Donnell G.M., Hamlet A.F. and Lettenmaier D.P. (2001): Hydrologic Sensitivity of Global Rivers to Climate Change, *Climatic Change*, 50: 143-175.

Oslen J.R. (2006): Climate Change and Flood Plain Management in the United States, *Climate Change*, 76: 407-426.

Pai N. (2008): A Report on Climate Change and National Security: Preparing India for New Conflict Scenarios, The Indian National Interest: Policy Brief.

Palmer T.N. and Raisanen J. (2002): Quantifying the Risk of Extreme Seasonal Precipitation Events in a Changing Climate, *Nature*, 415: 512-514.

Petrow T., Merz B., Lindenschmidt K.E. and Thieken A.H. (2007): Aspects of Seasonality and Flood Generating Circulation Patterns in a Mountainous Catchment in South-eastern Germany, *Hydrology and Earth System Sciences*, 11: 1455-1468.

Pielke R.A. Jr. and Downton M.W. (2000): Precipitation and Damaging Floods: Trends in the United States, 1932-97, *Journal of Climate*, 13: 3625-3637.

Ramesh K.V. and Goswami P. (2007): Reduction in Temporal and Spatial Extent of the Indian Summer Monsoon, *Geophysical Research Letters*, 34: L23704.

Rupakumar K., Sahai A.K., Krishna K., Parwardhan S.K., Mishra P.K., Revendeker J.V., Kamala K. and Pant G.B. (2006): High Resolution Climate Change Scenarios for India for the 21st century, *Current Science*, 90 (3): 334-345.

Sah M.P. and Mazari R.K. (2007): An Overview of the Geo-environmental Status of the Kullu Valley, Himachal Pradesh, India, *Journal of Mountain Sciences*, 4(1): 3-23.

Sanyal J. and Lu X.X. (2004): Application of Remote Sensing in Flood Management with Special Reference to Monsoon Asia: A Review, *Natural Hazards*, 33: 283-301.

Sathaye J., Shukla P.R. and Ravindranath N.H. (2006): Climate Change, Sustainable Development and India: Global and National Concerns, *Current Science*, 90(3): 314-325.

Singh P. (2003): Effect of Warmer Climate on the Depletion of Snow Covered Area in the Satluj Basin in the Western Himalayan Region, *Hydrological Science Journal*, 48: 413-425.

Singh P. and Bengtsson L. (2005): Impact of Warmer Climate on Melt and Evaporation for the Rainfed, Snowfed and Glacierfed Basins in the Himalayan Region, *Journal of Hydrology*, 300: 140-154.

Singh P. and Jain S.K. (2002): Snow and Glacier Melt in the Satluj River at Bhakra Dam in the Western Himalayan Region, *Hydrological Science Journal*, 47(1): 93-106.

Singh P. and Kumar N. (1997): Impact Assessment of Climate Change on the Hydrological Response of a Snow and Glacier Melt Runoff Dominated Himalayan River, *Journal of Hydrology*, 193: 316-350.

Singh P., Arora M. and Goel N.K. (2006): Effect of Climate Change on Runoff of a Glacierized Himalayan Basin, *Hydrological Processes*, 20(9): 1979-1992.

Singh P., Jain S.K. and Kumar N. (1997a): Snow and Glacier Melt Runoff Contribution in the Chenab River at Akhnoor, *Mountain Research and Development*, 17(1): 49-56.

U.N.E.P. (2007): Glaciers and Ice Caps. In: Global Outlook for Ice and Snow, United Nations Environment Programme, pp. 38.

U.N.E.P. (2009): Recent Trends in Melting Glaciers, Tropospheric Temperatures Over the Himalayas and Summer Monsoon Rainfall Over India, Division of Early Warning and Assessment (DEWA).

U.N.E.P. and WGMS (2008): Global Glacier Changes: Facts and Figures, United Nations Environment Programme and World Glacier Monitoring Service, pp. 88.

Wang J., Li H. and Hao X. (2010): Responses of Snowmelt Runoff to Climatic Change in an Inland River Basin, Northwestern China, Over the Past 50 Years, *Hydrology and Earth System Sciences*, 14: 1979-1987.

Wetherald R.T. and Manabe S. (2002): Simulation of Hydrologic Changes Associated with Global Warming, *Journal of Geophysical Research*, 107(D19): 4379.

White K.S. *et al.* (2001): Technical Summary in Climate Change 2001: Impacts, Adaptation and Vulnerability (eds. McCarthy JJ *et al.*), Cambridge University Press, Cambridge, United Kingdom, pp. 19-73.

Wohl E.E. and Cenderelli D. (1998): Flooding in the Himalaya Mountains, In: Flood Studies in India, (ed. Kale VS) Geological Society of India, Banglore, Karnataka, India, Memoir, 41: 77-99.

W.W.F. (2005): An Overview of Glaciers, Glacier Retreat, and Subsequent Impacts in Nepal, India and China, World Wild Fund for Nature, Nepal Programme, pp. 79.

W.W.F. (2008): Reducing Climate Change Induced Risks and Vulnerabilities from Glacial Lake Outburst Floods, World Wild Fund for Nature.

Xu C.Y. (2000): Modelling the Effects of Climate Change on Water Resources in Central Sweden, *Water Resources Management*, 14: 177-189.

Yamada T., Shiraiwa T., Kadota T., Watanabe T., Rana B., Ageta Y. and Fushimi H. (1992): Fluctuations of the Glaciers from the 1970s to 1989 in the Khumbu, Shorong and Langtang Regions, Nepal Himalayas, *Bulletin of Glacier Research*, 10: 11-19.

Pages: 23-38

CLIMATE CHANGE, DISASTER MANAGEMENT AND ENVIRONMENT
*Edited by:* Dr. Alka Chauhan; Dr. Pawan Kumar 'Bharti'
ISBN: 978-93-5056-784-5
*Edition:* 2016
*Published by:* Discovery Publishing House Pvt. Ltd., New Delhi (India)

# CHAPTER – 2

# Climate Change Disaster Risks
## *A Wakeup Call for Zimbabwe*

Onalenna Gwate

**ABSTRACT**

Climate change disaster risk is increasingly becoming a reality for Zimbabwe. Global Circulation Models (GCMs) are instrumental in developing scenarios that assist us in understanding future climate. Causes of climate change are well documented. Climate change is principally driven by anthropogenic activities. The present study sought to outline changing risk profiles for the communities due to climate change and to identify critical constraints to adaptation in Zimbabwe. Essentially, literature review was done to identify gaps in climate change adaptation.

Results indicated that the country is not adequately prepared to deal with climate change eventualities and conventional development

Lupane State University, Department of Geography and Population Studies
P. Bag AC 255, Raylton, Bulawayo, Zimbabwe.

planning does not factor in climate change disaster risks. The projected disaster risks aptly sum up the gross vulnerability of the country to climate change. Critical constraints to climate change adaptation revolve around poor governance for risk reduction. Therefore future development planning for Zimbabwe should be geared towards tackling disaster risks associated with climate change. Climate change adaptation could be achieved if broad based changes related to governance for risk management and mainstreaming disaster risk into development planning are done.

*Keywords:* Climate change, General Circulation Models, disaster risk reduction, governance, compensatory risk management, integrated climate risk management.

## INTRODUCTION

For the purposes of this paper climate change refers to the alterations in the state of the climate that can be identified (e.g., using statistical tests) by changes in the mean and/or the variability of its properties, and that persists for an extended period, typically decades or longer (Intergovernmental Panel on Climate Change (IPCC, 2007). It brings about corresponding changes to ecosystems and socioeconomic activity. Accordingly, fluctuations on periods shorter than a few decades, such as El Niño, do not represent climate change. United Nations Framework Convention on Climate Change defines climate change as "a change of climate which is attributed directly or indirectly to human activity that alters the composition of the global atmosphere. Climate change may be due to internal processes and/or external forcings.

Some external influences, such as changes in solar radiation and volcanism, occur naturally and contribute to the total natural variability of the climate system. Other external changes, such as the change in composition of the atmosphere that began with the industrial revolution, are the result of human activity. Climate change is distinguished from climate variability which refers to fluctuations about the mean of meteorological observations (Burroughs, 2001). A glut of disaster risks is inherent within climate change. A disaster is a serious disruption of the functioning of a society, causing widespread human, material, or environmental losses which exceed the ability of affected society to cope using only its own resources (Kotze and Holloway, 1996).

Risk is defined by United Nations Development Programme (UNDP, 2004) as the probability of harmful consequences or expected loss (of lives, people injured, property, livelihoods, economic activity disrupted or environment damaged) resulting from interactions between natural or human-induced hazards and vulnerable conditions. Therefore, climate change disaster risk relate to expected losses in the event that extreme projected impacts of climate change occur. Disaster risk reduction entails measures to curb disaster losses by addressing hazards and people's vulnerability to them (UNDP, 2004) within a broader sustainable development context.

General Circulation Models (GCM) are used in simulating the climate system in order to help mankind understand climate. Much of the knowledge relating to future trends of climate is derived from GCM. Climate change is a highly contested and debated topic with some school of thought arguing that climate is not changing at all. What is even more debatable are the disaster risks associated with climate change because the projected impacts are based on simulations. While both natural and anthropogenic activities are critical in climate forcing, there is a general scientific consensus that anthropogenic activities are key to fuelling rapid global temperature increase. Global warming is resulting in an increase in the frequency and severity of climatic extremes, which increases the frequency of weather-related disasters. There is a general paucity of climate change information in Zimbabwe. To the majority, knowledge of climate change is low but shifts in seasonal rainfall patterns have been acknowledged.

The need for building, supporting and strengthening communities' livelihoods so that they become more resilient during and after a hazard cannot be overemphasized. History is replete with various types of hazards, most of which turned into disasters on impact with the vulnerable communities. In such cases, mainstream and official prescriptions have focused on response and relief aid, without paying due regard to the need for reducing the vulnerability of affected communities by increasing their resilience through building their capacity. With the effects of climate change worsening globally, communities will be called to be even more responsive to these changes, as they affect them in newer and unique ways. Therefore extraordinary measures will have to be taken to enhance adaptation measures. It is against this background that a desk study was undertaken to identify gaps in climate change adaptation. This paper outlines changing risk profile caused by the changing climate. It also explores critical constraints to climate change disaster risk reduction. Consequently, an overarching strategy for climate change disaster risk reduction in Zimbabwe is proposed.

## METHODS

The present study sought to outline changing risk profiles for the communities due to climate change and to identify critical constraints to adaptation in Zimbabwe. Essentially, literature review was done to identify gaps in climate change adaptation. This enabled the development of appropriate recommendations.

## RESULTS

### Food Security

According to Chigwada, (2005), Zimbabwe is vulnerable to climate change principally through shifting rainfall patterns and extreme events. This is particularly true given that the country is essentially agro-based. Social, economic and political processes affecting human settlements, agricultural patterns and natural resources such as water, vegetation and forestry, are likely to exacerbate climate impacts. Drought already affects water supplies, agriculture and access to food which impact negatively on basic health and survival. Mano and Nhemachena, (2007) examined some simple climate scenarios to see how agricultural production in Zimbabwe would respond to climate change. These showed that:

1. A 2.5°C increase in temperature would result in a decrease in net farm revenues by US$0.4 billion for all farms and increase net revenue from farms with irrigation by US$0.3 billion.
2. A 5°C increase in temperature would result in a decrease in net revenues across all farms, dryland farms and farms with irrigation by US$0.4 billion, US$0.5 billion and US$0.003 billion respectively.
3. A 7% and a 14% decrease in precipitation would result in a decrease in net farm revenue by US$0.3 billion for all farms.

As temperatures continue to rise, however, the net effect on African farms becomes steadily more harmful. Where water is available, moving from dryland to irrigated agriculture would increase not only average net revenue per hectare but also the resilience of agriculture to climate change (Kurukulasuriya *et. al.*, 2006). Unfortunately in Zimbabwe there is not much irrigation infrastructure so our revenue trend from agriculture will be negative as shown in figure 2.1 below:

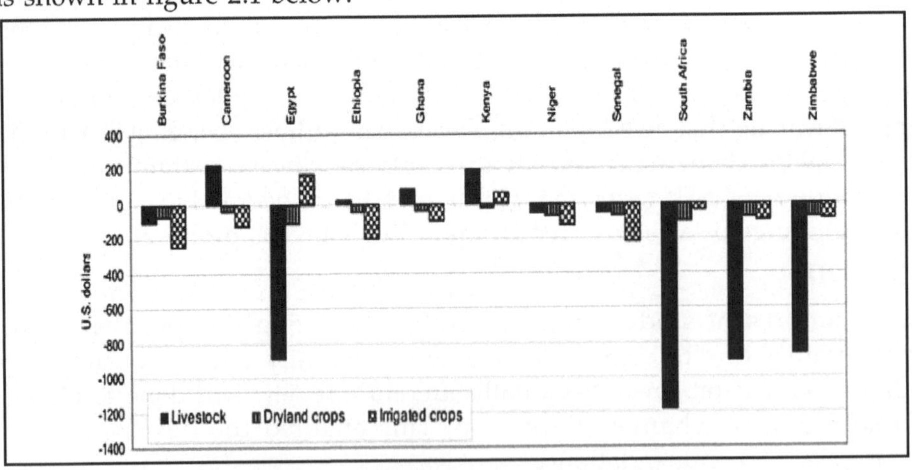


*Fig. 2.1:* **Projected Revenues from Farms in Africa**

***Source:*** **www.zimfarmer.org/environment/temperature-trends accessed 10/06/2011**

Matarira, Makadho and Mwamuka (2004) used the Global Climate Change Models (GCMs) and the PS123 crop growth model to assess the potential effects of climate change on maize production in Zimbabwe. Results showed that this crop is increasingly coming under stress due to high temperature and low rainfall conditions. Projected climate change causes simulated maize yields to decrease dramatically under dryland conditions in some regions. The reduction in modelled maize yields are primarily attributed to temperature increases that shorten the crop growth period, particularly the grain-filling period, causing dramatic negative effects on yields. Eriksen, O'Brien, and Rosentrater, (2008) further note that for Eastern and Southern Africa net productivity reductions of more than 10% for maize and other major crops such as sorghum, millet, sugar cane, and wheat would be experienced. Therefore, the above empirical cases show that climate change has indeed amplified disaster risks related to food security in the country. This will be exacerbated by a malfunction agricultural system due to poor governance and policy failures such as the fast track land reform programme.

Related to the foregoing, Cooper *et al.*, (1979) in Thompson, (1989) argue that for every 1% temperature rise there would be a yield increase of 6% in primary production efficiency. However Warnock (1988) in Thompson, (1989) notes that in the mid latitude cereal regions where an average warming of 2% may reduce potential yields by 3-17% does not recognize this. In addition it has been estimated that every 10ppm increase in carbon dioxide levels would enhance plant growth by between 0,5 and 2%. However the food quality of some plants would be reduced with carbon dioxide concentration (Thompson 1989). For example the leaves of soya beans will become richer in carbon components and deficient in nitrogen, which means insects, will destroy more foliage since they would be forced to eat more leaves in order to obtain enough nitrogen. Hence, Zimbabwe needs to brace for such new challenges.

## WATER SUPPLY

Levina, (2006) observed that for Zimbabwe drought is expected be the biggest problem facing Zimbabwe. Recent projections of precipitation and runoff in Africa suggest a drop of up to 10% in precipitation in most of southern Africa (including Zimbabwe) by 2050. Since some 80% of Zimbabwe's 13 million inhabitants are farmers, with 30% of them being city-dwellers but also engaged in agro-industry, the economic damage and human suffering associated with droughts are enormous. Also, 80% of Zimbabwe's electricity supply comes from the Lake Kariba dam, making not only agriculture but also electricity supply reliant on sufficient water. According to Zimbabwe's Initial National Communications under the United Nations Framework Convention on Climate Change (1998), likely impacts in Zimbabwe caused by present trends in climate change include: an increased water demand for irrigation due to increased evapotranspiration and a decrease by approximately 30–40 per cent in water yield per dam. The same source alleges that a doubling of carbon dioxide would cause the rivers in the Eastern Highlands of Zimbabwe that are today well watered and perennial to develop flow regimes similar to those currently experienced in the dry regions i.e seasonal rivers. Obviously, this would have serious repercussions on local industry. Eriksen, O'Brien, and Rosentrater, (2008) also observe that reduced runoff overall will exacerbate current water stress, reduce the quality and quantity of water available for domestic and industrial use, and limit hydropower production. The flight of industry from the city of Bulawayo could also be linked to water shortage also triggered by climate change. Water scarcity may also have international consequences and become a source of conflict particularly on shared water courses as the Zambezi case illustrate. Already the Matabeleland Zambezi Water Project (MZWP) which is an ambitious inter-basin transfer project has ruffled feathers among riparian countries.

According to the Zimbabwe Ministry of Mines, Environment and Tourism, (1998), the major form of water conservation in Zimbabwe is through the construction of dams. All urban centres and large-scale irrigation schemes depend on dams for water supply. The impact of climate change on future water supply from dams is a major indicator of the vulnerability of Zimbabwe to climate change. The amount of water that can be supplied by these dams with a reliability of 96% was estimated for the baseline and doubling of carbon dioxide scenarios. The costs of constructing reservoirs with such storage capacities were estimated using then the current construction costs of about Z$500 per 1 000 cubic metres of water stored. The analysis further shows that the yield of dams will decrease by about 30%-40%. If the same level of supply and reliability is desired, then there will be a need to either increase the storage of these dams or construct new ones. Increase in storage is not possible since all major dams are designed for their maximum yield.

## INCIDENCE OF EXTREME WEATHER EVENTS

UNDP, (2004) noted that climate change brings with it long-term shifts in mean weather conditions and the possibility of the increasing frequency and severity of extreme weather events. The coming warmer era would lead to the atmosphere becoming increasingly unstable with greater frequency of weather disasters and extreme events. Extreme weather events like the heat waves and droughts would become prevalent, for example, Thompson (1989) notes that there has been an increase in heat waves and droughts in the United States America from twice in six years in 1980s to four in 1990s. In addition, severe cold winters and more destructive tropical cyclones are expected to become the order of the day. The recurrence of droughts in Southern Africa and indeed Zimbabwe also points to the disastrous consequences of the warmer era. Eriksen, O'Brien, and Rosentrater, (2008) also corroborate the above view as they observe that intense rainfall events will increase the incidence of flooding in many areas. It has also been observed that global warming is resulting in an increase in the frequency and severity of climatic extremes, which increases the frequency of weather-related disasters. Climate change is likely to hit the poor hardest and is also likely to increase the displacement of people as a result of flooding or drought.

## EXTINCTION OF FAUNA AND FLORA

Burroughs, (2001) observed that the impacts of a warmer era would be mass extinction of many annual and plant species as they fail to adjust to environmental changes. The extinction of dinosaurs during the pre Cambrian era is testimony to possibilities of extinction. In addition this climate change disaster risk is further amplified by human activities of ecosystems modifications as a keystone species. Myers, (2003) identified anthropogenic activities as key to the on going Holocene extinction. The proportion of total land area covered by forest has been falling significantly, estimated to be 330 000 hectares per year (Ministry of Environment and Natural Resources Management, 2010). The same Ministry has identified the following medicinal plants as threatened among others; *Fluggea virosa, Dicoma anomala, Rhus dentate, Pterocarpus angolensis,* For Zimbabwe the extinction risk is further compounded by the on going plundering of natural resources as a result of the fast track land reform programme. However, it should be noted that some fauna and flora could manage to adapt as available evidence suggests that many life forms evolved in conditions, which were very different to those in which their descendants are now living. Nevertheless, it can be argued that life forms managed to adapt over time because these extinction events were essentially driven by geophysical forces rather than human activities. Hence, the extinction disaster risk is critical since regeneration has been rendered redundant owing to anthropogenic activities.

## SEA LEVEL RISES

Increased warming may result in sea level rises. A recent United Nations Environment Programme (UNEP) meeting in Yugoslavia predicted that the level of the Mediterranean Sea will rise by 13-55 cm before the year 2030 and by up to 2 m with in a century (Thompson, 1989). Such sea level would lead to the submersion of coastal areas. The countries like the Netherlands, which is below sea level, may be submerged. This could create ecological refugees and loss of property and life. While this may seem remote for Zimbabwe, stream hydrology may be adversely affected in terms of deposition and reversal of stream flow.

## GEOLOGICAL IMPACTS

The warmer era could also have disastrous geological impacts. Burroughs, (2001) notes that climate events like the waxing and waning of ice sheets, the desiccation of continental interiors or the drying up of oceans had major impacts on the geology of large parts of the earth. In addition climate change helps to release stresses in the earth's crust, for example, during the last ice age the eruption of volcanoes in the Mediterranean region appear to have occurred more often at times of rapid sea level changes. This changes the loading of the earth's crust by the build up and collapses of ice. Closer home, recurrent earth tremors in Zimbabwe towards the end of the 1990s decade were linked to changes in the weight of water at Lake Kariba which can also be linked to the effects of climate.

## AILMENTS AND DISEASES

Burroughs, (2001) also observes that the coming warmer era could lead to the spread of tropical diseases and the vectors to higher latitudes. Ebi *et al.*, (2005) used a range of future climate scenarios and found that climate suitability for malaria transmission in Zimbabwe is more likely to increase than decrease in the central plateau where the population is currently concentrated. They suggested that most of Zimbabwe could have near complete climate suitability for stable malaria transmission by 2050 under the scenario showing the greatest change (4.5 °C warming). Among all scenarios, the highlands become more suitable for transmission. Eriksen, O'Brien, and Rosentrater, (2008) also note that others argue, however, that malaria risk must be interpreted on the basis of local environmental and socioeconomic development, where land use decisions and the ineffectiveness of malaria control programmes may in fact be driving risk. Increased ultraviolet radiation in the atmosphere will cause eye ailments and will also interfere with fish farming. It may also cause abnormal development of larvae and killing of phytoplankton that is the primary source of the aquatic ecosystem. The United States Environmental Protection Agency predicts that each 2,5 % increase in CFCs, will cause one million additional skin cancers.. In addition incidences of epidemic diseases are also linked to climatic factors.

## VEGETATION PATTERNS

The warmer era could lead to the shifting of climate and vegetation belts. This means that desertification would become pronounced in some parts of the world. Hence, much of Zimbabwe could become a desert. Encroachment of the invasive desert plants such as *Opuntia fulgida* (E) in south western Zimbabwe is suggestive of this. This has serious implications for livelihoods for communities whose livelihoods are anchored around vegetation. At the same time some areas may become wet and have equatorial or temperate climate and vegetation type.

## CLIMATE CHANGE ADAPTATION: CRITICAL CONSTRAINTS

### Bottle Necks to Livelihood Diversification

Climate change disaster risk is increasingly becoming more real. Studies by JIMAT Development Consultants, (2008) in Chiredzi confirmed that communities appreciated that climate has changed (81% of respondents interviewed). As such adaptations mechanisms are being shaped. Chigwada, (2005) notes that communities have considerable experience in adapting to climate variability and deploy sophisticated livelihood diversification strategies if obstacles (lack of legal status, bank accounts) are removed and additional resources provided. As such adaptation could be achieved if bottlenecks related to bank accounts requirement and credit worthiness are removed. If such bottlenecks are removed, communities would be able to access credit to enable them to diversify livelihoods. It should, however, be noted that for Zimbabwe livelihood diversification is hindered by poor economic performance. Owing to a low income per capita people are general living from hand to mouth and as such the majority have no disposable income to venture into income generating activities. In addition owing to the decade long crisis to 2009, the banking sector which could have assisted in funding livelihood diversification had collapsed.

## INEFFECTIVE DEVOLUTION OF POWER

Regional and national policy makers have realised that by decentralizing authority to the local–traditional leaders, the natural resources of the country will be better protected than if determined externally on the basis of someone else's priorities. The Traditional Leaders Act of Zimbabwe is instructive. With respect to decentralization of authority, Mupedziswa, (2001), notes that the discrepancy between rhetoric and action may occur as a result of deliberate action by technocrats who tend to suffer from 'the ivory tower syndrome'. This syndrome is characterized by the tendency to look down upon the grassroots people, coupled with a reluctance to view them as normal and rational beings. In this case some technocrats may also view themselves as very knowledgeable and hence no need to consult the local communities. At the same time development practitioners have also been accused of reluctance to real hand over stick to local level structures. Therefore, such as attitude tends to kill any motivation for participation at the grass roots level to curb adverse impacts of climate change.

## NATURE OF INTERVENTIONS

Chigwada, (2005) also submits that financial interventions, where possible, should go directly to communities who should form legal entities or through organisations with grassroots connections that practice bottom-up approaches. In addition all new infrastructure should be "climate proofed", i.e. designed to take into account potential climate change impacts which are unlikely to resemble past impacts. Climate proofing may mean ensuring building standards are set for the construction of dams, bridges and roads and guarantee infrastructural development. While these submissions are critical to climate change adaptation, the realities of the Zimbabwean context are that aid goes via a third part viz; an Non Governmental Organisation (NGO), Rural District Council (RDC) or a government department. Meanwhile, there are no efforts to change policy framework to allow aid to flow directly to the grassroots. With respect to climate proofing lack of requisite expertise and financial resources to build such structures as well as lack of political will have been the major constraints.

## GOVERNANCE

Governance is seen by UNDP, (2004) as the exercise of economic, political and administrative authority to manage a country's affairs at all levels. It comprises the mechanisms, processes and institutions through which citizens and groups articulate their interests, exercise their legal rights, meet their obligations and mediate their differences. The characteristics of good governance — participation, rule of law, transparency, responsiveness, consensus orientation, equity, effectiveness, efficiency, accountability and strategic vision — are key for sustainable development and disaster risk reduction. The case of Zimbabwe might be instructive. With a 75% crop loss in 1992, Zimbabwe was able to manage subsequent food crises thanks to good governance (UNDP, 2004). In 2002, after unseasonably heavy rain and a long dry spell, half of the population of 13 million needed food aid. Yet unlike 1992, reservoirs were full of water and there was plenty of grazing for cattle. The UNDP attributed this to a combination of governance issues, economic crisis, widespread poverty and the spread of HIV/AIDS added human elements to a natural disaster. This was exacerbated by the collapse of commercial farming, thanks to the fast track land reform. Hence, good governance is a critical pillar for developing climate change risk reduction strategies. It can be argued that, poor governance is the main constraint to developing robust strategies for climate change disaster risk reduction in Zimbabwe. For example a disaster management bill has been on the cards for may years yet one of the major challenges faced in disaster risk reduction is lack of a responsive legislative and policy framework. A good lesson can be drawn from the South African disaster management framework. As with other development issues, disaster risk policy is sometimes hampered because of disjointed and uncoordinated policy-making. This very often has its roots in a fragmented governance structure. So poor governance is one of the critical constraints to climate change adaptation.

## INADEQUATE ANTICIPATORY ADAPTIVE MEASURES

According to the Ministry of Mines, Environment and Tourism (1998), at the national level, adaptive measures are anticipatory. Through its policies on infrastructure development, research and development, education, water resources management and product pricing, the government can plan and implement anticipatory adaptive measures. However, implementation is weak, rendering these measures redundant.

## INFRASTRUCTURE DEVELOPMENT POLICY

Based on the above document, the government of Zimbabwe contends that it has an ongoing investment programme to construct medium to large dams throughout the country. Increases in dam capacities and numbers will enhance the availability of water in future. Construction of these dams allows policy makers to establish irrigation projects, which facilitate a shift from subsistence agriculture to a cash crop economy and higher rural incomes. Technology of irrigation has to improve as well in order to minimize water costs. It should be submitted that this is a good policy document but on the ground there is no meaningful progress with respect to dam impoundment as a climate change mitigation strategy. For example, for Matabeleland South province which is one of the most vulnerable region in terms of water scarcity no dam has been constructed for over a decade. The only meaningful dam impoundment programme in the province was done under the auspices of the Give-a- Dam (GAD) campaign during the 1990s. GAD was a consortium of NGOs to construct dams in Matabeleland South province to alleviate the effects of drought (Matabeleland South Province Provincial Development Committee, 2006). The initiative has however, since died down. Hence, the projected benefits of dam construction enshrined in the infrastructure development policy of the government will remain a mirage in the interim making communities more vulnerable to climate change. In addition, efforts have not been done to quantify ground water in the country which could play a critical role in the adaptation to climate change. Governments of the poorest countries have often found that their relations with international finance institutions have discouraged rather than facilitated action to reduce risk from disasters and Zimbabwe is not an exception.

## RESEARCH AND DEVELOPMENT

The Government also contends that its policy and support for research and development considerably influences the agricultural production sector. Strategic research planning and a well directed research programme are needed to study crops, and livestock that are more droughts tolerant and disease resistant. Sustained research on short-season, high-yield crop varieties and livestock breeds is of paramount importance to adaptation. While this is an important vision, lack of requisite financial and technical resources have played together to hinder government from realizing the enunciated benefits of research development to adapt to climate change.

## INADEQUATE EXPOSURE TO AND INFORMATION ON CLIMATE CHANGE DISASTER ISSUES

There is a general paucity of information relating to climate change impacts in the country. This may stem from the fact that there has been little research on climate change in the country. Where research has been done, the distribution and communication of research findings has not been effective. More so, Philip, (2004) note that because disasters are often seen as an exclusively humanitarian concern, development professionals are rarely exposed to disaster risk reduction issues. Consequently information on climate change is unknown and not well disseminated so as to conscientise ordinary people of the adverse impacts of climate change. As such the majority of the grass roots remain unaware and vulnerable to climate change.

## INADEQUATE CLIMATE CHANGE ADAPTATION IN THE AGRICULTURAL SECTOR

Zimbabwe has gone steps in climate adaptation (Eriksen, O'Brien, and Rosentrater, (2008); IFPRI,(2008); Levina, (2006); JIMAT Development Consultants, (2008); Chigwada, (2005). While farmers are already deploying various adaption mechanism such as dry and early planting, rowing drought resistant crops, changing planting dates, and using irrigation (Mano, and Nhemachena, (2007), they often lack robust support mechanisms to fully realize their potential towards their endeavours. This leaves them still vulnerable to the vagaries of climate change and hence ill equipped to fairly and squarely tackle the challenges of climate change. While NGOs are doing a sterling job in terms of agricultural support, their efforts are just but a drop in the ocean given the overwhelming need in the country. In addition, their financial pipeline is susceptible to frequent breaking since they are dependent on donors. This ultimately has serious ramifications on projects as they may end prematurely. NGO activities are not sustainable and may not improve the position of farmers in the long run.

It is also poignant to note that the country seems to concentrate on mitigating agricultural impacts. While this is understandable because our economy is agro-based, it would have been more prudent to also tackle other equally projected impacts such as ailments and diseases, extinctions, water supply, ozone depletion, and geological impacts. While remarkable milestones could have been achieved in the agricultural sector, the broad based impacts of climate change have undoubtedly received little attention. Therefore, a broad based effort is required to address biodiversity loss, ozone layer depletion, shifts in vegetation patterns, health and geological impacts. Although, an ozone and climate change offices are there within the ministry of Environment, these are dependent on donor funds and hence they suffer from weaknesses highlighted above. There are also highly centralised at headquarters with a very thin staff complement resulting in critical constraints in the execution of their mandates.

## DISASTER PREPAREDNESS FRAMEWORK

From a national disaster preparedness perspective, the country has not yet developed robust capacity to assess vulnerability to all projected impacts of climate change as well as plan for climate change disaster. There is also a dearth of information systems to enable early warning and communication of climate change disaster related information to enable for requisite response. Public education and training in climate change is also weak . For example, climate change is not embedded in school curricular except for specialised courses at university level. The institutional framework is also very weak owing principally to inadequate enforcement of laws such as the Environmental Management Act. Therefore, a weak national disaster preparedness framework is at the core of increasing vulnerability to climate change risk.

## TOWARDS CLIMATE CHANGE DISASTER RISK REDUCTION IN ZIMBABWE

Taken together, the effects of climate change increase uncertainty and the complexity of risk for everyone. Changing natural hazard risks related to climate change will alter disaster risk patterns. Climatic disturbances that change hazard profiles demand changes in coping strategy. Given projected disaster risks and critical constraints highlighted, it goes without saying that Zimbabwe is seating on a time bomb. However, a robust response could save the day. Undoubtedly, challenges of climate change might best be met by building on current disaster risk reduction capacity. Interventions must be geared towards improving current risk management and adaptation. In order to adapt to climate change, it will be prudent to undertake broad based changes relating to governance for risk management, mainstreaming disaster risk into development planning, integrated climate risk management, managing the multifaceted nature of risk and compensatory risk management.

## GOVERNANCE FOR RISK REDUCTION

Appropriate governance for disaster risk management is a fundamental requirement if risk considerations are to be factored into development planning, and if existing risks are to be successfully mitigated. Governance has three legs: economic, political and administrative (UNEP, 2004). Economic governance includes the decision-making process that affects a country's economic activities and its relationships with other economies. It clearly has major implications for equity, poverty and quality of life. Political governance is the process of decision making to formulate policies, including national disaster reduction policy and planning. Administrative governance is the system of policy implementation and requires the existence of well-functioning organisations at the central and local levels. In the case of disaster risk reduction, it requires functioning enforcement of building codes, land-use planning, environmental risk and human vulnerability monitoring and safety standards. There is a need for robust institutional systems and administrative arrangements that link public, private and civil society sectors and build vertical ties between local, district, national and global scale actors. The country should strengthen the basic tenets of good governance in its conduct. These include participation, rule of law, transparency, responsiveness, consensus orientation, equity, effectiveness, efficiency, accountability and strategic vision. While legislation reform would be critical, enforcement and monitoring should be paramount in order to reduce risks related to climate change.

## MAINSTREAMING DISASTER RISK INTO DEVELOPMENT PLANNING

Development projects need to be regulated in terms of its impact on disaster risk. The Environmental Impact Assessment process is an attempt to mainstream disaster risk into development planning. Admittedly, Zimbabwe has adopted environmental impact assessment (EIA) strategy as key to managing risk, but enforcement and monitoring are weak with a consequent that prescribed development projects are implemented without going through the EIA process. This exacerbate climate change disaster risks as well. Therefore, government needs to strengthen enforcement and monitoring to improve project performance and also mitigate projected adverse impacts. It may also be instructive to make it mandatory for organisations involved in post disaster reconstruction to factor in disaster risk in planning relief and disaster recovery operations. However, even if enforcement is improved, government would still grapple with geographical equity issues in mainstreaming disaster risk into development planning. This relates to attributing responsibility for disaster risk experienced in one location, but created by actions in another location. For example, pollution induced climate change which may not necessarily emanate from countries that bear the backlash such as ozone depletion.

## INTEGRATED CLIMATE RISK MANAGEMENT

UNDP, (2004) submit that building on capacities that deal with existing disaster risk is an effective way to generate capacity to deal with future climate change risk. Therefore, it would be critical that guiding principles be established for ensuring the mainstreaming of climate change concerns within ongoing human development practices. Hence, key sectors of economic planning such as agriculture, tourism, land-use planning, public health, environmental management and basic infrastructure provision, will all need to take climate change into consideration. Such an arrangement would undoubtedly improve climate change disaster preparedness in the country. Integrated climate risk management could provide a framework to allow the disaster community to move beyond the dominant focus on preparedness and response and stimulate a move beyond the design of hypothetical future adaptation strategies. Integrated climate risk management would need to include elements of anticipatory risk management (ensuring that future development reduces rather than increases risk), compensatory risk management (actions to mitigate the losses associated with existing risk) and reactive risk management (ensuring that risk is not reconstructed after disaster events).

## MANAGING THE MULTIFACETED NATURE OF RISK

It should be noted that climate change induced natural hazard is one among many potential threats to life and livelihood. Often, those people and communities most vulnerable to natural hazards are also vulnerable to other sources of hazard. Therefore, the overarching government strategy should be to identify all risk drivers with a view of managing them to reduce adverse impacts on communities.

## COMPENSATORY RISK MANAGEMENT

There is need to improve disaster preparedness and response given, a legacy of risk accumulation that exists today in the country. In addition an reorientation towards the long-term management of disaster risk within the broader context of sustainable development should be done. This would include tools aimed at reducing exposure to hazard events through preparedness planning and early warning systems; tools that spread losses through insurance mechanisms, including mechanisms developed for low-income groups and informal settlement dwellers; and tools to help people bear disaster impacts, including policies aimed at enhancing livelihood sustainability. Such interventions are needed over the medium-term to contribute towards the meeting of the Millennium Development Goals which will ultimately lead to better adaptation to climate change.

## CONCLUSION

Changing natural hazard risks related to climate change will alter disaster risk patterns. Adaptation to climate disaster risk requires an overarching comprehensive disaster risk reduction strategy. However, institutional capacity and lack of requisite resources are essentially hindering effective adaptation to climate change. Nevertheless, good governance in disaster risk reduction would underpin sustainable climate change disaster risk reduction.

## REFERENCES

Burroughs T.J., (2001): Climate Change: A Multidisciplinary Approach, Cambridge University Press, UK.

Chenje M., Sola L. and Palecnzy D. (1998): The State of Zimbabwe's Environment, Government of Zimbabwe, Ministry of Mines, Environment and Tourism.

Chigwada J., (2005): 'Climate Proofing Infrastructure and Diversifying Livelihoods in Zimbabwe' IDS bulletin Vol. 36, No. 4.

Ebi, K.L., Hartman, J., Chan, N., McConnell, K. J.,Schlesinger, M. and Weyant, J. (2005): Climate Suitability for Stable Malaria Transmission in Zimbabwe Under Different Climate Change Scenarios. Climatic Change, 73, 375-393.

Eriksen, S., O'Brien, K. and Rosentrater, L., 2008, 'Climate Change in Eastern and Southern Africa. Impacts, Vulnerability and Adaptation', Global Environmental Change and Human Security (GECHS), Oslo.

FPRI, (2008): Micro-Level Analysis of Farmers' Adaptation to Climate Change in Southern Africa.

Intergovernmental Panel on Climate Change (IPCC 2007): Working Group I: The Physical Science Basis.

JIMAT Development Consultants (2008): 'Coping with Drought and Climate Change Project: Baseline Study', Final Report to EMA and UNDP, Harare.

Kotze and Holloway (1996): Reducing Risk: Participatory Learning Activities for Disaster Mitigation in Southern Africa, OXFAM.

Kurukulasuriya, P., R. Mendelsohn, R. Hassan, J. Benhin, M. Diop, H. M. Eid, K.Y. Fosu, Gbetibouo G., Jain S., Mahamadou A., El-Marsafawy S., Ouda S., Ouedraogo M., Sène I., Seo N., Maddison D. and Dinar A., (2006): "Will African Agriculture Survive Climate Change?" World Bank Economic Review 20: 367-388.

Levina, E., 2006, 'Domestic Policy Frameworks for Adaptation to Climate Change in the Water Sector Part II: Non-Annex I Countries. Lessons Learned from Mexico, India, Argentina and Zimbabwe', OECD, Paris

Mano. R, and Nhemachena, C., (2007): 'Assessment of the Economic Impacts of Climate Change on Agriculture in Zimbabwe: A Ricardian Approach' CEEPA Discussion Paper 11.

Matabeleland South Province Provincial Development Committee (PDC): Matabeleland South Province Disaster Preparedness Plan 2006) (unpublished).

Matarira C. H., Makadho J. M., Mwamuka (2004): Zimbabwe: Climate Change Impacts on Maize Production and Adaptive Measures for the Agricultural Sector, SIRDC, Harare.

Ministry of Mines, Environment and Tourism, (1998): 'Zimbabwe's Initial National Communication on Climate Change', prepared for the United Nations Framework Convention on Climate Change', Government of Zimbabwe, Harare.

Ministry of Environment and Tourism, (2010): Zimbabwe's Fourth National Report To the Convention on Biological Diversity, GoZ.

Mupedziswa R (2001): Land and Natural Resources Management in Southern Africa: A Review of Constraints to Civil Society Participation in Policy Formulation in Gaidzano ed. (2001): Policy Making in Zimbabwe in SAPES, Harare.

Pickering K. and Owen L. (1994): An Introduction to Global Environmental Issues, Routledge, London, United Kingdom.

Philip W. (2004): Disaster Risk Reduction: A Development Concern: A Scoping Study on Links Between Disaster Risk Reduction, Poverty and Development, Overseas Development Institute.

Thompson D.R. (1989): Short Term Climate Change: Evidence, Causes, Environmental Consequences and Strategies for Action in 'Progress in Physical Geography Vol. 13, No. 3.

UNDP (2004): Reducing Disaster Risk: A Challenge for Development: A Global, UNDP, New York.

Pages: 39-50

CLIMATE CHANGE, DISASTER MANAGEMENT AND ENVIRONMENT
*Edited by:* Dr. Alka Chauhan; Dr. Pawan Kumar 'Bharti'
ISBN: 978-93-5056-784-5
*Edition:* 2016
*Published by:* Discovery Publishing House Pvt. Ltd., New Delhi (India)

# CHAPTER – 3

# Climate Change and Brahmaputra Valley of North East India; Looking Through the Fisheries Perspective

Bhaskar J. Saud

***ABSTRACT***

Climate change stresses will have complex pressure on fisheries resources and threatened the fish production in Brahmaputra valley of Northeast India. This is visible in the form of temperature increase, enhanced anomalies in the rainfall pattern and frequency and severity of extreme events in the last decades. Consequently, changes in habitat temperatures significantly influence on fish metabolism, and hence growth rate, total production, reproduction seasonality and possibly reproductive efficacy, and susceptibility to diseases and toxins. It has been observed that the captures of the Indian Major Carps (*Catla catla, Labeo rohita, Cirhinus mrigala etc.*) from the Brahmaputra River has depleted down drastically in the last decade and is replenish by minor

Central Inland Fisheries Research Institute (CIFRI), Regional Centre, Guwahti HOUSEFED Complex, 4th Floor, Dispur Last Gate, Guwahati - 6, Assam, (India).

carps and economically low valued trace fishes. Climate change-induced temperature variations and extreme events will therefore have a much stronger impact on the spatial distribution of fishing and aquaculture activities and on their productivity and yields in this region of the country.

***Keywords:*** Climate change, Brahmaputra River, Fish and Fishery.

## INTRODUCTION

Climate change caused by global warming is one of the most intensely debated issue in today's world. The climate system is a very complex interactive system of the atmosphere, hydrosphere, biosphere, cryosphere, lithosphere and outer space. The change in climate will affect the whole ecosystems and human systems like agricultural, transportation, health and infrastructure severely. The report of Intergovernmental Panel on Climate Change (IPCC, 2007); an international body of over 3000 experts, projects that the global mean temperature may increase between 1.8°C to 4°C by 2100.

The recent global climate analysis has indicated that the climate change is likely to change stream flow volume and the distribution throughout the years over Asian region, imposing significant stress on the water resources in the region. The vulnerability of the Indian subcontinent to the impact of changing climate is of vital importance because the major impact of climate change in this continent would be on the hydrology, affecting water resources. The increased intensity of climate change in last 50 years is in accord with the significant effect on hydrology and water resources of entire India. The impacts of climate change in India are all apparent as the water supply in India is getting affected badly with Himalayan glaciers melting at the rate of 10-15 mts per year. The discharge in the Himalayan River generally consists of two parts, one which is resulting from melting of glaciers and another resulting from the monsoonal rainfall in catchment areas. And the substantial low rainfall, 40% below normal has triggered a significant consequence on riverine ecosystem.

However, a very little work has been carried out in India in particular to Assam on the impact of climate change on hydrobiolology. The major river systems of the North East Indian subcontinent, namely Brahmaputra (Plate - 3.1) is originate in the Himalayas, are expected to be vulnerable to climate change because of substantial contribution from snow and glaciers into this river system. Brahmaputra River basin is sturdily influenced by the melt of snow and ice in the upstream part due to global warming. As 60 percent of the basin area has an elevation of over 2000 m. Predictable rise in temperature will lead to increased glacial and snow melt, which could lead to increased summer flows in this river system for a few decades, followed by a reduction in flow as the glaciers disappear and snowfall diminishes

(Immerzeel, 2008). Immerzeel *et al.* (2010) stated that the Brahmaputra is most susceptible to reductions of flow, threatening the food security of an estimated 26 million people. This is particularly true for the dry season when water availability is crucial for the irrigation systems. Secondly, the Brahmaputra basin is highly influenced by extreme monsoon rainfall and flooding (Mirza, 2002; Warrick et al., 1996). This impact is very critical for Brahmaputra valley since more than 70 per cent of its population relying on Brahmaputra River for their livelihood (agriculture, fishery) directly or indirectly. The present chapter highlights the climate change and its impacts on the aquatic resources of Brahmaputra valley with a special emphasis on capture fishery.

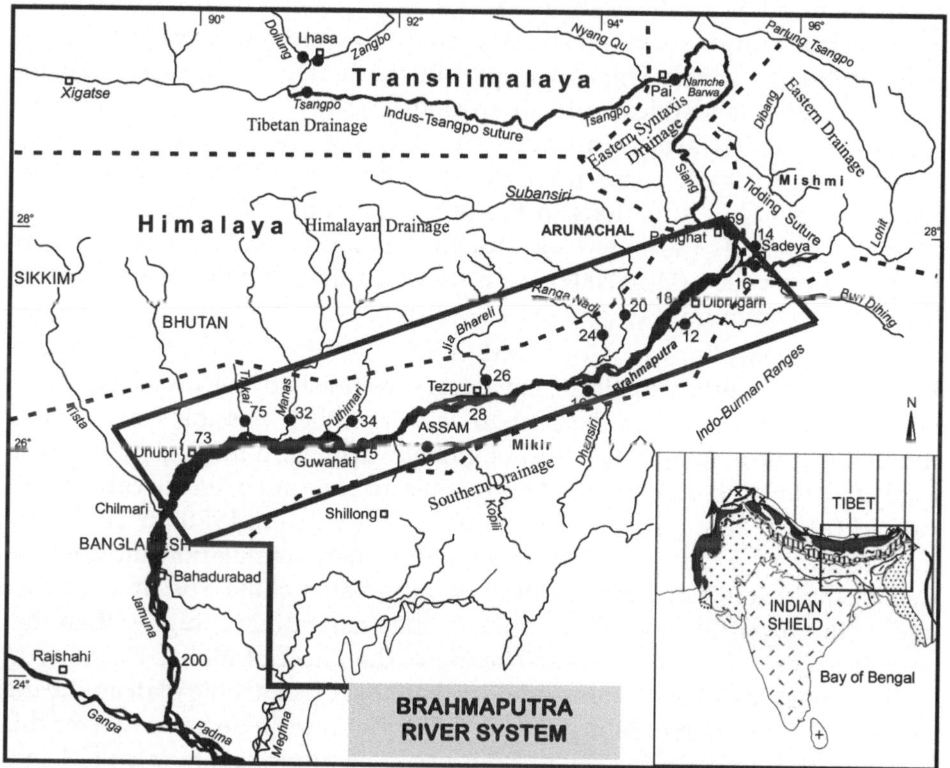


*Plate. 3.1:* **Map of Brahmaputra River System in the Brahmaputra Valley of Assam, India**

## EVIDENCE OF CLIMATE CHANGES IN BRAHMAPUTRA VALLEY

Climate change is considered as one of the major driving force causing changes in the nature of flooding and associated hazards in the Himalayan river basins. Of late significant changes have been observed in the hydro-climatic regime of the Brahmaputra valley resulting in changed nature of water induced hazards in the river basins like the siltation, erosion, flash flood etc.

Hundreds of villages with fertile agricultural land and important infrastructure have been lost to the rivers due to frequent shifting of the river courses and erosion of river banks. It has been observed that the monsoon precipitation is trendless and is mainly random in nature in the last decade while floods are now more intense and frequent in this part of the country.

The yearly mean rainfall showed considerable year to year fluctuation during the period of 1980 - 2010 showing ten peak and troughs (Fig. 3.2) in and around Guwahati city of Assam. The amount of rainfall experience by the region during this period ranged from 1314.8 mm in 2008 to 2250.2 mm in 1988 showing wide variation of 47.4 mm. No definite trends of variation were observed in the rainfall pattern in the region. Heavy spells of downpour occur more often, so do flash floods. Extreme precipitation events (heavy rain storm, cloud burst) may have their own impacts on the fragile geomorphology of this Himalayan part of the Brahmaputra valley causing more extensive landslides and soil erosion. Decadal departures in summer monsoon rainfall are found above and below the long-time average alternatively for three consecutive decades. (Mall *et al.*, 2006). On the other hand droughts like situations in the present decade (2001-02, 2005-06 and 2008-09) have also affected agricultural productivity considerably in Brahmaputra valley (Das, 2009). As a result all the agricultural practices of the riparian communities living in these areas have been significantly affected.

The researchers of Cold and Arid Regions Environmental and Engineering Research Institute have recently finished the investigation of climate change features in the past 26 years and their possible causes along the Brahmaputra Valley. The effect of global warming in the region had been analyzed through analyzing the changes of averaged temperature and precipitation along the Brahmaputra Valley from 1980 to 2005 and investigating the correlation between atmospheric circulation indices and their changes. It is found that the Brahmaputra Valley climate became warmer and wetter from 1980 to 2005, and the change magnitude is higher than that over the whole Tibetan Plateau. Therefore, the effect of global warming in the Brahmaputra Valley is more evident than that of the whole plateau during the period. The summer monsoon rainfall is found to be decreasing over this region significantly during the last century at an approximate rate of 11 mm per decade (Das 2004, Mirza *et al.*, 1998). The annual mean maximum temperatures in the region are rising at the rate of +0.11°C per decade. The annual mean temperatures are also increasing at a rate of 0.04°C per decade in the region (Das 2004, Saud, *et al.* 2012, 2014). Over the last 30 years (1980 2010) the annual mean maximum temperature showing an increase of 1°C in and around Guwahati. Similarly annual mean minimum temperature showing an increase in 0.7°C over the same period (Fig. 3.1).

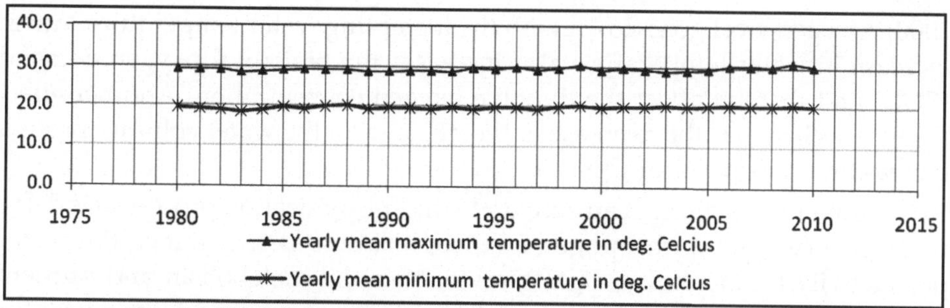


*Fig. 3.1:* **Time Series Change in the Yearly Mean Maximum and Minimum Temperature in and Arround Guwahati, Assam from 1980-2010**

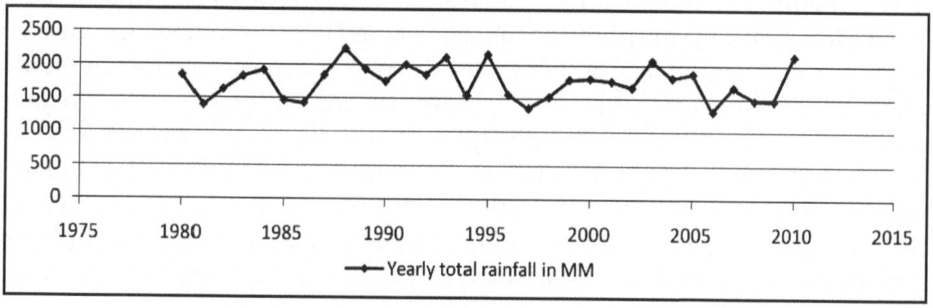


*Fig. 3.2:* **Time Series Change in the Yearly Total Yearly Rainfall in and Arround Guwahati, Assam from 1980-2010**

Our river and other natural water bodies hold a bounty of biological wealth in the form of highly nourishing protein rich fin and shell fish and other organisms for the human food basket and provide employment to a large number of people. The effects of climate change in mountain regions of the Brahmaputra basin coupled with siltation and shifting of river course may be indirect but significant in the scenario of the capture fishery dynamics of the Brahmaputra River system. The distribution and yield of fish stocks are observed to be affected owing to the processes such as habitat damage, disruption to precipitation, changes in river course etc. in the last three decades.

## IMPACTS OF CLIMATE CHANGE ON WATER CHEMISTRY

Climate change and extreme climatic events are likely to worsen the existing situation of Brahmaputra basin by further limiting water availability in the Brahmaputra during the dry season. Water temperature is one of the key influencing factors of most water chemistry parameters like dissolve oxygen, pH, nutrient concentration and toxicity of natural and anthropogenic pollutant. And dissolve oxygen concentration in a water body is perhaps the most critical aspect of water chemistry in the fisheries perspective. Oxygen solubility in water has an inverse relationship with water temperature (Kalff,

2000). Oxygen level goes down with the increasing water temperature. Again increase in water temperature also increases the biological oxygen demand (BOD) and thereby affect the dissolve oxygen concentration. Another effect of climate change is the decrease in the pH level of the water column through increasing atmospherical $CO_2$.

Temperature change can accelerate the eutrophication process and delay the recovery from anthropogenic eutrophication as it enhance the water productivity by increasing algal growth, bacterial metabolism and nutrient cycling rate (Klapper 1991). Increases in temperature may increase eutrophic conditions by stimulating explosive macrophyte growth. A biomass amplify of this magnitude would affect the system in various ways. First, because macrophytes take up the phosphorus sequestered in the sediment, the amount of phosphorus immediately available for other primary producers would decline. However, when the macrophytes die and decompose, they release nutrients such as nitrogen and phosphorus into the water column (Cooper 1996; Kankaala et al. 2002). This influx of nutrients can stimulate algal blooms and aid high macrophyte production. Additionally, the increased oxygen demand during the bacterial and fungal decomposition of these macrophytes increases the amplitude of the dial oxygen cycle. This can lead to depressed levels of DO in the system.

## IMPACTS OF CLIMATE CHANGE ON FISH PHYSIOLOGY

Fresh water fishes are poikilothermic or cold blooded aquatic vertebrates which can not regulate their internal body temperature through physiological means ( Moyle and Cech, 2004) and whose body temperature are identical or close to the environmental temperature at their specific location. All aspects of an individual fish's physiology include growth, reproduction and foraging activities are directly influence by changes in temperature. The ambient water temperature can alter the physical habitat availability to a species, primarily through thermal stratification and heterogeneity within a system.

Increase in temperature causes increase in metabolic rate, and a subsequent increase in the amount of energy needed. Food intake increases exponentially with temperature for fishes both in natural and laboratory conditions (Brett 1971; Elliot 1975a; Speczia'r 2002). Common carp cultured at 35.8 °C developed a vitamin C deficiency and grew more slowly than those cultured at 25.8°C when both experimental groups received the same rations (Hwang and Lin 2002).

Reproductive success of adults and recruitment of juveniles are also be affected by changing thermal regimes. Juvenile fishes often occupy different thermal niches than adults of the same species; higher temperatures encouraged faster growth in juvenile and decreased rate of mortality (Craig and Kipling 1983). However, these faster-growing had cohorts' lower reproductive potential than slow-growing ones (Craig and Kipling 1983).

Saud *et al.* (2012) mentioned that the advancement of breeding season of Indian Major Carp (IMC) i.e. *Catla catla, Labeo rohita* and *Cirrhinus mrigala* by almost one month due to raise in the mean temperature from the Assam region of Northeast India as compared to the previous decade.

## IMPACTS OF CLIMATE CHANGE ON AQUATIC FOOD CHAIN

Climate change impacts on inland aquatic ecosystems will range from the direct effects of the rise in temperature and $CO_2$ concentration to indirect effects through alterations in the food chain of the native ecosystem. The species composition will undoubtedly change, particularly those depending on cold water or torrential river water, are likely to decline. Major changes will be likely to occur in the species composition, seasonality and production of planktonic communities and their food web interactions resulting in changes in higher trophic niches. The seasonal migration patterns and routes of many migratory fish species will need to have change and some may be threatened with extinction (Hilsa fishery).

Higher temperatures will negatively affect micro-organisms and benthic invertebrates and the distribution of many species of fish. Species extinctions are expected when warm summer temperatures and anoxia (oxygen depletion) eliminate deep cold-water refuges. Due to changing climate alien species would expand into regions in which they previously could not survive and reproduce (Walther *et al.*, 2009). The present establishment of exotic species like grass carp, silver carp and common carps in the natural water bodies of the region proves the alteration in the nature eco-habitat. There may also be local movements within drainages where fish from lower elevations are able to move upstream which were previously too cold for them. These fish would compete for food and space in their new ecosystems, possibly at the expense of native species that share similar thermal requirements or in some cases have lower thermal tolerances (Carveth *et al.* 2006).

## IMPACT OF CLIMATE CHANGE ON THE PARASITE TRANSMISSION ON AQUATIC ORGANISM

As a result of the warming of water column, the number of bacteria living in high temperature and their disease causing capacities will increase more. For this reason, regional temperature increase poses danger for fishes from bacterial infection.

The toxicity of common pollutants (e.g., organophosphates and heavy metals) to fish generally increases at higher temperatures (Murty 1986b). These increases in toxicity may result from the increased production of bioactivated free radicals that are more toxic than the parent compound (Nemcsók *et al.* 1987) or from the increased uptake of the original toxin (Murty 1986a). The temperature-dependent accumulation of toxicants has large economic implications. For example, accumulation of endogenously produced ammonia and its metabolites is a serious issue in aquaculture systems. A combination of high temperature, low dissolved oxygen concentration, and sublethal ammonia concentrations have been shown to cause gill necrosis in common carp (Jeney and Nemcso´k 1992). Increased uptake of exogenous toxicants and the synergy existing between high temperatures, poor environmental conditions, and the presence of ammonia suggest that an increase in global temperatures has the potential to lower productivity in wild fish populations and in intensive aquaculture systems worldwide.

Parasite transmission depends on host condition, the presence of intermediate hosts water quality and temperature. Hence climate change may alter host-parasite dynamics by changing transmission opportunities and host susceptibility (Marcogliese 2001). Changing global temperatures will also affect fish vulnerability to disease because the immune function of fish is compromised in the presence of stressors and high temperatures, osmotic stress etc. For example, rates of bacterial disease such as furunculosis in aquaculture systems often peak at high temperature (Hefer and Pruginin 1981; Wedemeyer 1996). The observed thermal effects on parasites, fishes, and water quality suggest that global warming may well increase the virulence of certain fish pathogens and the transmission of some parasites (Wakabayashi 1991; Watson *et al*. 1998; Decostere *et al*. 1999; Cairns *et al*. 2005). Parasitism and disease outbreaks can cause increased mortality, slower growth rates, and lower marketability in fishes (Hefer and Pruginin 1981).

## IMPACTS OF CLIMATE CHANGE ON FISHERY SECTOR OF THE REGION

The Brahmaputra valley is endowed with rich and diversified inland water resources in the form of river, tributaries, hill- streams, flood-plain wetlands, swamp and man made reservoir, pond and tanks which harbor about 216 species of ichthyofauna with large numbers of endemic and ornamental species. The changed eco-climatic condition affect the pristine feeding and breeding ground of the native fish species, their population and composition structure, maturity condition, spawning etc. In the meantime, fishers are already being affected by changes that are ultimately driven by rising global atmospheric temperatures. For example, coastal fishers in Bangladesh face increased frequency and severity of hurricanes, coupled with the greater penetration of saline water into coastal land due to thermal expansion of the warming oceans (Unnikrishnan *et al*. 2006).

Climate change in the Brahmaputra valley leading to high erosion of the river bank and heavy siltation has led to habitat shrinkage of aquatic fauna in the river and the adjoining wetlands thus capture fisheries statistics has shown a sharp decline and wiped out of some commercially prized fish species from the region in the near future. It has been observed that the captures of the IMC s from the upper reaches of the Brahmaputra River has depleted down drastically in the last decade (Boruah and Biswas, 2002a & b) and are now available in the lower basin of the river only. Debnath et al (2015) mentioned the landing of IMCs decline from 13.68% in 1975 to only 3.85% in 2010. Minor carps catch become a major contribution ( about 50%) of total fish landings of Uzanbazar fish landing centre of River Brahmaputra showing a catch statitics of 52.926 kg in 2010 compared to 11.234 kg in 1975 (Debnath et al. 2015)While once abundant Mojor carps of the Brahmaputra basin is replenish by minor carps and economically low valued trace fishes.

IPCC third assessment report identify an average increase in global temperature of 0.4~0.8 °C in past century. Over the same period preliminary results show this temperature increase to be between 0.7~0.8 °C in regions like the Northeast India. The average rainfall has decreased and monsoon is also delayed; consequently, the climate change impact is being felt on the temperature of the inland water bodies and on the breeding behavior of fishes. It is well known that temperature is an important factor which strongly influence the reproductive cycle in fishes. Temperature, along with rainfall and photoperiod, stimulate the endocrine glands of fishes which help in the maturation of the gonads. In India, the inland aquaculture is centered on the Indian major carps, *Catla catla, Labeo rohita and Cirrhinus mrigala* and their spawning occurs during the monsoon (June-July) and extend till September. In recent years the phenomenon of IMC maturing and spawning as early as March is observed from this agro climatic condition of Brahmaputra valley, making it possible to breed them till the end of August of a year. Thus, there is an extended breeding activity as compared to a couple of decades ago (Saud *et al*, 2012; Dey *et al.*, 2007), which appears to be a positive impact of the climate change regime with a suspicion of its effect on the native ecosystem complex.

Warmer water leads eggs to hatch earlier in the year, so the young are smaller and more vulnerable to predators. Warmer conditions increase fish metabolism, taking energy away from growth and forcing the fish to find more food, but earlier hatching of eggs could put them out of sync with the food they eat, thus effecting the total production of fishery resources from the region.

## CONCLUSION

Climate change impacts on inland aquatic ecosystems will be caused by the direct effects of rising temperatures and rising $CO_2$ concentrations to indirect effects caused by changes in the regional or global precipitation and the melting of glaciers and ice cover. Water temperature comes to first in the list of most determinant factors of aquatic ecosystem since it is essential for the reproduction of fish species and the formation of an perfect living environment. In the stages of larva and juvenile, fish are quite susceptive to changes in the water temperature. The upstream movement of migratory fishes, particularly species bound to small streams and springs, which can not move further upstream, are greatly effected by climate change. Most fish of small rivers, especially those cold-adapted will be particularly affected by rising temperatures. The impacts of global climate change on the physical and chemical characteristics that determine the available niche for a fish species will likely prove to be the driving factors in determining the well-being and composition of fish communities.

It is difficult to estimate or predict the broader or aggregated effects of climate change at national and regional scales. Ecosystems that support fisheries, particularly wetlands and river basins, often lie downstream of other human activities (including forestry, agriculture, industrial etc.). Little attention has been given to the consequences of changing fisheries ecosystems on people, particularly so for the thousands of small-scale fisher folk of the region who are among the most vulnerable to climate change. Because the impacts could affect their food security and levels of poverty by elevating stress on fisheries production.

The detailed effects of climate change and direction of change on the physical and biological processes that affect individual fisheries are uncertain. Again variability in fisheries can lead to increased pressure on terrestrial ecosystems and biodiversity. Currently, the magnitude of global climate change is such that most of its effects on freshwater fisheries could be easily masked by or attributed to other anthropogenic influences, such as deforestation, overexploitation and land use change.

Since we do not have the chance to reverse the global warming and climate change phenomena, the only thing that needs to be done is to minimize the foreseen harms in the future. To this end, the native community needs to understand the global warming problem and have to adapt eco-friendly indigenous mitigation measure to combat with climate change in the region.

## REFERENCES

Boruah, S., and Biswas, S.P. (2002a): Ecohydrology and Fisheries of the Upper Brahmaputra Basin. *The Environmentalist*, 22(2): 119-131

Boruah, S., and Biswas, S.P. (2002b): Application of Ecohydrology in the Brahmaputra River. *Ecohydrology & Hydrobiology*, 2(1-4): 79-87.

B.J. Saud, M. Chetia, S. Borah, B.R. Chetia (2014): Climate Change Consequences and Possible Impacts in the Fish and Fisheries of Brahmaputra valley. *Aqua International*, 51-54.

Brett, J.R. (1971): Energetic Responses of Salmon to Temperature. A Study of Some Thermal Relations in the Physiology and Freshwater Ecology of Sockeye Salmon (Oncorhynchus nerka). *Am Zool.* 11: 99-113.

Cairns, M.A; Ebersole, J.L.; Baker, J.L.; Wigington, P.J.; Lavigne, H.R, Davis, S. M (2005): Influence of Summer Stream Temperatures on Black Spot Infestation of Juvenile Coho Salmon in the Oregon Coast Range. *Trans Am Fisher Soc.* 134: 1471-1479.

Carveth, C.J.; Widmer, A. M.; Bonar, S.A. (2006): Comparison of Upper Thermal Tolerances of Native and Nonnative Fish Species in Arizona. *Trans Am Fisher Soc.* 135: 1433-1440.

Cooper, S.D. (1996): Rivers and Streams. In: McClanahan RR, Young TP (eds) East African Ecosystems and Their Conservation. Oxford University Press, New York, pp. 133-170.

Craig, J.F.; Kipling, C. (1983): Reproduction Effort Versus the Environment; Case Histories of Windermere Perch, Perca Fluviatilis L., and Pike Esox lucius L.J Fish Biol 22: 713-727.

Das, P.J., (2009): Water and Climate Induced Vulnerability in Northeast India: Concerns for Environmental Security. WATCH Research Report 1. AARANYAK. Guwahati, Asssam, India. www.aaranayak.org (accessed October 25, 2009).

Das, P.J., (2004): Rainfall Regime of Northeast India: A Hydrometeorological Study with Special Emphasis on the Brahmaputra Basin. Unpublished Ph.D. Thesis. Gauhati University (Accessed October 25, 2009).

D. Debnath, B.J. Saud, B.K. Bhattacharjya, S. Yengkokpam, A.K. Yadav (2015): Percieved and Probable Impact of Climate Change on Fisheries Ecology of River Brahmaputra in Assam, India. *Fishing Chimes.* Vol. 34(12), 48-51.

Dey, S., Srivastava, P.K., Maji, S., Das, M. K., Mukhopadhyay, M.K., & Saha, P. K. (2007): Impact of Climate Change on the Breeding of Indian Major Carps in West Bengal. *J. Inland Fish. Soc. India*, 39, 1, 26-34.

Decostere, A.; Haesebrouck, F.; Turnbull, J. F.; Charleir, G. (1999): Influence of Water Quality and Temperature on Adhesion of High and Low Virulence Flavobacterium Columnare Strains to Isolated Gill Arches. *J. Fish Dis.* 22: 1-11.

Elliot, J.M. (1975a): The Energetics of Feeding, Metabolism and Growth of Brown Trout (Salmo trutta) in Relation to Body Weight, Water Temperature, and Ration Size. *J Anim Ecol* 45: 923-946.

Hefer, B.; Pruginin, Y. (1981): Commercial Fish Farming: With Special Reference to Fish Culture in Israel. Wiley and Sons, New York.

Hwang, D.; Lin, T. (2002): Effect of Temperature on Dietary Vitamin C Requirement and Lipid in Common Carp. Comp Biochem Physiol Part B 131: 1-7.

Immerzeel, W. (2008): Historical Trends and Future Predictions of Climate Variability in the Brahmaputra Basin, *Int. J. Climatol.*, 28, 243-254.

Immerzeel, W.W.; Van Beek, L.P.; and Bierkens, M.F.P. (2010): Climate ChangeWill Affect the AsianWater Towers, *Science*, 328, 1382-1385.

IPCC (2007): Fourth Assessment Report - Climate Change 2007: Synthesis Report, 2007.

Jeney G., Nemcso´k J (1992): Acute Effect of Sublethal Ammonia Concentrations on Common Carp (Cyprinus carpio L.). II. Effect on Ammonia on Blood Plasma Transaminases (GOT, GTP), G1DH Enzyme Activity, and ATP Value. Aquaculture 104: 149-156.

Kallff, J. (2000): Limnology, Prentice Hall, Upper Saddle River, New Jersy.

Kankaala, P.; Ojala, A.; Tulonen, T.; Arvola, L. (2002): Changes in Nutrient Retention Capacity of Boreal Aquatic Ecosystems Under Climate Warming: A Simulation Study. Hydrobiologia 469: 67-76.

Klapper, H. (1991): Control of Eutrophication in Inland Waters. Ellis Horwood Ltd., West Sussex, UK.

Mall, R.K., Akhilesh Gupta, Ranjeet Singh, R.S. Singh and L.S. Rathore (2006): Water Resources and Climate Change: An Indian perspective. *Current Science*, 90(12).

Marcogliese, D.J. (2001): Implications of Climate Change for Parasitism of Animals in the Aquatic Environment. *Can J Zool* 79: 1331-1352.

Mirza, M.M.Q.; Warrick, R.A.; Ericksen, N.J. and Kenny, G.J. (1998). Trends and Persistence in Precipitation in the Ganges, Brahmaputra and Meghna River Basins. *Hydrological Sciences-Journal-des Hydrologiques*, 43(6): 845-858.

Mirza, M.M.Q. (2002): Global Warming and Changes in the Probability of Occurrence of Floods in Bangladesh and Implications, *Glob. Env. Change*, 12, 127-138.

Moyle, P.B.; and J.J. Cech. (2004): Fish: An Introduction to Ichthyology, 5th Edition, Prentice Hall, Englewood Cliffs N.J.

Murty, A.S. (1986a): Toxicity of Pesticides to Fish. I. CRC Press, Boca Raton, FL.

Murty, A.S. (1986b): Toxicity of Pesticides to Fish. II. CRC Press, Boca Raton, FL.

Nemcso´k J, Orba n L, Aszalos B, Vig E (1987): Accumulation of Pesticides in the Organs of Carp, Cyprinus Carpio L., at 4 and 20 C. *Bull Environ Contam Toxicol* 39: 370-378.

Saud, B.J., B.K. Bhattacharjya, V.K. Verma, D. Kumar, D. Debnath, M.K. Das and A.P. Sharma (2012): Effect of Climate Change on Aquatic Lives with Special Reference to North-east Region of India. *J. Environ & Ecol.*, Vol. 30 (4A): 1534-1537.

Unnikrishnan, A.S., Kumar, K.R., Fernandes, S.E., Michael, G.S. and Patwardhan, S.K. (2006): Sea Level Changes Along the Indian Coast: Observations and Projections. *Current Science.* 90, 362-368.

Walther, G.R.; Roques, A.; Hulme, P.E.; Sykes, M.T.; Pysek, P.; Kühn, I.; Zobel, M.; Bacher, S.; Botta-Dukat, Z.; Bugmann, H.; Czucz, B.; Dauber, J.; Hickler, T.; Jarosik, V.; Kenis, M.; Klotz, S.; Minchin, D.; Moora, M.; Nentwig, W.; Ott, J.; Panov, V. E.; Reineking, B.; Robinet, C.; Semenchenko, V.; Solarz, W.; Thuiller, W.; Vila, M.; Vohland, K.; & Settele, J. (2009): Alien Species in a Warmer World: Risks and Opportunities. *Trends Ecol Evol.*, 24, 12, 686-693.

Warrick, R.A.; Bhuiya, A.H.; and Mirza, M.Q.: The Greenhouse Effect and Climate Change, in: The Implications of Climate and Sea-Level Change for Bangladesh, Edited by: Warrick, R.A. and Ahmad, Q.K., Kluwer Academic Publishers, Dordrecht, Briefing Document 1, 1996.

Watson, L.R.; Milani, A.; Hedrick, R.P. (1998): Effects of Water Temperature on Experimentally-induced Infections of Juvenile White Sturgeon (Acipenser Transmontanus) with the White Sturgeon Iridovirus (WSIV). *Aquaculture.* 166: 213-228.

Wedemeyer, G. (1996): Physiology of Fish in Intensive Culture Systems. Chapman and Hall, New York Wakabayashi H (1991) Effect of Environmental-conditions on the Infectivity of Flexibacter-columnaris to Fish. *J Fish Dis.* 14: 279-290.

Pages: 51-71

CLIMATE CHANGE, DISASTER MANAGEMENT AND ENVIRONMENT

*Edited by:* Dr. Alka Chauhan; Dr. Pawan Kumar 'Bharti'

ISBN: 978-93-5056-784-5

*Edition:* 2016

*Published by:* Discovery Publishing House Pvt. Ltd., New Delhi (India)

# CHAPTER – 4

# Weather Forecasting and Indian Agriculture

Alok Kumar Patra[1] and Pulak Kumar Patra[2]

**ABSTRACT**

Despite impressive advances in agricultural technology, agricultural production is still dependent on weather and climate. The farmers are adversely affected by climate risks in their farming, which include increase in temperature, decrease in rainy days, increase in precipitation intensity and amount, shorter winter periods, decreased ground water availability, increased occurrence of drought and floods, increased duration of water logging, *etc.* which in turn result in yield losses. Decision making in agricultural operations for well grown crops or crops endangered by pests, diseases and/or other environmental disasters needs weather forecasting and climate prediction to the

1 Associate Professor (Agronomy), All India Coordinated Research Project on Integrated Farming Systems, Orissa University of Agriculture and Technology, Bhubaneswar - 751 003, Odisha, (India).

2 Associate Professor, Department of Environmental Studies, Institute of Science, Visva-Bharati, Santiniketan - 731 235, West Bengal, (India).

required accuracies. A number of crop monitoring systems and yield forecasts are now being implemented worldwide and upscaling to regional scales are being attempted. In these, commercial crops like soybean, maize, wheat, sorghum, *etc.* are continuously monitored and forecasted. Though India has acquired the relevant sophisticated technologies but these are yet to be fully translated to the benefits of the farming community.

## INTRODUCTION

Agriculture plays a significant role in the overall socio-economic fabric of India. However, agricultural production is highly dependent on weather, climate and water availability, and is adversely affected by weather and climate related disasters. In many developing countries like India, where rainfed agriculture is the norm, a good rainy season means good crop production, enhanced food security and a healthy economy. Failure of rains and occurrence of natural disasters such as floods and droughts can lead to crop failures, food insecurity, famine, loss of property and life, mass migration, and negative national economic growth (Sivakumar, 2006). Much of the developed world is less vulnerable to climate now-a-days than in the past. They have applied climate knowledge and early warning systems to allow adaption to mitigate the impacts of extreme events.

Weather forecasting is the application of science and technology to predict the state of the atmosphere for a given location. Weather forecasts are made by collecting quantitative data about the past and current state of the atmosphere on a given place and using scientific understanding of atmospheric processes to project how the atmosphere will evolve on that place. Weather warnings are important forecasts because they are used to protect life and property. Forecasts based on temperature and precipitation is important to agriculture.

Farming in many parts of the world, especially in the arid and semiarid regions is risky, because climate is highly variable. In some developing countries as much as 80% of the variability in agricultural production is due to the variability in weather conditions. This production variability in agriculture has immediate and important macroeconomic impacts. A timely seasonal forecast of favourable conditions could permit farmers to adjust cropping patterns and input use in order to benefit fully from these conditions. Also a timely forecast could give the marketing system and downstream users, such as the food processing industry, time to prepare for a bountiful harvest (Arndt, *et al.*, 2000). It is important to remember that under rainfed conditions, even a less reliable, but earlier forecast may be more valuable than an accurate but late forecast (Mjelde, *et al.*, 1998).

In about 340 B.C., Aristotle described weather patterns in *Meteorologica*. Later, Theophrastus compiled a book on weather forecasting, called the *Book of Signs*. Ancient weather forecasting methods usually relied on observed patterns of events, also termed pattern recognition. This experience was accumulated over the generations to produce weather knowledge. However, not all of these predictions prove reliable, and many of them have since been found not to stand up to rigorous statistical testing.

Two officers from of British Royal Navy, Francis Beaufort and Robert FitzRoy formed the basis for all of today's weather forecasting knowledge by middle of 19th century. A terrible storm in 1859 inspired FitzRoy to develop charts to allow predictions to be made, which he called 'forecasting the weather', thus coining the term 'weather forecast'. The 'Weather Book' which FitzRoy published in 1863 was far in advance of the scientific opinion of the time.

With the invention of the telegraph and telephone, the study of weather systems took off. Scientists could then study masses of weather and how such large systems could move and in what direction. By the early 20th century, scientists had begun to believe that weather forecasting could be predicted based on mathematical methods. Computers were first used to create surface analyses in 1992 and by 1998 digital imagery were used for satellite, radar and surface observations, encompassing nearly every factor of weather interpretation. Modern technology, particularly computers and weather satellites, and the availability of data provided by coordinated meteorological observing networks, has resulted in enormous improvements in the accuracy of weather forecasting.

## METEOROLOGICAL AND CLIMATOLOGICAL FORECASTS

The meteorological forecasts are defined as forecasts of the state of the atmosphere, particularly the near surface atmosphere, from the present up to 15 days into the future. These forecasts may be contrasted with climatological forecasts which are defined as a forecast of the mean atmospheric conditions more than 15 days into the future (Hollinger, 2009).

The major differences between the two forecasts are the lead time and the length of time for which the forecast represents. Lead time is defined as the duration of gap between the time of delivery of forecast and the effective time of occurrence of the forecast event. Meteorological forecasts are made hours to days before the effective time of the forecast, while climatological forecasts are made months to years before the effective time of the forecast. Meteorological forecasts provide estimates of actual temperature; humidity; precipitation probability, type and amount; wind speed and direction; and sky conditions. However, climatological forecasts are given in terms of deviation from normal, such as above normal, normal, or below normal. Thus, the forecast is incomplete without the knowledge of the normal temperature and precipitation conditions for the time and location of the forecast. Normals are defined by thirty years of daily weather observations, and are updated every 10 years.

Meteorological and climatological forecasts can be 'general' or 'applied'. A general forecast represents the conditions without reference to a particular activity, while an applied forecast takes the general forecast and applies it to an activity such as agricultural and animal production, or aviation. Meteorological and climatological forecasts for agricultural production differ from general meteorological and climatological forecasts in their application. For agricultural production the general forecasts are interpreted to indicate how the forecast conditions may impact the growth and development of crops, diseases, insect pests, and livestock; and how the conditions will affect production management practices. Thus, meteorological and climatological forecasts for agricultural production require knowledge of the circulation of the atmosphere and the factors that cause the day-to-day changes in the weather, and how agricultural organisms respond to short and long term atmospheric conditions. Crop canopies develop a microclimate and it is within these conditions that the crop interacts with the soil, pests, and diseases. Therefore, the micrometeorological conditions must be related to the synoptic-scale meteorological forecast (Hollinger, 2009).

The meteorological or climatological forecast is to be provided with a reasonable degree of accuracy and enough lead time so that a farmer can take the necessary actions to protect his crop or livestock. He must be able to change his management practices to take advantage of favourable weather conditions, or mitigate unfavourable conditions. A perfect forecast has the potential to have the most value, or even an imperfect forecast can have some value if the forecast is in the right direction and provided with enough lead time for management practices to be effected. However, a highly accurate forecast may have no value if appropriate management practices could not be applied to the crop or livestock before the forecast event.

## TYPES OF WEATHER FORECASTING

The product or result of a weather forecast can be expressed in a variety of forms, which are called type of forecast. The forecast may be of quantitative, qualitative and probabilistic in nature. Depending on the spatial and temporal scales of atmospheric systems and the details of the accuracy desired, the weather forecasts are usually referred to nowcasting, short range, medium range and long range.

### Nowcasting

Prediction on the time scale of minutes to hours is called nowcasting. This type of weather forecasting is issued for less than 12 hours. It is concerned with severe weather events such as tornadoes, hail, and flash floods, which are manifestations of intense mesoscale weather systems. Nowcasting techniques use highly automated computers and image analysis systems to integrate data rapidly from a variety of sources.

**Short Range Forecasting**

It comprises of forecast and warning of weather elements which is valid for 24 hours and an outlook for the subsequent two days. It includes the day-to-day prediction, usually concerned with the more ordinary weather events and changes in the synoptic-scale weather systems. The short range forecast includes cloud spread, rainfall distribution, heavy rainfall warning, maximum and minimum temperature, relative humidity, duration of sunshine, heat and cold waves, low pressure areas, cyclone warning, hail or thunderstorm, snow, frost and likelihood of maximum wind speed. The information is sufficiently accurate. Though it helps in scheduling irrigation, adjusting time of agricultural operations and protecting plants from frost, this type of forecast is not much beneficial to the farmers because the lead time of the forecast is too short to take preventive measures against the adverse weather effects. The short range forecast is issued twice daily. This forecast information is available through television, radio and newspapers. It may also be obtained *via* the telephone from the forecasting agencies. A short range forecasting is based on a detailed analysis of the physical processes occurring in the atmosphere.

**Medium Range Forecasting**

It is a forecast and warning of weather elements which is valid for 3 to 10 days. It is also known as extended forecast. This forecast includes cloud amount, rainfall distribution, sequence of rainy days and weekly cumulative rainfall, extended dry or wet spells, maximum and minimum temperature, and average wind speed. The forecast information is sufficiently accurate. The extended weather forecast is most effective and useful in agriculture as it gives sufficient lead time for both planning and executing farm operations. It helps to determine sowing time and depth of sowing, in planning of irrigation schedules, in making decisions on harvesting and time of spraying to get higher efficiency and in managing labourers and equipments. The forecasting procedure is fundamentally same as for short range forecasting. This method involves the production of a number of forecasts using the same computer model but slightly altering the initial conditions within the error range of the observational instruments. It involves enormous numerical computations. Medium range forecasting is receiving considerable attention worldwide, particularly in agriculture sector. In India, the National Centre for Medium Range Weather Forecasting (NCMRWF) has been established in New Delhi during 1988, to develop only medium range weather forecasting for 3 to 10 days ahead. At present the NCMRWF is giving the forecast along with agroadvisories twice a week for all the 127 NARP (National Agricultural Research Project) agroclimatic zones of the country.

### Long Range Forecasting

The forecast valid for more than 10 days is knows as long range forecasting. There is no rigid definition for long range forecasting. Generally the forecast period ranges from a week to the limits of technical feasibility. Improvement in seasonal climate prediction is one crucial factor that could reduce the vulnerability of agricultural systems to severe impacts of extreme interannual climate anomalies (Mavi and Tupper, 2004). The India Meteorological Department (IMD) started issuing long range forecasting since 1988 on total monsoon rainfall of the country by 25th May every year. It has emphasised on abnormality of temperature and precipitation. The seasonal predictions can be described as above normal, near normal or below normal. This forecast will be helpful in deciding soil moisture management, irrigation scheduling, selection of crops, managing irrigation with limited water supply and deciding cropping pattern and crop yield. These forecasts can be used for predicting likely trends in agricultural production before the beginning of the *kharif* season. The methods used for long range forecasting include climatology, statistics, numerical models and subjective judgement.

### Climate/Agroclimate Forecasting

The trends in rainfall, its variability and probability of distribution over a season can be determined weekly by using the historical data on rainfall for a good number of years at a particular location. This information is useful to the farmers as crop growth periods can be adjusted depending upon the rainfall probability. This forecasting predicts the impact of climatic variability on the agricultural production over a period of time. By analysing and computing the past data on rainfall and evapotranspiration of a locality the periods of water surplus and deficit can be predicted. This information will be helpful in selecting crops and adjusting their growth periods, irrigation scheduling during the dry spells, and facilitating proper drainage during water surplus. The past biological data of crops in a specific location can be interrelated to the meteorological data pertaining to the period and location. This information will help in adopting suitable agronomic management practices that can mitigate the adverse effects of weather aberrations. There are some fundamental differences in predicting weather and climate. Weather prediction is largely restricted to the consideration of dynamic and physical processes internal to the atmosphere. In climate prediction interactions between the atmosphere and other elements of the climate system are taken into account (Patra, 2012).

## TOOLS OF WEATHER FORECASTING

The weather forecasting requires several basic inputs such as area coverage under the network of meteorological stations, collection of meteorological data on cloud cover, sunshine, radiation, rainfall, temperature, wind and pressure, and upper air data on wind, humidity and temperature at various heights (Rao and Pillai, 2012). It requires an international effort even while making forecast for a small region. The World Meteorological Organisation (WMO) under the auspices of the United Nations oversees the collection of weather data across the globe from its 179 member nations. The WMO collects data through its global observing system called World Weather Watch (WWW) which comprises of 10,000 land stations, some 7,000 ship stations and 600 moored and drifting buoys with automatic weather sensors. The weather data thus collected at different observation stations from all countries are sent to the three world meteorological centres at Washington DC, Moscow and Melbourne, which in turn disseminate the data to all member countries. The member nations of the WMO maintain their own meteorological agencies that obtain and process the data and issue regional and national forecasts. The weather forecasting agencies use various tools for collection of the weather data, coding and plotting of these voluminous data to prepare charts. They also need information on the state and stage of crops to give weather forewarnings. The crop weather calendar is required to deliver weather services like forecasting with agroadvisories (Rao, 2008).

**Pilot Balloons**

The pilot balloons are small balloons usually made of a highly flexible latex material inflated with a gas lighter than air, *i.e.*, hydrogen or helium. These are generally launched to determine wind speed and wind direction at different heights in the atmosphere using a theodolite. Sometimes they may also be used for a wide variety of observations. The theodolite is an optical telescope that measures horizontal and vertical angles of the ascending balloons over a specific time interval. High accuracy is obtained when using a dual theodolite set-up. The ascent rate can be controlled by the amount of gas with which the balloon is filled. The path of the balloon is determined from the data observed through graphical techniques.

The balloons are provided in different colours to provide better sighting depending on the sky background. White balloons are used when there is a clear sky, black balloons are used when there is a low overcast and red balloons are used when there is high overcast, or there is a white or gray background. The radio-theodolites are also used to track the balloon when the sky is obscured.

**Radiosonde**

Radiosondes are small lightweight boxes equipped with weather instruments and a radio transmitter attached to the ascending balloons. As the radiosonde rises at about 300 metres/minute, sensors on the radiosonde measure profiles of pressure, temperature, and relative humidity. These sensors are linked to a battery powered 300 milliwatt or less radio transmitter that sends the sensor measurements to a sensitive ground tracking antenna on a radio frequency. The meteorological instruments contained in the radiosonde are designed to register temperature ranging from about +40 to –90° C, relative humidity from 15 to 100% and barometric pressure from 1040 to 40 mb or less. The radio signals received by the tracking antenna are converted to meteorological values and from these data significant levels are selected by a computer, put into a special code form, and then transmitted to data users.

The advantage of radiosonde is that the data are available very fast with it. Usually a complete radiosonde ascent takes about two hours and can ascend to over 35 km and drift more than 300 km from the release point. The radiosonde is suspended 25 to 35 metres below the balloon to minimise contamination of the temperature measurements from heat shedding off the balloon skin. A radiosonde that is dropped from an airplane and falls, rather than being carried by a balloon is called a dropsonde. Balloons meant to stay at a constant altitude for long periods of time are known as transosondes. Specialized radiosondes are used for measuring particular parameters, such as the ozone concentration. Radiosondes are essential sources of meteorological data, and hundreds of them are launched all over the world daily.

**Weather Satellites**

Weather forecasting has been greatly benefited from major advances in remote sensing. For viewing large weather systems on a worldwide scale, weather satellites are invaluable. Geostationary and polar orbiting satellites show cloud formations, large weather events such as hurricanes, and other global weather systems.

There are two types of sensors. One is a visible light sensor called the 'imager', which works like a camera in space and helps gather information on cloud movements and patterns. This sensor can only be used during daylight hours, since it works by capturing reflected light to create images. Since different surface features reflect light in distinctive ways, they can be distinguished from each other in the images. Water reflects very little light, making it appear black on the satellite image. Land masses tend to appear as grey shades, depending on their temperature and moisture. The second sensor is called the 'sounder'. It is an infrared sensor that reads temperature. The higher the temperature of the object, the more energy it emits. This sensor allows satellites to measure the amount of energy radiated by earth's surface, clouds, oceans, air, and so on. Infrared sensors can be used at night, a helpful feature for forecasters, considering that the imager can only pick up data during daylight hours.

In addition to providing visual images, satellites can also provide data that allow calculation of atmospheric temperature and moisture profiles and other environmental variables. This is done using a variety of instruments, including atmospheric sounders, which measure quantities at various levels in atmospheric columns. The data retrieved from sounder measurements taken from a satellite can be utilised in a way similar to radiosonde observations, with the major advantage that the satellite data are more complete spatially, filling in gaps between weather ground stations, which often are hundreds or even thousands of kilometres apart.

There are very few upper air stations over the oceans that cover 70% of the earth's surface. Satellites are now providing some observations of wind and temperature profiles over the oceans. However, the signals received by the satellites are affected by the distribution of humidity and cloud cover. Therefore, information on wind and temperature derived from satellites suffer from a certain amount of uncertainty. Nevertheless, due to their large spatial coverage, this information is valuable in making weather forecasts.

**Radar**

Doppler radar is another essential meteorological tool. Radar is an acronym that stands for Radio Detection and Ranging. It works a little differently from satellite sensors. Instead of reading reflected light or energy, radar measures reflected sound waves. When sound waves are broadcast from a radar antenna, they may come into contact with objects in their path, such as dust particles or ice crystals. If they come into contact with an object that is moving away from the radar, the sound waves will be reflected back at a decreased frequency. If the object they come in contact with is moving towards the radar, the sound waves will be reflected back at an increased frequency. This effect was discovered in 1842 by Christian Doppler. Later, scientists applied Doppler's principle to weather radar. Using Doppler radar, meteorologists can get a picture of precipitation that allows them to track a storm's progress over time. The radar is used for detecting tropical cyclones and their movements. The IMD has been operating radar systems in the east and west coasts of the country.

Some radiosondes are tracked by radar as they ascend through the atmosphere, to determine the wind speed and direction in the middle and upper atmosphere. Radiosondes tracked by radar are called rawinsondes. Over the whole globe there are about 1100 such stations but only about 600 of these provide regular observations twice a day at noon and midnight Greenwich Mean Time.

Upper level information is obtained from other sources as well. Many commercial aircrafts are equipped with weather sensors that automatically monitor the atmosphere throughout their flights. Weather satellites supplement the upper level database by determining temperature and humidity at several depths throughout the atmosphere. Aircrafts and satellites provide data from locations far away from any radiosonde site, particularly over the oceans.

## Weather Maps

An enormous volume of meteorological data is being collected from all over the world, continuously round the clock, through various telecommunication channels. To assess, assimilate and analyse the vast data, they have to be suitably presented. For this purpose, the observations are plotted on maps using standard weather codes (Table 4.1). These maps are called synoptic maps or charts and are the most valuable tool for weather forecasting. Weather forecasting requires analysing the atmospheric condition both at the surface and upper air. Hence meteorologists use two types of synoptic maps namely the surface maps and upper-level maps.

**Table 4.1: Some of the Codes Used on Weather Charts**

| Codes | Weather Parameters |
|---|---|
| TTT | Dry bulb temperature in degree Celsius |
| TdTdTd | Dew point temperature in degree Celsius (plotted in red colour) |
| TxTxTx | Maximum temperature |
| TnTnTn | Minimum temperature |
| ww | Present weather |
| VV | Visibility |
| PPP | Barometric pressure reduced to sea level |
| ddd ff | Wind direction and speed |
| $C_L$ | Types of low cloud |
| $C_M$ | Types of medium clouds |
| $C_H$ | Types of high clouds (plotted in red colour) |
| N | Total amount of cloud |
| h | Height of the base of low cloud |
| Nh | Amount of cloud reported under h |
| RRR | Amount of rainfall in mm (plotted in green colour) |

Synoptic charts display the weather conditions at a specified time over a large geographical area. The surface synoptic charts plotted for different synoptic hours depict the distribution of pressure, temperature, dew point, clouds and winds. The upper air charts are prepared at the 850, 700, 500, 300 and 200 mb pressure levels of the atmosphere, which correspond to nearly 1.5, 3, 5.6, 9 and 12 km above mean sea level, respectively. The pressure, wind and temperature data are plotted at each level. The surface charts together with the upper air charts provide a composite three dimensional weather picture pertaining to a given time. The pattern of pressure distribution is brought out by drawing isobars, troughs, ridges, lows, highs, depressions, cyclones, fronts and discontinuities. Charts are updated at least every six hours. The meteorological observations are plotted according to standard station models prescribed by WMO. The synoptic charts together with the satellite pictures on cloud spread are the basic material needed to understand the initial state of the atmosphere. These systems are clearly marked and labelled by using appropriate symbols (Table 4.2).

**Table 4.2: Standard Symbols Used on Weather Charts**

| Symbol | Precipitation | Symbol | Cloud Cover | Symbol | Wind Speed |
|---|---|---|---|---|---|
| , | Drizzle | ○ | Clear sky | ◎ | Calm |
| ▽ | Shower | ⦶ | *One okta* |  | 1-2 knots |
| ● | Rain | ◔ | Two oktas | 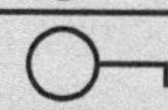 | 5 knots |
| ✱ | Snow |  | Three oktas | 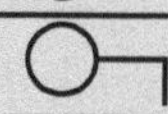 | 10 knots |
| △ | Hail | ◑ | Four oktas |  | 15 knots |
| 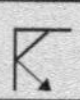 | Thunderstorm |  | Five oktas |  | 20 knots |
| •<br>• • | Heavy rain | ◕ | Six oktas | 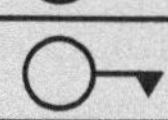 | 50 knots or more |
| •<br>✱ | Sleet |  | Seven oktas | | |
| ✱<br>▽ | Snow shower | ● | Eight oktas | | |
| ═ | Mist | ⊗ | Sky obscured | | |
| ≡ | Fog | | | | |

## Crop Weather Calendar

In order to provide the farmers with an efficient weather service, it is essential that the weather forecaster should be familiar with the crops that are grown in a particular agroclimatic zone. The type of forewarnings to be given depends on the stages of the crop. The users of the forecasts, *viz.*, farmers should become familiar with weather based agro-bulletins and learn how to interpret them. To meet the above requirement, the detailed information collected from the agricultural departments has been condensed by the IMD and presented in a pictorial form known as crop weather calendar.

The crop weather calendars consist of three parts, *viz.*, crop husbandry, normal weather requirements and weather warnings. At the bottom is the typical life history of the crop, from the sowing window to the period of maturity, in the form of a diagram. Important crop phases like sowing, germination and seedling, transplanting, vegetative growth, flowering, grain formation and maturity are indicated against the standard agrometeorological weeks. The phenological stages of the crop cover certain time intervals indicated by horizontal arrows, which depend on variations in crop variety, sowing date from place to place and from year to year, and the nature of the crop itself. For ready reference, the months and standard weeks are marked at the bottom of the diagram.

Middle part of the calendar gives information regarding normal weather condition required for active crop growth. It is divided into different sections according to rainfall, rainy days, minimum temperature, maximum temperature, pan evaporation and sunshine hours. The normal weather conditions are determined from long term averages. Normal phasewise water requirements of the crop are determined from potential (or reference crop) evaporation multiplied by appropriate crop coefficients. The uppermost portion of the calendar indicates the weather conditions favourable for incidence of pests and diseases and the nature of the weather warnings that can be given. The uppermost portion of the calendar gives information related to the weather abnormalities and to take precautionary measures to be taken. This part is divided into different sections according to dry spell length, high wind, heavy rainfall and cloudy weather.

These calendars are useful for crop planning, irrigation scheduling and plant protection measures. Information on normal weather conditions, water requirement of crops, *etc.* are of vital importance for effective crop planning and for maximising and stabilising food production in the country. The diagrams in the calendar help the weather forecaster to see, at a glance, what warnings are to be issued for a particular district during a given weather situation during a particular phase of a crop. The calendars are being subjected to periodical checking and revision. A sample of crop weather calendar is presented in Fig 4.1.

## WEATHER FORECASTING METHODS

The methods in use for weather forecasting can be divided into three broad categories, *viz.*, conventional or synoptic, statistical and numerical weather prediction. The method that can be utilized for forecasting depends on the length of forecast, the type of information desired and how much is known about the current state of atmosphere.

### Synoptic Methods

It is the traditional approach in weather prediction. This primary method continued to be in use until the late 1950s.The present state of the atmosphere is observed and surface and upper air synoptic charts are prepared. Synoptic means the observation of different weather elements at a specific time. The inferences on expected movement of weather systems are drawn by using previous and present charts. In order to have an average view of the changing pattern of weather, a modern meteorological centre prepares a series of synoptic charts every day. Such synoptic charts form the very basis of weather forecasts. From the careful study of weather charts over many years, certain empirical rules were formulated. These rules helped the forecaster in estimating the rate and direction of the movement of weather systems. The experience of the meteorologists is the knowledge gathered over years of observations and the background theory on weather. Given a background condition, a particular weather pattern, *e.g.*, a low pressure area, tends to evolve on the average in a certain way. This may be termed as mean or 'climatological' behaviour. Also atmospheric fluctuations have a certain amount of 'persistency'. In other words, once a low pressure is formed, it persists for a while. Forecasts made by meteorologists based on 'climatology' and 'persistence' and empirical knowledge about evolution of weather systems are known as synoptic forecasts. Before the advent of computers, this was the only method of weather forecasting. Up to 12 hours or 24 hours in advance, the meteorologists can actually make very good forecasts based on this technique. But beyond that this type of forecast is not useful. In addition to synoptic charts, satellite pictures also supply considerable information on cloud spread to the forecaster in issuing short range forecasts. Short range forecasts are issued by using the past analogous situations on the presumption that a current situation will evolve on the lines of the past analogous one.

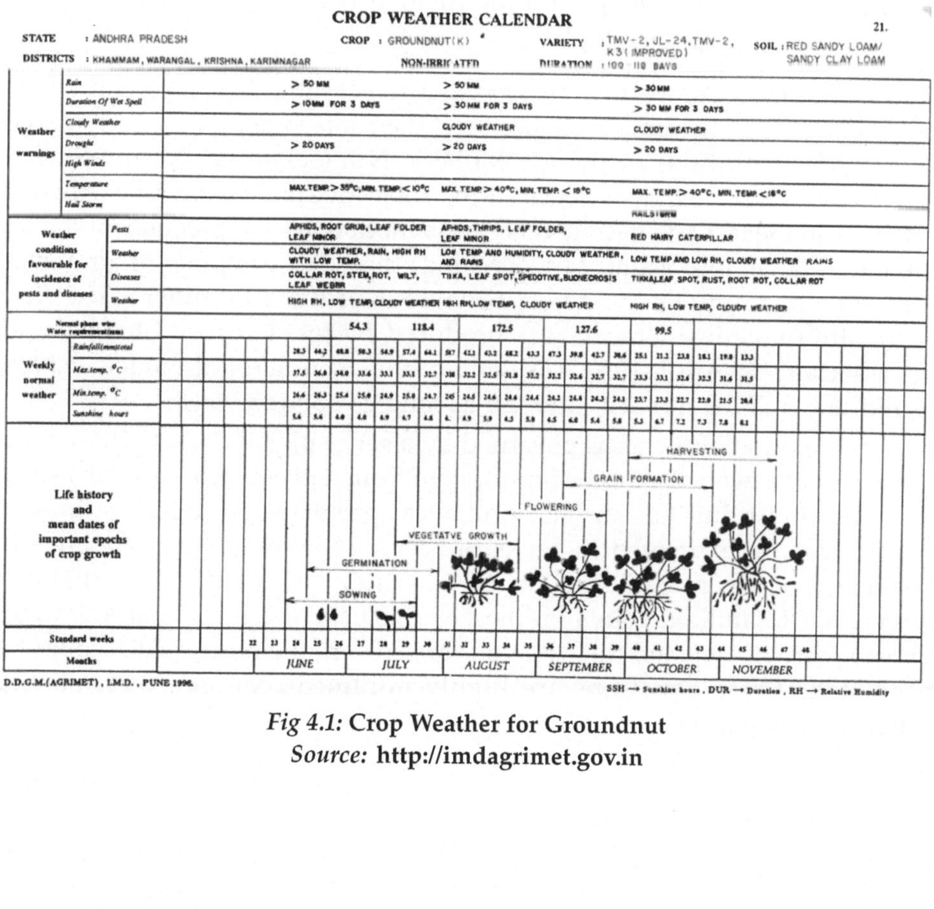


*Fig 4.1:* **Crop Weather for Groundnut**

*Source:* **http://imdagrimet.gov.in**

### Statistical Methods

The statistical methods are used mostly in long range and seasonal climate forecasts. These methods use the past records of weather data on the assumption that future will be a repetition of the past weather. The main purpose of studying the past weather data is to find out those aspects of the weather that are good indicators of the future events. After establishing these relationships, correct data can be safely used to predict the future conditions. Only overall weather can be predicted in this way. It is particularly of use in projecting only one aspect of the weather at a time.

Statistical techniques such as multiple regression and ARIMA (auto regressive integrated moving average) models are used for predicting Indian monsoon rainfall based on 16 global-land-ocean-atmospheric variables. A new 10 parameter Power Regression model is being used since 2003 for estimating monsoon rainfall at the national level. IMD advances the long range forecast by 40 days and generates a quantitative forecast update by mid-July. This information is very much useful for contingency planning. Forecasts can also be attempted in the absence of any data about current weather, provided that long term information is available.

### Numerical Weather Prediction

Until the 1950s, weather analysis and forecasting depended entirely on the experience of the meteorologists and their interpretation of current and recent past conditions of the atmosphere. Numerical weather prediction (NWP) models have largely replaced the subjective and statistical prediction methods in the last few decades and these models are the preeminent tool of modern weather forecasting. NWP method is based on computer programmes that attempt to mimic the actual behaviour of the atmosphere. The first successful numerical forecast was produced by Jule Gregory Charney and his associates in April, 1950. The state-of-the-art numerical models exhibit significant skill for forecast intervals as long as about a week.

The motion of the air is governed by a set of physical laws. These laws determine the evolution of the atmosphere from a given state to some future state. For most, but not all, meteorological problems the relevant laws of physics can be expressed in terms of seven equations which govern the behaviour of seven variables. The NWP requires enormous computations with about 1.3 million points for these variables. If the initial states of these variables are known and the equations are solved, the future states could be predicted. These equations are highly nonlinear coupled with partial differential equations.

**Table 4.3: Variables and Equations that Define the State of Atmosphere**

| Variables | Equations | Applications |
|---|---|---|
| Pressure ($P$) | Gas law or equation of state | Relates temperature, pressure and density |
| Temperature ($T$) | First law of thermodynamics | Relates temperature changes to external heating or cooling due to radiative balance and latent heat released during cloud formation |
| Density ($\rho$) | Continuity equation for air | Expresses conservation of mass of air |
| Water vapour ($q$) | Continuity equation for water vapour | Expresses rate of change of water vapour in terms of source (evaporation) and sink (precipitation) and diffusion due to turbulent eddies |
| West to east component of wind ($u$) | Newton's second law (force = mass × acceleration) | Applied to west-east direction; the pressure gradient force, the Coriolis force, gravitational force and frictional force |
| South to north component of wind ($v$) | Newton's second law | Applied to south-north direction; the pressure gradient force, the Coriolis force, gravitational force and frictional force |
| Vertical component of wind ($w$) | Newton's second law | Applied to vertical direction; the pressure gradient force, the Coriolis force, gravitational force and frictional force |

Weather agencies around the world develop their own models and typically maintain a suite of models which are continually updated. Although there are large differences among models, the general procedure is the same for all numerical models and each has three phases *i.e.*, analysis, prediction and post processing. In the analysis phase, observations are used to supply values corresponding to the starting state of the atmosphere for all the variables carried in the models. Analysis involves integration of the latest available observations, past values and outputs from other models to generate uniform initial values throughout the atmosphere over land and ocean. In the prediction phase, the values delivered by the analysis phase are used in the governing equations to obtain new values a few minutes into the future. The process is then repeated, using the output from the first step as input for the next set of calculations. This procedure is performed over and over as many times as necessary to reach the end of forecast period. Governing equations cannot be solved directly and are broken down into simple operations that computers can perform. The forecast conditions at regular intervals (*e.g.*, every 12 hours) are represented on a grid for mapping. In the post processing phase, such maps for each period from different models are studied to recognise the pattern and the final forecast is to be made.

The NWP technique is used mostly in medium range weather forecasting. This method has a practical limit of 3 to 5 days in the tropical region and about 10 days in mid-latitudes. The NCMRWF, New Delhi gives medium range weather forecasting by using supercomputers. The NWP techniques are also used for short range forecasting of meteorological parameters.

## APPLICATION OF AGROMETEOROLOGICAL FORECASTS

Meteorological forecasts for agricultural production can be provided for making strategic, tactical, and operational decisions. Lead time and number of days the forecast represents are the variables that determine whether a forecast is used for strategic, tactical, or operational decisions. Climatological forecasts are used in making strategic decisions. Both meteorological and climatological forecasts are used in making tactical decisions, and only meteorological forecasts are used in making operational decisions (Hollinger, 2009).

### Strategic Decision

Strategic agricultural climatological forecasts provide the data and information for planning agricultural practices that change on a time scale of months to years. These include selection of crop or livestock species, crop rotation, size of farm, size and type of equipment, tillage practices, planting date and spacing, cultivar selection, livestock stocking of pasture or range, design of livestock facilities, and investment decisions such as purchase of land, irrigation systems, and storage facilities. Crop forecasts for strategic decisions require application of crop models to either existing climate data or forecast climate data. In practice, either historical daily weather data or weather data from 'weather generators' are used with the assumption that the historical or generated data represent the future weather mean and variance. 'Weather generators' are computer programmes that create sequences of daily weather data fitting to the known distribution of each weather variable.

### Tactical Decision

Tactical agricultural meteorological forecasts provide meteorological data with lead times of months. These forecasts can be used to plan final changes in crop cultivar selection, timing of planting and harvest, planting density and spacing, timing of pest and disease control measures, intercultural operations, irrigation schedules, nutrient management, pre-season crop marketing decisions, and purchase or disposal of livestock.

### Operational Decision

The transition of forecasts from tactical to operational decisions is, in some cases, difficult to define. This is because forecasts for both tactical and some operational agricultural production decisions include current weather observations, with forecasts of the important variables into the future. A major difference is that the decisions being made in an operational framework are generally days into the future, rather than weeks to months for tactical decisions. Such decisions can include timing of planting, cultivation, and harvest; irrigation scheduling; fertilizer and pesticide application; and livestock movement between pastures, or to shelter.

## WEATHER SERVICES TO FARMERS

Accurate forecasts are vital for the farming because weather deeply affects agricultural operations like risk assessment, crop planning, sowing, pest management, manuring, harvesting and storage. Accurate long term forecasts prompt efficient crop planning. The medium range forecasts focussing on major weather events can allow a farmer to more precisely plan critical decisions such as sowing, pesticide and fertilizer application, and harvesting. To meet the farmers' need in real-time the India Meteorological Department (IMD) has started Integrated Agromet Advisory Service (IAAS) in the country involving all the concerned organisations, *viz.*, Indian Council of Agricultural Research (ICAR), Ministry of Agriculture (both Centre and State), State Agricultural Universities (SAUs) and other agencies from April 2007.

### National Agromet Advisory Bulletin

National Agromet Advisory Service Centre (NAASC) has been set up in Agrimet Division of IMD at Pune to act as the nodal centre and headquarters of state Agromet Advisory Services (AAS) units of IMD. Since

July 2004 this centre has been preparing All India Agromet Advisory Service bulletins on Thursday for issuing the same to the Ministry of Agriculture, Ministry of Earth Sciences and to the members of Crop Weather Watch Group (CWWG), who meet every Friday at Krishi Bhavan, Ministry of Agriculture, Govt. of India, New Delhi. Based on these inputs, important decisions on short time crop planning in various parts of the country are taken in this meeting. Besides, these bulletins are also uploaded on real time basis of the Agricultural Meteorological Division, IMD, Pune. Monthly and seasonal reports on Agromet Advisory Services are also prepared.

**State Level Composite Bulletin**

The state level composite AAS bulletins are issued twice a week (Tuesday and Friday) from 23 AAS units of IMD located at different state capitals on operational basis in consultation with the Director of Agriculture of the respective states to prepare state level agricultural planning and management. The bulletins are disseminated in English as well as in local languages through radio, television, newspaper, internet, *etc*. The state level bulletin is a composite of district bulletins helping to identify the distressed district of the state as well as plan the supply of appropriate farm inputs such as seeds, irrigation water, fertilizer, pesticides, *etc*.

**District Agromet Advisory Service Bulletin**

IMD has started issuing quantitative district level weather forecast up to 5 days from 1st June, 2008. The products comprise of quantitative forecasts for 7 weather parameters *viz*., rainfall, maximum and minimum temperatures, wind speed and direction, relative humidity and cloudiness. In addition, weekly cumulative rainfall forecast is also provided. IMD, New Delhi generates these products based on a Multi Model Ensemble technique using forecast products available from models developed in India and other countries. The products are communicated to 130 Agromet Field Units (AMFUs) located at SAUs and ICAR institutes covering all agroclimatic zones of the country. On receipt of the forecasts, AMFUs prepare the medium range weather forecast based agrometeorological advisories in vernacular language in consultation with a panel of experts in various disciplines of agriculture. These agroadvisories which are crop specific, weather event specific and farm operation specific are disseminated to the farmers through all possible mass media like newspaper, radio, television and also through personal contacts by extension workers. The advisories are kept as simple as possible both in terms of the language and terminology, in view of literacy level of the farming community. In addition to the farmers, these bulletins are also provided to authorities of concerned departments like those of Agriculture, Horticulture, Irrigation, Soil Conservation, Animal Husbandry, *etc*. to enable them to take necessary measures for effective utilization of the advisories.

## CHALLENGES AND COMPLEXITIES OF WEATHER FORECASTING

Weather observation techniques have improved and there have been technological advancements in predicting the weather in recent times. On average, a five-day weather forecast of today is as reliable as a two-day weather forecast 20 years ago. Despite this major scientific and technical progress, many challenges remain unsolved regarding long-term weather predictability. Weather forecasts for today or tomorrow are likely to be more dependable than predictions about the weather about two weeks from now. Sometimes it is also felt that weather forecast accuracy falls significantly beyond about 10 days. The accuracy of individual weather forecasts varies significantly.

Weather forecasting is a complex and often challenging skill that involves observing and processing vast amounts of data. Forecasting is a three step process; observing, forecasting, and communicating. Short range forecasting, looking to a few hours into the future, typically depends on closely observing how weather systems are currently evolving and tracking, and projecting their movement into the future based on what is understood about dynamics of the atmosphere. Forecasting beyond a day rely more on numerical weather modelling. Numerical forecast models compile data from surface observations, weather balloons and satellite imagery to create a computer generated simulation of the weather into the future. The model simulations use dynamic equations that express how the atmosphere will respond to changes in temperature, pressure and humidity over time. However, the earth's atmosphere is a complicated system that is affected by many factors and can react in different ways.

Much research has gone into characterisation of various crop environments, quantification of crop-weather interactions in relation to crop yield, crop weather modelling and crop-pest-weather dynamics. Now it is time to consolidate these findings in different locations, make use of this information and reach the farmers through agroadvisories on a larger scale in a more realistic way. These advisories are to be more farmer-friendly. A more accurate forecast along with actionable agroadvisories is required at block level. Remote sensing aided weather based agroadvisories may be a promising way which would enable the farmers to take the most appropriate actions on real time basis. Satellite remote sensing technology is increasingly gaining recognition as an important source of many agricultural applications as it is superior to the traditional methods in terms of accuracy and saving of time. Geographic Information Systems technology is becoming an essential tool for combining various maps and satellite information sources in models that simulate the interactions of complex natural systems.

Once a forecast is created with reasonable confidence, the next role of the forecaster is to deliver that forecast in a way that the users can understand and appropriately respond to. The timeliness of issuing the forecast to provide adequate response to users is also one of the concerns. The medium range weather forecasting based agroadvisories should be location specific so that suitable actions can be taken timely for altering or prompting the agricultural operations. The most important challenges that the forecasters face today are to improve the skill of forecasting through better understanding of atmospheric phenomena and thus improving the relevant processes, and to increase the lead time of the agrometeorological forecast from the present 3 to 4 days to at least one week. This will be useful in the field of agriculture and animal husbandry in a big way.

## CONCLUSION

Despite the technological advances, Indian farmers are mostly dependent on seasonal rains which are highly variable in time and space. Thus, weather forecasts are of great importance to agricultural activities. The fields of interest of weather forecasting include agricultural and horticultural production, forestry, animal husbandry, fisheries, agricultural planning, processing, transport and storage of food, poverty reduction and sustainable development aspects of the livelihood of farmers. The use of climate in land-use planning, scheduling agricultural activities and preparing crop calendars as well as in crop, forest and livestock protection have benefited the agricultural communities of many regions. Information like return periods, frequencies of occurrences and intensities of extreme events and assured rainfall in different growing periods are valuable in choices for preparedness strategies. An appropriate, preferably integrated pest management system using meteorological and microclimatological information can reduce pre- and post-harvest losses appreciably. The tactical use of weather information in the prediction of pest and disease development allows for near optimum use and timing of pesticides and/or release of predators.

Lot of research has been done in various aspects of weather forecasting and it is time to consolidate the results and translate them to actionable weather based agroadvisories. In addition to weather predictions, the forecasters should be able to estimate the likelihood of unusual weather events and their potential impacts on crops and animals through quantitative analysis, which will be a great challenge.

## REFERENCES

Arndt, C., Hazell, P. and Robinson, S. (2000). Economic Value of Climate Forecasts for Agricultural Systems in Africa. *In*: Sivakumar, M.V.K. (ed.) *Climate Prediction and Agriculture*. Proceedings of START/WMO International Workshop, Geneva, Switzerland, September 27-29, 1999. International START Secretariat, Washington, DC, pp. 157-180.

Hollinger , S.E. (2009). Meteorological Forecasting for Agricultural Production. *In*: Ting. K.C., Fleisher, D.H. and Rodriguez, L.F. (eds.) *Systems Analysis and Modelling in Food and Agriculture*. EOLSS Publishers Co. Ltd. UK.

http://en.wikipedia.org/wiki/Weather_forecasting

http://www.imd.gov.in

http://www.imdagrimet.gov.in

http://www.indiaweather.gov.in

http://www.preservearticles.com/what-are-the-methods-used-for-weather-forecasting.html

http://www.theweatherprediction.com/habyhints

http://www.worldwatch.org

Mavi, H.S. and Tupper, G.J. (2004). Agrometeorology: Principles and Applications of Climate Studies in Agriculture. Food Products Press, Binghamton, New York.

Mjelde, J.W., Hill, H.S.J. and Griffiths, J.F. (1998). A Review of Current Evidence on Climate Forecasts and Their Economic Effects in Agriculture. *American Journal of Agricultural Economics* 80: 1089-1095.

Patra, P.K. (2012). A Text Book on Climatology. Kalyani Publishers, Ludiana. 255 pp.

Rao, G.S.L.H.V.P. (2008). Agricultural Meteorology. Prentice-Hall of India Pvt. Ltd., New Delhi. 364 pp.

Rao, G.S.L.H.V.P. and Pillai, P.B. (2012). Weather Forecasting. *In*: Varshneya, M.C. and Pillai, P.B. (eds.) *Text Book of Agricultural Meteorology*. Indian Council of Agricultural Research, New Delhi. pp. 180-190.

Sivakumar, M.V.K. (2006). Climate Prediction and Agriculture: Current Status and Future Challenges. *Climate Research* 33: 3-17.

Pages: 72-92

CLIMATE CHANGE, DISASTER MANAGEMENT AND ENVIRONMENT

*Edited by:* Dr. Alka Chauhan; Dr. Pawan Kumar 'Bharti'

ISBN: 978-93-5056-784-5

*Edition:* 2016

*Published by:* Discovery Publishing House Pvt. Ltd., New Delhi (India)

# CHAPTER – 5

# Spatial-temporal Analysis of Rainfall Trends in Changing Scenario of Uttar Pradesh, India

Avadhesh Kumar Koshal

***ABSTRACT***

Uttar Pradesh is situated between 23°52′N-30°24′ N latitude and 77°05′E-84°38′E longitude. It located in the north-central part of the country. The present study is based on secondary sources of time series data (total, actual and normal rainfall) obtained 50 years from 1961 to 2010 is used for analysis and model formulation. The different type of statistical data analysis viz. coefficient of variation (CV), correlation of coefficient ($R^2$) and trend analysis to given important scenario of change pattern of time series data. The use of ARIMA and Box Cox model also makes it possible to predict for changing pattern of rainfall. The high rainfall 1272 mm noticed in 2008 and lowest rainfall 568 mm noticed in 1987. The average annual rainfall is noticed as 899.1 mm.

Research Associate (GIS), NICRA Project, P.D.F.S.R., Modipuram, Meerut, U.P. Pin - 250 110

The coefficient of variation varied with the season. The standard deviation from mean annual rainfall was 182.7mm. The decreasing trends of annual rainfall@-2.36mm/year. The prediction map of actual data of year wise long term rainfall data (1961-2010) used for study. In the created maps were observed in year 1961-1970 most of the districts cover > 1050mm rainfall decadal but in year 2001-2010 rainfall covered less districts area. In year 1991-2000 rainfall covered districts are too much less than other decadal year. The statistical and geo statistical analysis of time series and decadal data of rainfall study is useful to understand rainfall variability and decadal pattern scenario of study area.

***Keywords:*** ARIMA, GIS, Interpolation, Polynomial interpolation & Trend analysis.

## INTRODUCTION

Rainfall is non-linear and vital source of hydrological cycle. Rainfall influenced on the agriculture. Agriculture pattern are dependent on distribution of rainfall. It is a basic source of water cycle. The rainfall distribution in Uttar Pradesh is divided in two zones namely irrigated and Rainfed zones. The majority of districts in Bundelkhand, Vindhyan region are Rainfed region rest districts are belongs to irrigated zone. The Indian content South-west monsoon has great influence on crops. More than 75% water get soil through this monsoon (Gautam *et al.*). The changes of hydrological- meteorological properties are dynamic climatic pattern of natural and un-natural process. Climate change is great impact on cropping pattern and cropping systems of India as well as U.P. Rainfall has change of the scenario of cropping pattern and also providing opportunities for improvements in terms of develop improved (drought or salt tolerant) varieties and water management. Rice- wheat system is pre-dominant system of Uttar Pradesh and provides basic food to livelihood in rabi and kharif season. Rice (*Oryza sativa L.*) and wheat (*Triticum aestivum L.*) contribute about 77% of the total cereal production and are the backbone of India's food security (Bhatia *et al.*2012) Rice is grown in the wet season (July to October) and wheat is grown in the dry season (November to March). The water loving crop rice is dependent on rainfall. Agriculture systems/pattern is dependent on distribution of rainfall, so Indian agriculture is highly dependent on the spatial and temporal distribution of monsoon rainfall (Kumar *et al.* 2004).

GIS is very important and widespread tool serving a variety of functions in many environmental sciences including meteorology and climatology (Tveito *et al.* 2000). GIS is used for regional level planning (Hartkamp *et al.*1999; Heinemann *et al.* 2002) and large scale land use planning (Lal *et al.*1993; Smith 2000). The interpolation method used to estimates the values at locations where no measured values are available. The spatial interpolation is widely used for creating continuous data which are collected at discrete locations. The vector based GIS software package ARC GIS was used to map and analyze the spatial data. It was also used for the generation of various interpolated and thematic maps. The Geostatistical analyst uses sample points take at different locations in landscape and interpolates a continuous surface (Geostatistical Analyst, 2001). The deterministic interpolation method is used as the best interpolation technique, use exploratory spatial data analysis tools. Local Polynomial (LPI) is a moderately quick interpolator; it provides prediction, prediction standard error and condition number surfaces. It is useful for capture the short-range variation and sensitive to the neighbourhood distance may create empty areas in the prediction surface. Rainfall prediction is necessity of meteorological work its play vital role for analysis.

Statistical techniques are essential tools for analyzing large datasets. It also helps us to identify which of the many pieces of information derived from observations of the climate system are worthy of synthesis and interpretation. Chow (1954) investigated of the lognormal distribution, suggested relationships for calculating the mean and variance without taking the logarithms of all the data. Brakensiek (1958) also discussed a least squares procedure for estimating the parameters of the long normal distribution. The linear regression line was fitted using the most common method of least squares. This method calculates the best fitting line for the observed data by minimizing the sum of the squares of the vertical deviations from each data point to the line. In order to fit regression lines of the in rainy season monthly average Rainfall (dependent variables) against time (independent variable) in years were plotted. Linear regression lines were then fitted to determine the trends of rainfall.

The statistical softwares are *viz.* Statistix, Excel and XLSTAT consist of special method and tools for dealing with and interpreting such data (Chandel, 2001). The primary and secondary data are used for understanding of behaviour of related data and back to future planning. That software has specific tools for special analysis to provide fast and reliable information with easy steps. The climatic factors model analyses are give information about future planning and management to go right direction accordingly. Time series forecast is an important tool for resource management field. It is used for meteorological forecasting purpose. The time series variations studied by ARIMA (AutoRegressive Integrated Moving Average) approaches (Suhartono, 2011; Ali, 2013). ARIMA model is basically a linear statistical technique for modelling the time series and rainfall forecasting which ease to develop (Somvanshi, 2006). *Autoregressive Integrated Moving* Average (ARIMA) *model* was first proposed in 1976 for time series analysis. It is also called Box-Jenkins method (Box and Jenkins, 1970). Mahalakshmi *et al* (2014) used for rainfall forecast with ARIMA-ANN and the Hybrid model were compared on the basis of the error values.

The natural or human-induced factors are cause of climates change. The statistics model considers the past and can help predict future climate change. In the study area, most of the cropping systems are depend on the distribution of rainfall to planning irrigation management (Fig 5.1). It is based on GIS and past relationships are used to forecast future prospect with stastical analysis. The aim is to provide state level overview of long trends of rainfall pattern.

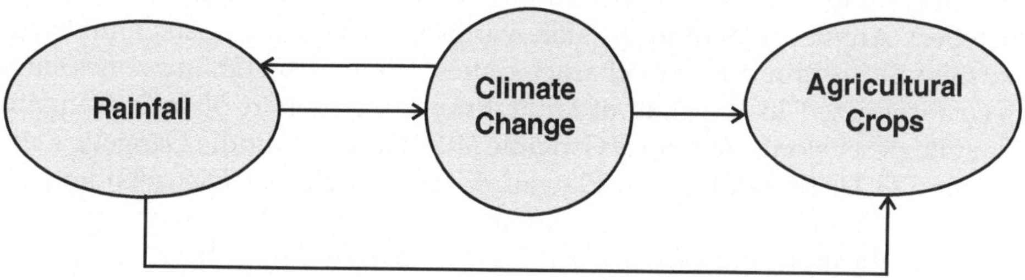


*Fig. 5.1:* **Interrelationship Between Agriculture and Rainfall**

## MATERIALS AND METHODS

### Study Area

Uttar Pradesh is situated between 23°52′N-30°24′ N latitude and 77°05′E-84°38′E longitude (FSI, 2011). Uttar Pradesh has a geographical area of 2,40,928 km² which constitutes 7.3% of the total area of the country (Fig 5.2).

*Fig. 5.2:* **Study Area**

It located in the north-central part of the country and shares border with nine states as well as international border with Nepal. The state is divided two physiographic zones namely: the vast Gangetic Plains and its tributaries (part of the Indo-Gangetic Plain) and smaller southern uplands. Based on IMD classification, UP has the following three predominant seasons (Upkar, 2008) Winter season (November to February), summer season (March, April and May) and South-west Monsoon (June, July, August, September and October). Annual rainfall in the state varies from 1,000mm-1,200 mm. Based on rainfall, terrain and soil characteristics, nine agro-climatic zones have been recognized in the state of Uttar Pradesh. It is part of Indo Gangetic Plain Region belongs to Upper Gangetic (40 Districts), Middle Gangetic Plain Region (23 Districts), Central Plateau & Hills Region (7 Districts) and six Subzones (Singh, 2007 & Planning commission 1989) and based on ecological land classification, out of 127 NARP zones of India, nine NARP zones are belongs to Uttar Pradesh state (NARPZONES).

### Data Collection

The present study is based on secondary sources of time series data (total, actual and normal rainfall) obtained 50 years from 1961 to 2010 is used for analysis and model formulation. The data set used in this study is derived from the time series of annual and monthly precipitation from 70 districts in Uttar Pradesh. The rainfall data were collected from the published records, Bulletin of the Directorate of Agricultural Statistics, Indian Meteorological Department and the Institute of State Planning, U.P., India Water Portal, ICAR and other national level institutes. The data are also collected in different authentic meteorological websites (Rainfall data Info). The geo-referencing/rectified, masking the area (Uttar Pradesh) in ARC GIS 10.2.2 software and time series data analysis through geostatistical method. The decadal rainfall maps were generated from rainfall data using standard methods in Arc GIS. The base maps of the study area have been generated based on survey of India digital map. The statistical information on crop area, production and productivity form the backbone of agricultural statistical system. The different type of statistical data analysis *viz.* Coefficient of Variation (CV), Linear regression ($R^2$) and Trend Analysis to given important scenario of change pattern of time series data. The statistical analysis are Mean, Coefficient of Variation, Standard Variation, $R^2$, ARIMA and other analysis of data in MS Excel, Statistix and XLSTAT softwares.

The GIS, GPS remote sensing is integrating technology to management of rainfall data. Arc GIS (ver. 10.2.2.) was used for the spatial data preparation and analysis. The base maps of the study area have been generated based on the survey of India digital map. The time series monthly rainfall data of Uttar Pradesh state's districts wise for a period of 50 years were analyzed. The trend pattern of normal rainfall data in the study area boundary feature file was used for GIS layer and integrated MS excel generated *.dbf to. shp file for geostatistical analysis. The most important and common tool of geostatistics is local estimation and prediction in ARC GIS. The decadal maps of the study area have been generated from rainfall data using standard methods in Arc GIS. The statistical analysis of data observed decadal linear regression value. The coefficient of variation and standard deviation values are also observed. The time series analysis of rainfall data in Statistix and XLSTAT softwares are used for modelling analysis. ARIMA (autoregressive integrated moving average) models are generalizations of the simple AR model that use for modelling the serial correlation in the disturbance Jovanovski, (2007). The MA, or moving average forecasting model uses lagged values of the forecast error to improve the current forecast. The inter- annual and inter-decadal variability of rainfall are examined using the coefficient of variation. The detail methodologies are used for further analysis (Fig. 5.3)

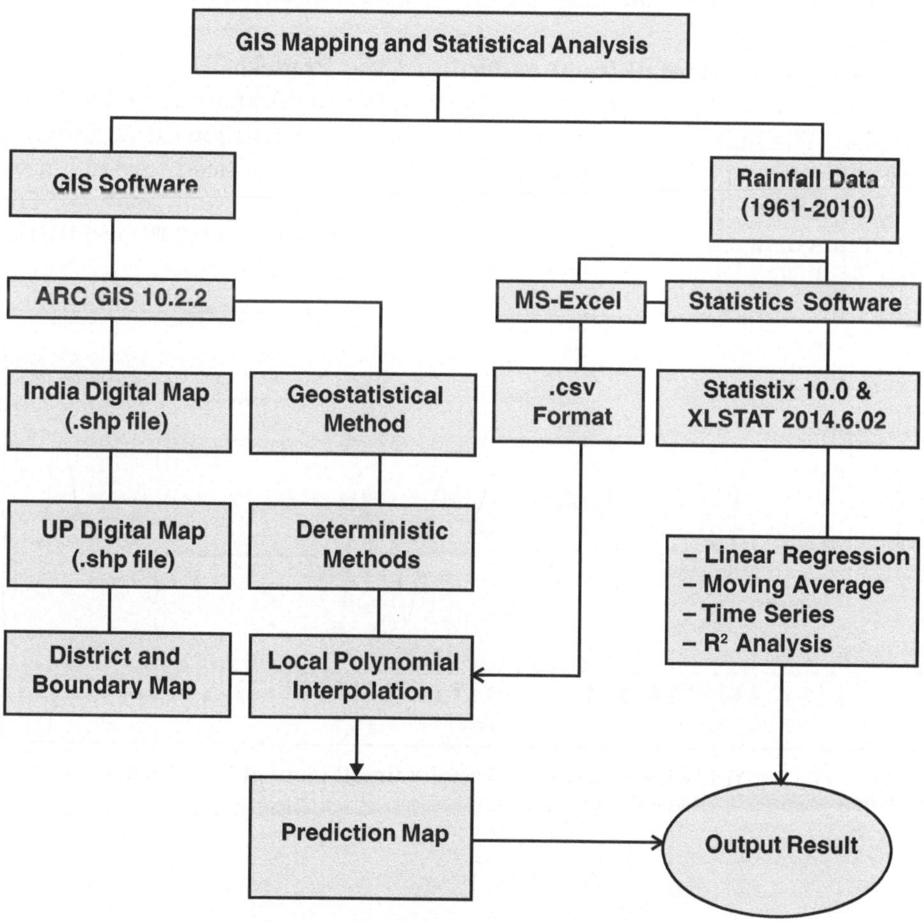


*Fig. 5.3:* **Methodology for Analysis**

## RESULTS OR FINDINGS

The long term data analysis for overall and decadal pattern of rainfall studies are divided in two parts:

*(i)* Statistical Analysis

*(ii)* Geo-statistical analysis

### Statistical Analysis

The different type of statistical data analysis viz. coefficient of variation (CV), correlation of coefficient ($R^2$) and trend analysis to given important scenario of change pattern of time series data. More than 60% of the cropped area in India still depends solely on monsoon rainfall (13). In India, the onset of the southwest monsoon is expected in June to July, depending on location. The statistical analysis of rainfall to estimated and prediction of data for better analysis and result oriented study The statistical analysis of long term spatial and temporal data is an effective tool for understanding the rainfall pattern of area.

**Fifty years rainfall (mm) pattern of Uttar Pradesh:** The districts wise fifty years (1961-2010) data were collected and trend analysis (Table 5.1 & Fig. 5.4). The high rainfall 1272 mm noticed in 2008 and lowest rainfall 568 mm noticed in 1987. The average annual rainfall is noticed as 899.1 mm. Normal rainfall 959.5 mm observed after normal rainfall data analysis. The fifty years data analysis coefficient of variation is observed 0.20% and $R^2$ 0.40 after analysis

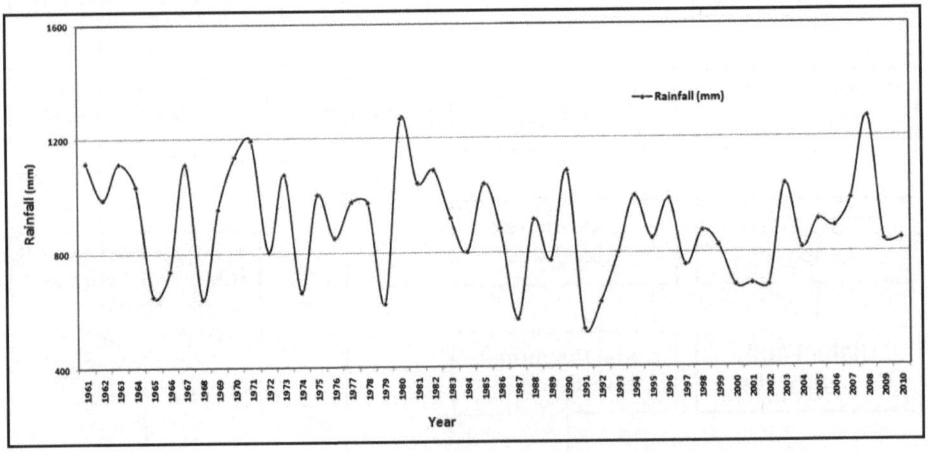


*Fig. 5.4:* **Year wise Actual and Normal Rainfall (mm) of Uttar Pradesh**

**Table 5.1: Districts wise Normal Rainfall & Average (Fifty Years) Rainfall of Uttar Pradesh**

| District | Normal Rainfall (mm) | 50 Year Average Rainfall (mm) |
|---|---|---|
| Gorakhpur | 1364.8 | 1017.5 |
| Maharajganj | 1364.1 | 1141.8 |
| Basti | 1264.0 | 937.0 |
| Sant Kabir Nagar | 1264.0 | 900.5 |
| Siddharthnagar | 1264.0 | 1078.2 |
| Pilibhit | 1242.0 | 1028.2 |
| Gonda | 1171.6 | 961.3 |
| Balrampur | 1155.3 | 1065.1 |
| Bahraihich | 1149.3 | 962.7 |
| Sonbhadra | 1148.5 | 1049.5 |
| Shrawasti | 1147.8 | 1056.4 |
| Bijnor | 1146.6 | 808.3 |
| Deoria | 1145.1 | 1012.7 |
| Kushinagar/Padrauna | 1145.1 | 1036.3 |
| Mirzapur | 1134.1 | 991.7 |
| Bareilly | 1125.9 | 953.0 |
| Lakhimpur (Kheri) | 1075.7 | 1094.7 |
| Sitapur | 1059.5 | 928.0 |
| Varanasi | 1058.6 | 932.8 |
| Chandauli | 1056.4 | 972.1 |
| Ghazipur | 1055.6 | 924.5 |
| Rabidas Nagar | 1052.3 | 889.6 |
| Barabanki | 1034.0 | 886.0 |
| Ambedkarnagar | 1032.1 | 788.3 |
| Faizabad | 1031.6 | 906.0 |
| Ballia | 1027.5 | 917.9 |
| Shahjahanpur | 1021.5 | 832.6 |
| Azamgarh | 1021.3 | 933.8 |
| Mau | 1021.3 | 956.1 |
| Sultanpur | 1010.2 | 899.2 |
| Jaunpur | 997.9 | 945.0 |
| Lucknow | 989.3 | 858.8 |
| J.B.P.Nagar | 988.8 | 859.3 |
| Allahabad | 983.1 | 949.7 |
| Pratapgarh | 980.9 | 901.7 |

(Table Contd...)

| District | Normal Rainfall (mm) | 50 Year Average Rainfall (mm) |
|---|---|---|
| Kaushambi | 975.9 | 936.0 |
| Moradabad | 973.2 | 856.6 |
| Banda | 966.5 | 996.8 |
| Sahranpur | 955.0 | 992.8 |
| Rampur | 944.3 | 1002.9 |
| Chitrakoot | 940.0 | 991.4 |
| Raebareli | 936.0 | 925.2 |
| Badaun | 935.2 | 684.1 |
| Fatehpur | 927.7 | 928.1 |
| Hardoi | 897.1 | 856.1 |
| Jhansi | 894.1 | 821.5 |
| Lalitpur | 880.1 | 1020.5 |
| Hamirpur | 877.9 | 944.8 |
| Unnao | 864.4 | 854.8 |
| Mahoba | 850.7 | 1001.9 |
| Farrukhabad | 823.6 | 824.6 |
| Jallaun | 813.6 | 896.0 |
| Kanpur (Nagar) | 801.5 | 869.4 |
| Kanpur (Dehat) | 801.5 | 860.3 |
| Kannauj | 795.4 | 813.6 |
| Muzaffarnagar | 773.9 | 764.4 |
| Etawah | 759.2 | 774.0 |
| Ghaziabad | 756.4 | 701.3 |
| Auraiya | 752.4 | |
| Mainpuri | 740.6 | 780.3 |
| Meerut | 731.7 | 761.0 |
| Bagpat | 721.2 | 1050.4 |
| Gautam Buddha Nagar | 719.7 | 682.9 |
| Etah | 701.6 | 738.6 |
| Bulandshahr | 679.0 | 731.4 |
| Aligarh | 670.2 | 706.7 |
| Hathras (Mahamaya Nagar) | 662.8 | 698.6 |
| Firozabad | 662.5 | 731.1 |
| Agra | 661.1 | 740.1 |
| Mathura | 591.4 | 689.1 |

(Table Contd...)

| Statistical Analysis | Normal Rainfall (mm) | 50 Year Average Rainfall (mm) |
|---|---|---|
| Average | 959.5 | 898.6 |
| MIN | 591.4 | 682.9 |
| MAX | 1364.8 | 1141.8 |
| SD | 182.7 | 113.7 |
| CV | 0.19 | 0.13 |
| CV% | 19.0 | 12.6 |

## Districts Rainfall (mm) Pattern of Uttar Pradesh

The recoded monthly and annual rainfall data, standard deviation, coefficient of variability is presented in Table 5.2. The average annual rainfall of fifty years was estimated 898.6 mm whereas normal rainfall 959.5mm. The maximum rainfall was observed in Maharajganj district 1141.8 mm while minimum rainfall (682.9 mm) in GautamBuddha Nagar. The coefficient of variation varied with the season. The standard deviation from mean annual rainfall was 182.7mm. A decreasing trend of annual rainfall@-2.36mm/year has been noticed but without any statistical significance. The fifty years double moving trend of rainfall was observed forecast trend rising status but actual trend is decreasing status (Fig. 5.5).

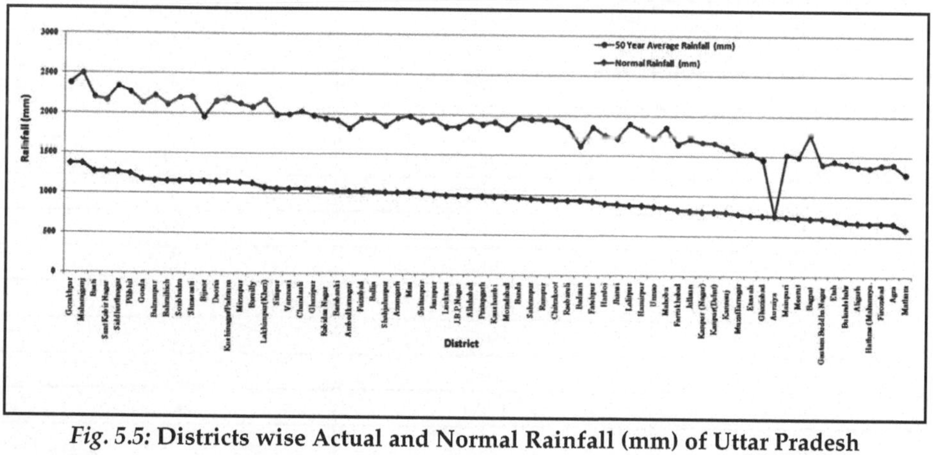


*Fig. 5.5:* **Districts wise Actual and Normal Rainfall (mm) of Uttar Pradesh**

## Trend Analysis of Uttar Pradesh

Trend analysis of a time series consists of the magnitude of trend and its statistical significance. The annual rainfall time series dataset (1961 to 2010) correspond interpolated regression line is also plotted (Fig. 5.6). The variability around the average value, that is ranges 900 to 1000mm. A decrease line of the annual rainfall graph had shown the slope of the regression line. The slope of the yearly time series is about -2.36mm/10 years. The $R^2$ 0.035 observed in the period 1961-2010.

**Table 5.2: Fifty Years Rainfall (mm) in All Districts of Uttar Pradesh**

| Sl. No. | Year | Rainfall (mm) |
|---|---|---|
| 1. | 1961 | 1119 |
| 2. | 1962 | 990 |
| 3. | 1963 | 1116 |
| 4. | 1964 | 1035 |
| 5. | 1965 | 651 |
| 6. | 1966 | 737 |
| 7. | 1967 | 1112 |
| 8. | 1968 | 642 |
| 9. | 1969 | 955 |
| 10. | 1970 | 1138 |
| 11. | 1971 | 1196 |
| 12. | 1972 | 804 |
| 13. | 1973 | 1076 |
| 14. | 1974 | 663 |
| 15. | 1975 | 1004 |
| 16. | 1976 | 851 |
| 17. | 1977 | 977 |
| 18. | 1978 | 974 |
| 19. | 1979 | 621 |
| 20. | 1980 | 1268 |
| 21. | 1981 | 1044 |
| 22. | 1982 | 1089 |
| 23. | 1983 | 922 |
| 24. | 1984 | 801 |
| 25. | 1985 | 1041 |
| 26. | 1986 | 883 |
| 27. | 1987 | 568 |
| 28. | 1988 | 914 |
| 29. | 1989 | 773 |
| 30. | 1990 | 1086 |
| 31. | 1991 | 533 |
| 32. | 1992 | 628 |
| 33. | 1993 | 799 |
| 34. | 1994 | 997 |
| 35. | 1995 | 849 |
| 36. | 1996 | 985 |
| 37. | 1997 | 755 |

(Table Contd...)

| Sl. No. | Year | Rainfall (mm) |
|---|---|---|
| 38. | 1998 | 874 |
| 39. | 1999 | 825 |
| 40. | 2000 | 684 |
| 41. | 2001 | 691 |
| 42. | 2002 | 685 |
| 43. | 2003 | 1039 |
| 44. | 2004 | 815 |
| 45. | 2005 | 912 |
| 46. | 2006 | 890 |
| 47. | 2007 | 986 |
| 48. | 2008 | 1272 |
| 49. | 2009 | 842 |
| 50. | 2010 | 846 |
| **Average** | | **899.1** |
| **Std. Dev.** | | **182.5** |
| **CV%** | | **0.20** |
| **Minimum rainfall in year 1991** | | **532.7** |
| **Maximum rainfall in year 2008** | | **1272.4** |
| **50 Year** | **Regression Line** | **$R^2$** |
| | -25.35x+975.1 | 0.404 |

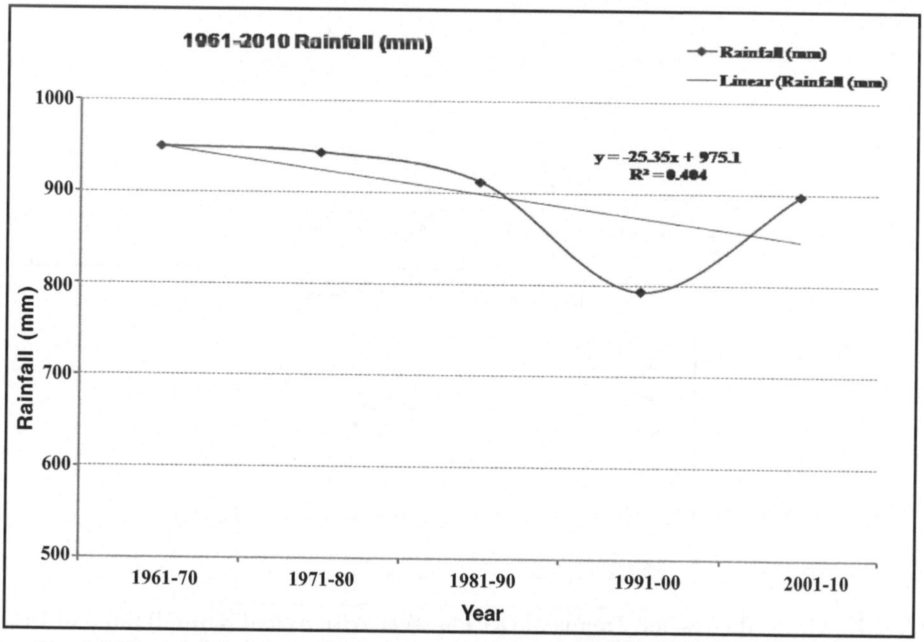


*Fig. 5.6:* Decadal Pattern of Rainfall (mm) of Uttar Pradesh (1961-70-80-90-00-10)

## Decadal Study of Rainfall Data

After analysis of decadal data of fifty years rainfall study divided in five decum series viz. 1961-70, 1971-1980,1981-1990, 1991-2000 and 2001-2010. The dataset series are based on fifty years district wise annual rainfall data (Fig.5.7). The average maximum rainfall is 949.4mm in 1961-1970 whereas minimum rainfall is 793 mm in 1991-2000 in decadal data series study. The CV (%) maximum observed 22.4 % in year 1971-80 and lowest in 1991-00 of the dacum series (Table 5.3). The study of decadal trend pattern analysis (Table 5.4) minimum $R^2$ value (R2=0.001) in 1971-80 and maximum ($R^2$=0.194) in 2001-2010.

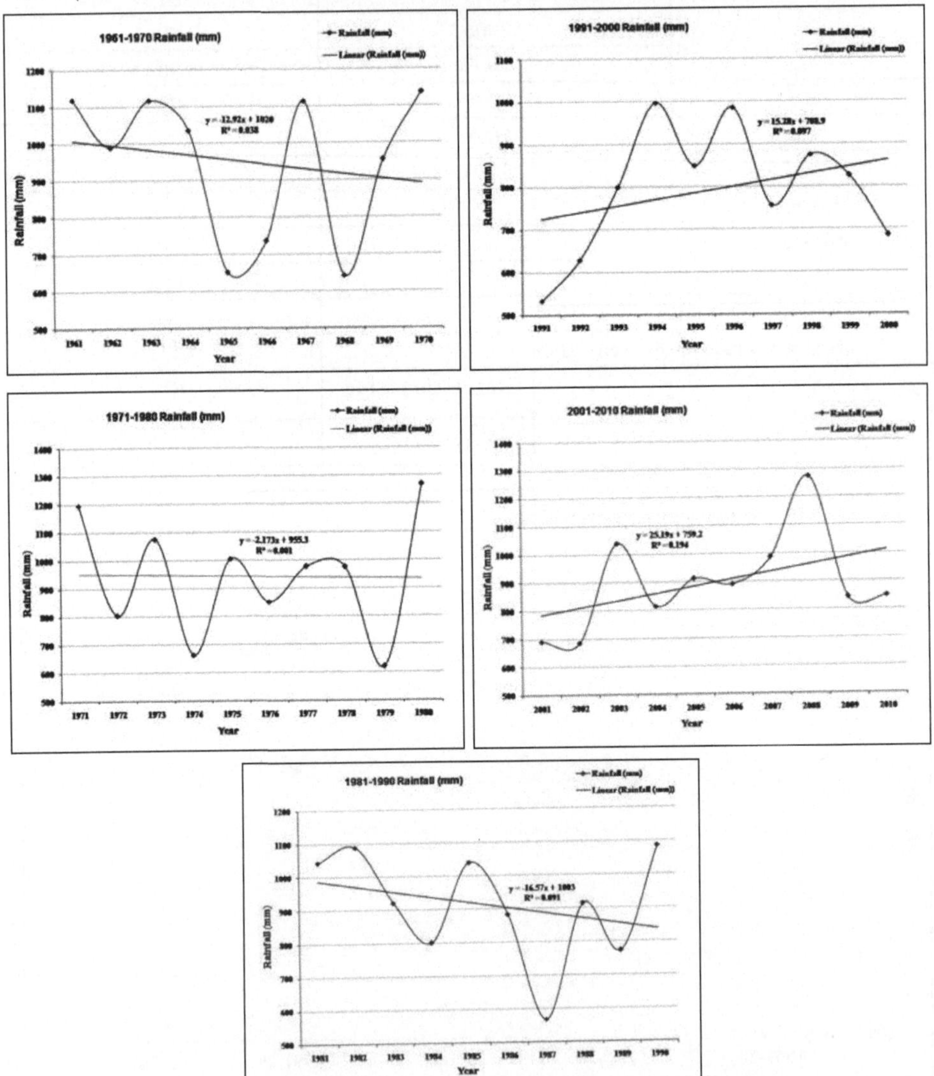


*Fig. 5.7:* **Linear Regression Trends of Decadal Year Wise Actual Rainfall (mm) of Uttar Pradesh (1961 to 2010)**

**Table 5.3: Statistical Summary of Decadal Rainfall (mm) in All Districts of Uttar Pradesh**

| Sl. No. | 1961-70 | 1971-80 | 1981-90 | 1991-00 | 2001-10 |
|---|---|---|---|---|---|
| 1. | 1119.2 | 1196.0 | 1043.8 | 532.7 | 690.9 |
| 2. | 990.2 | 804.1 | 1088.9 | 628.4 | 685.2 |
| 3. | 1115.9 | 1075.8 | 921.6 | 799.1 | 1038.6 |
| 4. | 1035.0 | 663.1 | 800.7 | 997.0 | 814.7 |
| 5. | 650.6 | 1004.4 | 1041.2 | 849.4 | 911.8 |
| 6. | 736.5 | 850.9 | 882.9 | 985.0 | 890.4 |
| 7. | 1112.4 | 976.7 | 567.7 | 755.2 | 985.9 |
| 8. | 641.6 | 974.3 | 913.5 | 874.2 | 1272.4 |
| 9. | 955.1 | 620.5 | 772.7 | 825.0 | 841.6 |
| 10. | 1137.6 | 1267.8 | 1085.6 | 683.8 | 846.4 |
| **Mean** | **949.4** | **943.4** | **911.9** | **793.0** | **897.8** |
| **Std. Dev.** | **199.1** | **211.7** | **165.6** | **148.2** | **172.8** |
| **CV** | **0.21** | **0.22** | **0.18** | **0.19** | **0.19** |
| **CV%** | **21.0** | **22.4** | **18.2** | **18.7** | **19.3** |

**Table 5.4: Linear Regression Equations of Decadal Rainfall (mm) in All Districts of Uttar Pradesh**

| Decadal Year | Regression Line | $R^2$ |
|---|---|---|
| **1961-70** | -12.92x+1020 | 0.038 |
| **1971-80** | -2.173x+955.3 | 0.001 |
| **1981-90** | -16.57x+1003 | 0.091 |
| **1991-00** | 15.28x+708.9 | 0.097 |
| **2001-10** | 25.19x+759.2 | 0.194 |

## Statistical Software used for Data Analysis

The two statistical software (Statistix10.0 & XLSTAT2014.6.02) used for analysis of rainfall data, the linear regression of fifty years data observed at coefficient interval at 95% is 2.36 mm/year. But that is observed in trend line $R^2$ value 0.40 and rainfall pattern decreasing -25.35 alarming rate.

In regression line were plotted on time series data (fifty years) and five decadal studies with total districts actual rainfall sum in a year collected over the fifty years. The rainfall (dependent variables) against time (independent variable) in years was plotted in Statistix 10.0. software. The linear regression line was fitted to determine the trends of rainfall observed from year 1990 to 1980. The decadal study, fitting of the regression lines were done in Microsoft Excel (Fig. 5.8).The Least Squares Linear Regression of Rainfall study observed statistical information $R^2$ 0.0358, Mean Square Error (MSE) 32771.2, Adjusted $R^2$ 0.0157and Standard Deviation 181.028. The statistical analysis results are shown in Fig. 5.9.

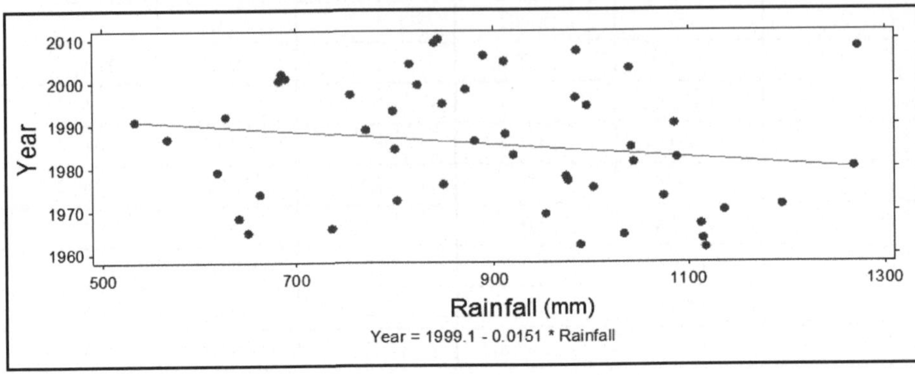


*Fig. 5.8:* **Linear Regression Fitted Line Between Year (Decadal) and Rainfall (mm)**

Statistix 10.0 (30-day Trial) arimal.sx, 2/8/2015, 9:33:56 PM

**Least Squares Linear Regression of Rainfall**

| **Predictor Variables** | **Coefficient** | **Std Error** | **T** | **P** |
|---|---|---|---|---|
| Constant | 5601.32 | 3522.49 | 1.59 | 0.1184 |
| Year | -2.36826 | 1.77406 | -1.33 | 0.1882 |

| | | | |
|---|---|---|---|
| $R^2$ | 0.0358 | Mean Square Error (MSE) | 32771.2 |
| Adjusted $R^2$ | 0.0157 | Standard Deviation | 181.028 |
| AICc | 524.35 | | |
| PRESS | 1.71E+06 | | |

| **Source** | **DF** | **SS** | **MS** | **F** | **P** |
|---|---|---|---|---|---|
| Regression | 1 | 58400 | 58400.1 | 1.78 | 0.1882 |
| Residual | 48 | 1573020 | 32771.2 | | |
| Total | 49 | 1631420 | | | |

Cases Included 50 Missing Cases 0

*Fig. 5.9:* **Statistical Output After Analysis of Time Series Data (Year 1961 to 2010)**

The double moving averages analysis of data used for actual as well as forecast of data from 1981 to 2021 in hypothetical lines/points (ten years) with rising pattern of rainfall with range of rainfall 900 to 1100 mm (Fig. 5.10 & Fig. 5.11).

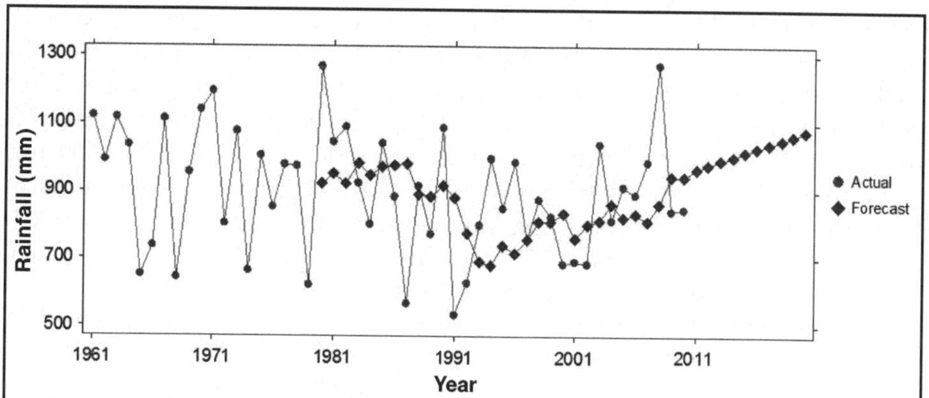


*Fig. 5.10:* **Double Moving Averages Forecast and Actual Plot for Rainfall (mm)**

Statistix 10.0 (30-day Trial) arimal.sx, 2/8/2015, 9:09:34 PM

**Double Moving Averages for Rainfall**

| | |
|---|---|
| Moving Average Length | 10 |
| Sum of Squared Errors (SSE) | **1073593** |
| Mean Squared Error (MSE) | 34632.0 |
| Standard Error (SE) | 186.097 |
| Mean Absolute Deviation (MAD) | 148.655 |
| Mean Abs Percentage Error (MAPE) | 17.68 |
| Mean Percentage Error (MPE) | -0.96 |
| Number of Cases | 50 |

| **Load** | **95% C.I. Lower Bound** | **Forecast** | **95% C.I. Upper Bound** |
|---|---|---|---|
| 1. | 600.688 | 965.438 | 1330.19 |
| 2. | 612.986 | 977.736 | 1342.49 |
| 3. | 625.284 | 990.033 | 1354.78 |
| 4. | 637.581 | 1002.33 | 1367.08 |
| 5. | 649.879 | 1014.63 | 1379.38 |
| 6. | 662.177 | 1026.93 | 1391.68 |
| 7. | 674.475 | 1039.22 | 1403.97 |
| 8. | 686.772 | 1051.52 | 1416.27 |
| 9. | 699.070 | 1063.82 | 1428.57 |
| 10. | 711.368 | 1076.12 | 1440.87 |

*Fig. 5.11:* **Double Moving Averages Output of Time Series Data (Year 1961 to 2010)**

The linear forecasting method is the ARIMA model used for rainfall data study; it is also called Box-Jenkins method. It is a flexible model used for time series pattern. That constructive a univariate ARIMA model for time series data observed linear trend line down fall 6.9 to 6.7 BoxCox rainfall series from year 1960 to 2010. The $R^2$ 0.028 value observed (Fig. 5.12 & 5.13). The time series analysis is used for random mechanism study and also for predict future series based on past data. Forecast was done using ARIMA model for a period 2010 to 2020. After study of the data observed may be forecasting view to rise rainfall status between ranges 900 to 1100 mm continuously based on actual data study collected from secondary dataset. But study in data in excels graph study during the period of 1961 to 2010 dataset observed the rainfall -25.35mm/10 year significantly decrease. The $R^2$ =0.40 observed in linear regression study.

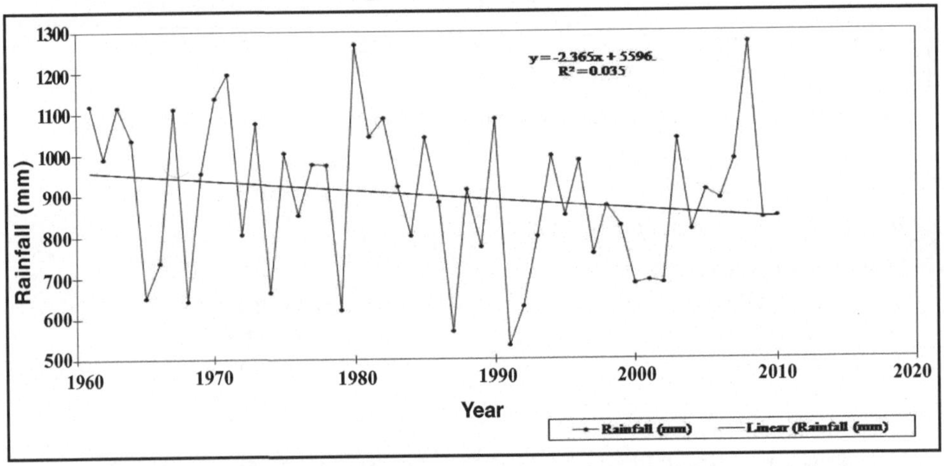


*Fig. 5.12:* **Decadal Trend Analysis of Average Rainfall of Uttar Pradesh**

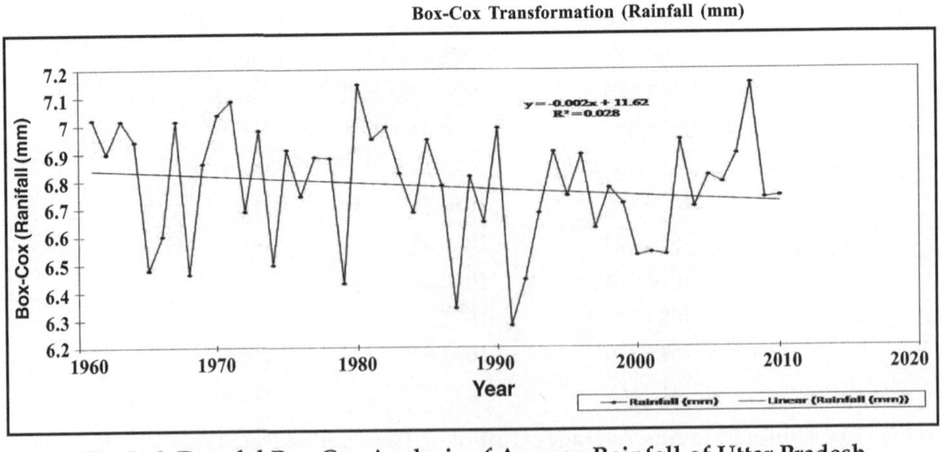


*Fig. 5.13:* **Decadal Box-Cox Analysis of Average Rainfall of Uttar Pradesh**

## Geo-statistical Analysis

The local polynomial interpolation (LPI) is deterministic method of Geostatistical analysis; it provides prediction, prediction standard error and condition number surfaces. It interpolated values (rainfall value) to every location (district point) as a result of surrounding measured values and mathematical formulas to create a surface from a point data. These decadal maps are created in within a study boundary. That is having ability to determine accuracy of the resulting predicted surface. In this prediction method assumes the variation in statistically homogenous point throughout all locations in the surface. The local polynomial interpolation is used to obtain an estimated of the spatial variation of the surrounding locations. The actual rainfall of all districts of Uttar Pradesh taken (1961-2010) for decadal change pattern analysis in ARC GIS 10.0; prediction maps were created. The rainfall data are classified in five equal classes after analysis. The initial value <650 to >1050 values with every class have 100 values differentiate. Every range/class is shown in a specific colour; low value range in yellow to maximum value is in red colour shown in legend. In the created maps were observed in year 1961-1970 most of the districts cover > 1050mm (red color) rainfall decadal but in year 2001-2010 rainfall covered less districts area. In year 1991-2000 rainfall covered districts are too much less than other decadal year. The rainfall distribution pattern west to east rising pattern but in current scenario give up down to uprising pattern with less covered districts having much rainfall. Very less rainfall (<650mm, yellow colour) pattern seen in western UP and rising in alarming rate (Fig. 5.14).

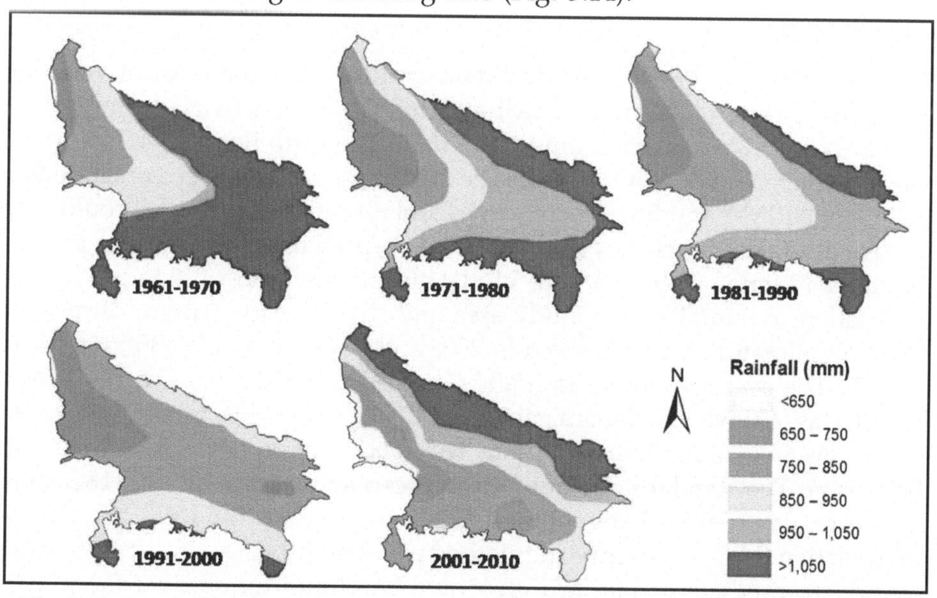


*Fig. 5.14:* **Geostatistical Analysis of Decadal Rainfall (mm) Pattern in Uttar Pradesh**

The prediction map of actual data of year wise long term rainfall data (1961-2010) used for study. The actual rainfall is giving the current scenario to distribution of rainfall pattern in all district cover area within the boundary. The prediction map of normal rainfall showed where west to eastern side rainfall decrease to increase pattern. The general trend of rainfall in the study area but in comparison to actual data rainfall pattern scenario is different, the high rainfall value is covered small area in range >1050 (red tone) and the sea green tone covered maximum district range is 850 to 950mm rainfall. The pattern of normal rainfall study found low rainfall in Bundelkhand-Jhansi region whereas study of actual rainfall is maximum it may be cause of climatic change (Fig. 5.15). The crops and cropping systems also be change due to change of rainfall pattern.

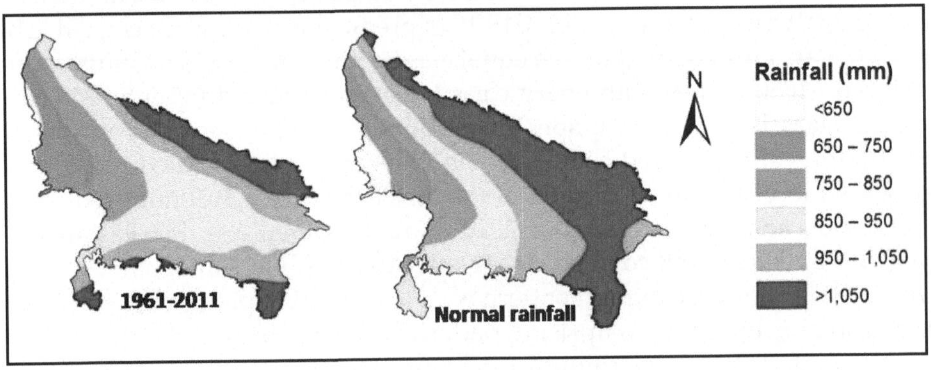


*Fig. 5.15:* **Geostastical Analysis of Fifty Years Rainfall (mm) and Normal Rainfall Pattern**

## CONCLUSION

The different type of statistical data analysis viz. coefficient of variation (CV), correlation of coefficient ($R^2$) and trend analysis to given important scenario of change pattern of time series data. The Auto-Regressive Integrated Moving Average (ARIMA) model is the starting series. It can be conclude that the use of ARIMA and Box Cox model as tool for predicting rainfall could help in agricultural research development and in predicting the rainfall pattern decadal and time series data. This model also makes it possible to predict the implication of rainfall in the study area and changing the pattern of rainfall. The high rainfall 1272 mm noticed in 2008 and lowest rainfall 568 mm noticed in 1987. The average annual rainfall is noticed as 899.1 mm. The maximum rainfall was observed in Maharajganj district 1141.8 mm while minimum rainfall (682.9 mm) in GautamBuddha Nagar. The coefficient of variation varied with the season. The standard deviation from mean annual rainfall was 182.7mm. The decreasing trends of annual rainfall@-2.36mm/year. The local polynomial interpolation (LPI) is deterministic method of Geostatistical analysis; it provides prediction, prediction standard error and condition number surfaces. It is useful for capture the short-range variation and sensitive to the neighbourhood distance may create empty areas in the prediction surface. The prediction map of actual data of year wise long term rainfall data (1961-2010) used for study. In the created maps were observed in year 1961-1970 most of the districts cover > 1050mm rainfall decadal but in year 2001-2010 rainfall covered less districts area. In year 1991-2000 rainfall covered districts are too much less than other decadal year. The actual rainfall is giving the current scenario to distribution of rainfall pattern in all district cover area within the boundary. The prediction map of normal rainfall showed where west to eastern side rainfall rising status but in actual rainfall data study high rainfall covered area low and rising direction down to up side area.

The statistical and geo statistical analysis of time series and decadal data of rainfall study is useful to understand rainfall variability and decadal pattern scenario of study area. That change also affects the crops and cropping systems and pattern which are grown in rabi and kharif season in the study area. The Indian agriculture are depend on rainfall and rainfall distribution pattern are changing due to climatic change it may be due to an urbanization, deforestation and rising of polluted material in the environment.

## REFERENCES


Bhatia, A., Aggarwal, P.K., Jain, N. and Pathak, H. (2012). Greenhouse Gas Emission from Rice and Wheat-growing Areas in India: Spatial Analysis and Upscaling. Greenhouse Gas Sci Technol. 2: 115-125. (DOI: 10.1002/ghg)

Box, G.E.P., & G.M. Jenkins. (1970), Time-series Analysis: Forecasting and Control. Rev. ed. San Francisco: Holden-Day.

Brakensiek, G.P.D. & Wallen C.C. (1963). A Study of Agroclimatology in Semi-arid and and Zones of the Near East. WMO Technical Note No. 56, Geneva.

Chow, V.T. (1954). The Log-probability Law and its Engineering Applications. Proc Am Soc Civil Eng 80: 536-1-536-25.

Chandel. S.R.S. (2001). A Handbook of Agricultural Statistics. Achal Prakashan Mandir. Kanpur. pp. 543.

Guha; G.S. & D.N. Basu: Agro-Climatic Regional Planning in India (Vol. I: Concept and Applications). pp. 127-131.

Gautam, H.R., Sharma, H.L., Kumar, R. & Bhardwaj, M.L. (2014). Effect of El Nino on Southwest Monsoon Rainfall and Agriculture in India. Current Science, 107(11): 1778-1779.

Hartkamp, A.D., White, J.W., & Hoogenboom, G. (1999). Interfacing Geographic Information Systems with Agronomic Modelling: A Review. *Agronomy Journal, 91*, 761-772.

Heinemann, A.B., Hoogenboom, G., & De Faria, R.T. (2002). Determination of Spatial Water Requirements at Country and Regional Levels Using Crop Models and GIS. *Agricultural Water Management,* 52, 177-196.

India State of Forest Report. (2011). Forest Survey of India, Ministry of Environment & Forests, Govt. of India, Dehradun. pp. 230.

Jovanovski, T.D. (2007). Auto-regressive Integrated moving Average (ARIMA). Modelling of Rainfall Process: Estimation and Forecast Geophysical Research Abstracts, 9: 02154.

Kumar, V., Jain, S.K. & Singh, Y. (2010). Analysis of Long-term Rainfall Trends in India. Hydrol. Sci. J. 55(4): 484-496. http://www.currentscience.ac.in/Volumes/107/11/1778.pdf

Khanna, S.S. (1989) The agroclimatic approach. The survey off Indian Agriculture. pp. 28-35. http://planningcommission.nic.in/aboutus/committee/wrkgrp11/wg11_agrclim.pdf

Lal, H., Hoogenb oom, G., Calixte, J. P., Jones, J. W., & Beinroth, F. H. (1993). Using crop simulation models and GIS for regional productivity analyses. Transactions of ASAE, 36(1), 175–184.

Mahalakshmi, N., P.R. Umarani & Samuel Selvaraj, R (2014). Forecasting the Tamil Nadu Rainfall Using Hybbrid ARIMA-ANN Model. International Journal of Recent Scientific Research, 5( 3):566-569.

**NARP ZONES:**

http://www.imdagrimet.gov.in/node/3535

Panjab Singh. Final Report of the Working Group on Agro-climatic Zonal Planning Including Agriculture Development in North-Eastern India for XI Five Year Plan (2007-2012). Volume I – Main Report. pp. 1-258.

**Rainfall Data Sources:**

http://indiawaterportal.org/met_data/ (1901-2002)

http://www.indiawaterportal.org/articles/district-wise-monthly-rainfall-data-list-

raingauge-stations-india-meteorological-department (2004-2010)

Smith, M. (2000). The Application of Climate Data for Planning and Management of Sustainable Rainfed and Irrigated Crop Production. Agricultural Forest Meteoroogy, 103, 99-108.

Somvanshi, V.K., Pandey, O.P., Agrawal, P.K., Kalanker, N.V., Ravi Prakash, M. & Chand, R. ( 2006). Modelling and Prediction of Rainfall Using Artificial Neural Network and ARIMA Techniques. J. Ind. Geophys. Union 10 (2):141-151.

Suhartono (2011). Time Series Forecasting by Using Seasonal Autoregressive Integrated Moving Average: Subset, Multiplicative or Additive Model, J. of Mathematics and Statistics, 7(1): 20-27.

Tveito, O.E., Forland, E.J., Heino, R., Hanssen- Bauer, I., Alexandersson, H., Dahlstroe, B., Dreb, A., Kern-Hansen, C., Jonsson, T., Vaarby-Laursen, E. & Westmann, Y. (2000) Nordic Temperature Maps, DNMI KLIMA, No. 9.

Using ArcGIS Geostatistical Analysis, (2001). The Principle of Geostastical Analysis. ESRI, USA. page 49-79.

Upkar Prakashan (2008). *Uttar Pradesh General Knowledge*. Upkar Prakashan. pp. 26. ISBN 978-81-7482-408-0. Retrieved 9 March 2011.

Pages: 93-107

CLIMATE CHANGE, DISASTER MANAGEMENT AND ENVIRONMENT

*Edited by:* Dr. Alka Chauhan; Dr. Pawan Kumar 'Bharti'

ISBN: 978-93-5056-784-5

*Edition:* 2016

*Published by:* Discovery Publishing House Pvt. Ltd., New Delhi (India)

# CHAPTER – 6

# Livestock Production in a Changing Climate *Impacts and Mitigation*

Alok Kumar Patra

**ABSTRACT**

Climate change, particularly global warming will have far-reaching consequences for dairy and meat production, especially in vulnerable parts of the world where it is vital for nutrition and livelihoods. Responses to climate change include adaptation to reduce sensitivity to climatic changes and mitigation to reduce the magnitude of climate change impact in the long run. However, neither adaptation nor mitigation alone can avoid all climate change impacts. To respond to this threat it is necessary to focus on both mitigation, to reduce the level of emission of gases contributing to global warming, and adaptation, to support local communities deal with the impacts. The effects of climate change on livestock and the impacts of thermal stress on animal health, reproduction, milk production and meat production

Associate Professor (Agronomy), All India Coordinated Research Project on Integrated Farming Systems, Orissa University of Agriculture and Technology, Bhubaneswar- 751003, Odisha, (India).

are reviewed in this article. Adverse impacts of climate on livestock production can be reduced through production adjustments, improved management practices, genetic improvement for adaptation, institutional and policy changes and capacity building for livestock keepers.

Ruminant animals, such as cattle, sheep, buffalo, and goats have special digestive systems called enteric fermentation, produces methane ($CH_4$), a potent greenhouse gas that can contribute to global climate change. It is estimated that nearly 20 per cent of $CH_4$ and 35 per cent of $N_2O$, another important green house gas come from livestock production. These adverse impacts of animal farming can be reduced through selection of fast growing breeds, improved feeding management, improved waste management and grazing management.

## INTRODUCTION

Climate change is a global phenomenon and its negative impacts are more severely felt by poor people in developing countries who rely heavily on the natural resource base for their livelihoods. The possible effects of climate change on food production are not limited to crops and agricultural production. Climate change will have far-reaching consequences for dairy, meat and wool production, mainly arising from its impact on grassland and rangeland productivity. Heat distress suffered by animals will reduce the rate of animal feed intake and result in poor growth performance (Rowlinson, 2008). Lack of water and increased frequency of drought in certain countries will lead to a loss of resources.

The IPCC predicts that by 2100 the increase in global average surface temperature may be between 1.8° C and 4.0° C. With increases of 1.5° C to 2.5° C, approximately 20 to 30 per cent of plant and animal species are expected to be at risk of extinction (FAO, 2007) with severe consequences for food security in developing countries.

## EFFECTS OF CLIMATE CHANGE ON LIVESTOCK

Weather and climate have a great influence on farm animal production. The environment in which an animal lives is referred to as its habitat. A habitat includes both biotic (living) and abiotic (non-living) components of the animals' environment. Abiotic components of an animal's environment include temperature, humidity, oxygen, wind, soil composition, day length and elevation.

The direct effects of climate change include higher temperatures and changes in rainfall patterns, which may increase the spread of existing vector-borne diseases and macro parasites of animals as well as the emergence and spread of new diseases. The major indirect effect of climate change is the reduction in availability and quality of animal feed and fodder. The changes in feed resources are linked to the carrying capacity of rangelands, the buffering abilities of ecosystems, increased desertification processes, increased scarcity of water resources, lower production of grain, *etc.* Other important indirect effects are linked to the potential shortage of feed due to a rapid increase in production competition among food, feed, fuel and land use systems.

Thornton, *et al.* (2008) examined some of the direct and indirect impacts of climate change on livestock and livestock systems. These are summarized in Table 6.1.

**Table 6.1: Direct and Indirect Impacts of Climate Change on Livestock and Livestock Systems**

| Factor | Impacts |
|---|---|
| Water | Water scarcity is increasing at an accelerated pace and affects between 1 and 2 billion people. Climate change will have a substantial effect on global water availability in the future. Not only will this affect livestock drinking water sources, but it will also have a bearing on livestock feed production systems and pasture yield. |
| Feeds | ***Land use and systems change***<br>As climate changes and becomes more variable, niches for different species alter. This may modify animal diets and compromise the ability of smallholders to manage feed deficits. |
| | ***Changes in the primary productivity of crops, forage and rangeland***<br>Effects will depend significantly on location, system and species. In $C_4$ species, a rise in temperature to 30-35° C may increase the productivity of crops, fodder and pastures. In $C_3$ plants, rising temperature has a similar effect, but increases in $CO_2$ levels will have a positive impact on the productivity of these crops. For food-feed crops, harvest indexes will change, as will the availability of energy that can be metabolized for dry season feeding. In semiarid rangelands where the growing season is likely to contract, productivity is expected to decrease. |
| | ***Changes in species composition***<br>As temperature and $CO_2$ levels change, optimal growth ranges for different species also change; species alter their competition dynamics, and the composition of mixed grasslands changes. For example, the proportion of browse in rangelands will increase in the future as a result of increased growth and competition of browse species due to increased $CO_2$ levels. Legume species will also benefit from $CO_2$ increases and in tropical grasslands the mix between legumes and grasses could be altered. |
| | ***Quality of plant material***<br>Rising temperatures increase lignifications of plant tissues and thus reduce the digestibility and the rates of degradation of plant species. The resultant reduction in livestock production may have an effect on the food security and incomes of smallholders. Interactions between primary productivity and quality of grasslands will require modifications in the management of grazing systems to attain production objectives. |

(Table Contd...)

| Factor | Impacts |
|---|---|
| Biodiversity (genetics and breeding) | In some places there will be an acceleration in the loss of the genetic and cultural diversity already occurring as a result of globalization, in crops as well as domestic animals. This loss will also be evident in crops and domestic animals. A 2.5° C rise in global temperature would cause extinction of 20 - 30 per cent of all plant and animal species assessed (IPCC, 2007). Ecosystems and species display a wide range of vulnerabilities to climate change, depending on the imminence of exposure to ecosystem-specific critical thresholds.<br>Local and rare breeds could be lost as a result of the impact of climate change and disease epidemics. Biodiversity loss has global health implications and many of the anticipated health risks driven by climate change will be attributable to a loss of genetic diversity. |
| Livestock (and human) health: | Vector-borne diseases could be affected by (i) the expansion of vector populations into cooler areas (in higher altitude areas: malaria and livestock tick-borne diseases) or into more temperate zones (such as bluetongue disease in northern Europe); and (ii) changes in rainfall pattern during wetter years, which could also lead to expanding vector populations and large-scale outbreaks of disease. Temperature and humidity variations could have a significant effect on helminth infections. Changes in crop and livestock practices could produce effects on the distribution and impact of malaria in many systems, and schistosomiasis and lymphatic filariasis in irrigated systems (Patz, *et al.*, 2005). |

*Source:* Thornton, *et al.*, 2008.

Birds and mammals are warm-blooded (endotherms or homeotherms), possessing a thermoregulatory system that maintains a stable body temperature and uniform internal environment (homeostasis) by converting food energy into heat. All metabolic processes generate substantial heat and much of this is retained within the body of homeotherms by insulating layers of fat, feathers or fur. Dairy cattle, like other warm-blooded animals, function most efficiently in environments where they can maintain their body temperature at around 38° C. Tissue and cellular metabolism and the underlying biochemical reactions that sustain life and productive functions need body temperature to be maintained within very narrow limits. Relatively small increases in body temperature result in the breakdown of body protein and a significant depression in production.

Heat stress is one of the greatest climatic challenges faced by the domestic animals and global climate warming may further aggravate the condition and even provoke thermal stress condition. Global warming has two way effects on animal production system. In one hand it directly affects the health, reproduction, nutrition *etc.* of the animals resulting in poor performance, inferior product quality, outbreak of diseases, *etc.* while on the other hand there are indirect effects on animal production due to change in soil fertility, decrease in preferred vegetation, rangeland degradation, desertification and decrease in production of feed stuffs (Bajagai, 2011). Dairy cattle are particularly more susceptible to increased ambient temperature than other ruminants because of their high metabolic rate and poor water retention mechanism in kidney and gastrointestinal tract.

Many diseases of farm animals and poultry are caused or carried by parasites like worms, flies, lice, and ticks. These parasites and many parasitic diseases are influenced by climate. Diseases spread by insects are encouraged when climatic conditions like temperature and excessive moisture favour the propagation of the vector (Mavi and Tupper, 2004).

## EFFECT OF HEAT STRESS ON CATTLE

All animals have a range of ambient environmental temperatures termed the thermo neutral zone. This is the range of temperatures that are conducive to health and performance. The upper critical temperature is the point at which heat or thermal stress effects begin to affect the animal. The environmental factors that contribute to heat stress include high temperature, high humidity and sunlight. Heat stress can be simply defined as the point where the cow cannot dissipate an adequate quantity of heat to maintain body thermal balance.

The environmental conditions that induce heat stress can be calculated using the temperature humidity index (THI). A THI is a single value representing the combination of air temperature and humidity associated with the level of thermal stress. The THI was developed during early 1990s as a weather safety index to monitor and reduce heat stress-related losses. Utilizing both humidity and temperature is important compared with utilizing temperature or humidity alone to evaluate heat stress. THI is calculated from air temperature and relative humidity using the following equation.

THI = Dry bulb temperature in degree Celsius + (0.36 x dew point temperature in degree Celsius) + 41.2

The dew point is the temperature at which the water vapour in a sample of air at constant barometric pressure condenses into liquid water at the same rate at which it evaporates. Heat stress begins to occur in dairy cattle when the THI is $> 72$. The THI threshold values for beef cattle, swine and poultry are 72-75, 72-74 and 70-78, respectively.

### Impacts of Thermal Stress on Animal Health

Thermal stresses have both direct and indirect effects on animal health. Direct effects of thermal stress include simple physiological disturbances, organ dysfunction and death.

Reduction in feed intake together with diversion of more energy to maintain normal body function creates negative energy balance which deteriorates animal health conditions. These animals with poor health are prone to infectious diseases. The high ambient temperature and moisture level creates the environment suitable for fungus growth in feed and feedstuffs which may lead to mycotoxicosis in animals due to mycotoxin produced by fungi.

**Table 6.2: Effect of Heat Stress on Dairy Cattle Based on Temperature Humidity Index**

| THI | Stress Level | Comments |
|---|---|---|
| < 72 | None | — |
| 72-79 | Mild | Dairy cows will adjust by seeking shade, increasing respiration rate and dilation of the blood vessels. The effect on milk production will be minimal. |
| 80-89 | Moderate | Both saliva production and respiration rate will increase. Feed intake may be depressed and water consumption will increase. There will be an increase in body temperature. Milk reduction and reproduction will be decreased. |
| 90-98 | Severe | Cows will become very uncomfortable due to high body temperature, rapid respiration and excessive saliva production. Milk production and reproduction will be markedly decreased. |
| > 98 | Danger | Death of cow may occur. |

*Source:* Hahn, 1999 and West, 2003.

### Impacts of Thermal Stress on Reproduction

Thermal stress causes imbalance in secretion of reproductive hormones. High ambient temperature increases incidence of ovarian cysts and reduces fertility of cattle. Conception rates are less in cattle under thermal stress as compared to those in thermo-neutral zone. Thermal stress prior to and immediately after artificial insemination causes reduction in conception rate in high producing lactating cows. Similarly, climatic warming also affects reproductive performance in bulls.

### Impacts of Thermal Stress on Milk Production

Reduction in milk production is one of the major economic impacts of climatic stress in dairy cattle. Reduction in milk yield is further intensified by decrease in feed consumption by the animals. Reduced milk production due to thermal stress is attributable only partly to decrease in feed intake. Actually 35% of reduced milk production is due to decreased feed intake while remaining 65% is attributable to direct effect of thermal stress (Bajagai, 2011). Milk production in cow has been found to be reduced when ambient temperature and temperature humidity index increase above critical threshold. The yield and composition of milk are affected by the temperature of the environment. Environmental temperatures lower and higher than the comfort zone temperatures reduce yield and alter many of the components of milk. At all India level an estimated annual loss due to direct thermal stress on livestock is about 1.8 million tonnes of milk, that is, nearly 2% of the total milk production in the country. This decrease can be either transitory or long term depending on the length and severity of heat stress. The decline in milk production will be higher in crossbreds followed by buffalo and indigenous cattle.

## EFFECT OF CLIMATE ON POULTRY BIRDS

Hot weather can have a severe impact on performance of poultry. The climate in poultry houses influences the health of the birds. Respiratory, digestive and behavioural disorders are more likely to occur in houses in which the climatic conditions are not up to standard. Production efficiency can be affected long before the temperature reaches a level at which survival becomes a concern.

**Table 6.3: Effect of Ambient Temperature on Adult Poultry Birds**

| Temperature Range (in degree Celsius) | Effect on adult poultry birds |
|---|---|
| 13-24 | Thermal neutral zone. The temperature range in which the bird does not need to alter its basic metabolic rate or behaviour to maintain its body temperature. |
| 19-24 | Ideal temperature range. |
| 24-30 | A slight reduction in feed consumption can be expected, but if nutrient intake is adequate, production efficiency is good. Egg size may be reduced and shell quality may suffer as temperatures reach the top of this range. |
| 30-33 | Feed consumption falls further. Weight gains are lower. Egg size and shell quality deteriorate. Egg production usually suffers. Cooling procedures should be started before this temperature range is reached. |
| 33-35 | Feed consumption continues to drop. There is some danger of heat prostration among layers, especially the heavier birds and those in full production. At these temperatures, cooling procedures must be carried out. |
| 35-38 | Heat prostration is probable. Emergency measures may be needed. Egg production and feed consumption are severely reduced. Water consumption is very high. |
| > 38 | Emergency measures are needed to cool birds. Survival is the concern at these temperatures. |

*Source:* Anderson and Carter, 2007.

The layers are warm blooded with a body temperature of 41-42.2° C. Body temperature is kept quite constant and is regulated by part of the chicken brain. It takes some time before heat regulating mechanisms start functioning in newborn chicks and therefore they need a higher ambient temperature than adult birds do. Furthermore, the ratio between the surface area and weight of young chicks is unfavourable and they do not have any fat reserves. The comfort zone is defined as the temperature zone in which the birds are able to keep their body temperature constant with minimum effort. Behaviour of birds will change when temperatures rise to above or decrease to below the comfort zone.

The thermo-neutral zone is defined as the temperature zone in which the birds are able to keep their body temperature constant with the help of physical heat regulation. The lowest temperature in the thermo-neutral zone is called the lowest critical temperature. If temperatures fall to under this temperature the bird will start to use feed energy to warm itself and will consequently consume more feed. The highest temperature in the thermo-neutral zone is called the highest critical temperature. If the temperature rises above this temperature the birds can no longer dissipate their heat. They will start to consume less feed and production will drop as a result. The highest and lowest critical temperature of a bird depends on its age and bodyweight, housing system, feeding level, relative humidity and air velocity. The critical temperature for layers is 20° C. For every 1° C lower than 20° C, the birds require an extra 1.5 g of feed per day. The most efficient temperature for layers lies between 20 and 24° C. When temperature rises above 24° C, shell quality and egg weight will reduce. The critical temperature for broilers and rearing birds is highly dependent on age.

Relative humidity in poultry houses is measured to determine its impact on respiratory disorders. If the relative humidity is too high, condensation may accumulate in the house which leads to wet litter. This has a direct effect on the growth of microorganisms. Humidity is controlled by the intense heating or cooling of air inside the house in response to the temperature outside the house. The ideal relative humidity for poultry is 60-80%.

**Table 6.4: Recommended Temperature and Relative Humidity for Poultry Birds**

| Age of the Bird (in days) | Recommended Ambient Temperature (°C) | Recommended Relative Humidity (%) |
|---|---|---|
| 1 | 33 | 50 |
| 7 | 31.5 | 50 |
| 14 | 28.5 | 60 |
| 21 | 28.5 | 65 |
| 28 | 26 | 70 |
| 42 | 23 | 85 |

*Source:* Hulzebosch, 2006.

### Optimum Temperature for Ducks

At the time of hatching, ducklings require a high temperature of about 30° C. They are not yet able to regulate their body temperature and require supplemental heat such as that provided by a brooder. As they grow older they become better able to produce and conserve heat, and regulate their body temperature. After a duckling is fully covered with feathers, they are able to maintain proper body temperature even when the outside temperature is low.

**Table 6.5: Recommended Temperatures for Ducks**

| Age of Ducks in Days | Temperature (°C) |
|---|---|
| 1 | 30 |
| 7 | 27 |
| 14 | 23 |
| 21 | 19 |
| 28 | 15 |
| 35 | 13 |
| 42 | 13 |
| 49 | 13 |
| Developing breeders | 13 |
| Laying breeders | 13 |

*Source:* Scott and Dean, 1991.

## REDUCING IMPACTS OF CLIMATE ON LIVESTOCK PRODUCTION

Livestock producers have traditionally adapted to various environmental and climatic changes by building on their in-depth knowledge of the environment in which they live (Calvosa, *et al.*, 2009). However, the expanding human population, urbanization, environmental degradation and increased consumption of animal source foods have rendered some of those coping mechanisms ineffective (Sidahmed, 2008). In addition, changes brought about by global warming are likely to happen at such a speed that they will exceed the capacity of spontaneous adaptation of both human communities and animal species.

For an animal to maintain homeothermy (no change in body temperature, other than normal circadian rhythms), the ambient environment and the animal must exchange heat at a rate that permits balancing the metabolic heat production and the energy gains/losses through the four transfer modes, *i.e.*, radiation, convection, conduction and evaporation. Ruminant animals primarily adjust evaporative heat loss to maintain homeo-thermy during brief exposures to adverse weather, but will reduce feed intake to lower heat produc-tion during prolonged hot weather. Swine and poultry primarily adjust heat production to main-tain homeothermy. To alter the microclimate of an animal effectively through housing or environmental modification the following factors should be considered (WMO, 2010).

The following have been identified by several experts (FAO, 2008; Thornton, *et al.*, 2008; Sidahmed, 2008) as ways to increase adaptation in the livestock sector.

**Production Adjustments**

Changes in livestock practices include (i) diversification, intensification and/or integration of pasture management, livestock and crop production; (ii) changing land use and irrigation; (iii) altering the timing of operations; (iv) conservation of nature and ecosystems; (v) modifying stock routings and distances; (vi) introducing mixed livestock farming systems, such as stall-fed systems and pasture grazing.

**Livestock Management Systems**

A lower number of more productive animals lead to more efficient production and lower green house gas (GHG) emissions from livestock farming. Changes in livestock/herd composition may be sometimes beneficial and more productive. Improved management of water resources through the introduction of simple techniques for localized irrigation like drip and sprinkler irrigation, accompanied by infrastructure to harvest and store rainwater, such as tanks connected to the roofs of houses and small surface and underground dams.

**Site Selection**

The selection of a site for housing of animals is the most important factor to minimise the effects of local weather. Climatic factors vary with height above the ground at a specific location. Observations of the microclimates in a general location will reveal much variation in thermal conditions resulting from terrain features, differential exposure, wetlands, rivers, type and height of vegetation, human activities and other factors. Proper selection of a site to emphasise factors for enhanced heat dissipation will have long-term protection benefits.

**Windbreaks**

Windbreaks have an important role to reduce the climatic impacts on animals in tropical and subtropical regions. Grazing animals are protected from strong winds, especially during cold weather. Structures or trees can markedly reduce wind speed and can be beneficial to the survival of exposed animals, especially the newborns. A windbreak acts as a barrier that lowers the wind speed near the ground surface and diverts and splits the air stream. The protection achieved is deter-mined by the configuration, height, density and thickness of the trees in a belt. The use of leguminous trees or shrubs can be a practical means to counteract the effects of wind and heat stress, as well as to improve animal diet.

### Shades

Shades may be provided for protecting farm animals in hot climates. In a tropical region, the solar irradiance is high even during the winter. It is reported that when dairy cows are given access to adequate shades, milk production is increased. Enclosed shelters are not recommended for tropical climates because of the decreased natural air veloc-ity and sanitation. In temperate regions, partially enclosed shelters can reduce the thermal radiation received by animals during hot weather.

### Genetic Improvement for Adaptation

Many local breeds are adapted to harsh living conditions and they are able to survive, grow and reproduce in conditions of poor nutrition, parasites and diseases. Any population must be genetically heteroge-neous in order to be able to survive under the challenges of the changing environment. Adaptation strategies address not only the tolerance of livestock to heat, but also their ability to survive, grow and reproduce in conditions of poor nutrition, parasites and diseases (Hoffmann, 2008). Thus, adaptation strategy should be identifying and strengthening local breeds that have adapted to local climatic stress and feed sources and improving local genetics through cross-breeding with heat and disease tolerant breeds. This is the basis for genetic improvement in livestock. If climate change is faster than natural selection, the risk of survival and adaptation of the new breed is greater (Hoffmann, 2008). Working towards a better understanding of the impacts of climate change on livestock, developing new breeds and genetic types, improving animal health and enhancing water and soil management would support adaptation measures in the long term.

### Institutional and Policy Changes

Removing or introducing subsidies, insurance systems, income diversification practices and establishing livestock early warning systems and other forecasting and crisis-preparedness systems – could benefit adaptation efforts. The agriculture market could be enhanced by, for example, the promotion of interregional trade and credit schemes.

### Capacity Building for Livestock Keepers

There is a need to improve the capacity of livestock producers and herders to understand and deal with climate change increasing their awareness of global changes. In addition, training in agroecological technologies and practices for the production and conservation of fodder improves the supply of animal feed and reduces malnutrition and mortality in herds (Calvosa, *et al.*, 2009).

## CONTRIBUTION OF LIVESTOCK TO CLIMATE CHANGE

Ruminant animals, such as cattle, sheep, buffalo, and goats have special digestive systems that can convert otherwise unusable plant materials into nutritious food and fibre. This helpful digestive process, called enteric fermentation, however, produces methane ($CH_4$), a potent greenhouse gas that can contribute to global climate change. Enteric fermentation is a digestive process by which carbohydrates are broken down by microorganisms into simple molecules for absorption into the bloodstream of an animal. It is one of the factors in increased methane emissions. Enteric fermentation occurs when methane is produced in the rumen as microbial fermentation takes place.

Livestock production systems can also emit other greenhouse gases such as nitrous oxide ($N_2O$) and carbon dioxide ($CO_2$). In recent years the increasing use of intensive live-stock production systems has become a source of solid, liquid and airborne emissions that can be both a nuisance and environmentally harmful. In spite of the low amount of $CH_4$ in the atmosphere relative to that of $CO_2$, its importance as a pollutant is considered to be 21 times greater than that of $CO_2$, while that of $N_2O$ is 310 times greater (Hartung, 2003).

It is estimated that nearly 20 per cent of $CH_4$ and 35 per cent of $N_2O$ come from livestock production. According to the European Environment Agency, nearly 50 per cent of the overall amount of $CH_4$ released in Europe originates from agriculture and stems mainly from ruminant animals (EEA, 2001).

**Table 6.6: Relative Contribution of Various Sources to the Global Emission of Methane ($CH_4$) and Nitrous Oxide ($N_2O$)**

| Gas | Natural Sources | Anthropogenic Sources | |
|---|---|---|---|
| | | Livestock Production | Others |
| $CH_4$ | 30 | 20 | 50 |
| $N_2O$ | 55 | 35 | 10 |

*Source:* Monteny, 2003.

Manure of cattle is a much more important source of $CH_4$ emission than enteric fermentation. This problem is due to liquid manure storage in tanks or pits. The amount and surface area of the stored manure, and the ambient and core manure temperature are the major factors that determine the quantity of $CH_4$ gas emission (Hartung and Monteny, 2000).

**Table 6.7: Methane Emission from Livestock Production (kg/animal/year)**

| Species | Enteric Fermentation | Manure |
|---|---|---|
| Dairy cows | 100 | 345 |
| Pigs | 1 | 32 |
| Poultry | 0.1 | 2.4 |

*Source:* Hartung, 2003.

Thus, the livestock sector which will be a sufferer of climate change is itself a large source of methane emissions. In India, although the emission rate per animal is much lower than the developed countries, due to vast livestock population the total annual methane emissions from Indian livestock ranged from 7.26 to 10.4 million tons/year. In India more than 90% of the total methane emission from enteric fermentation is being contributed by the large ruminants (cattle and buffalo) and rest from small ruminants and others.

## REDUCING IMPACTS OF LIVESTOCK PRODUCTION ON CLIMATE

Methane is generated mainly as a by-product of the fermentation of the digestible organic matter in ruminants; especially those with forage-based diets. The grain-based diets reduce the emission of $CH_4$. Thus, animal diet composition is an important influencing factor to determine the volume of $CH_4$ gas emission. Mitigation of GHG emissions in the livestock sector can be achieved through various activities (FAO, 2008 and WMO, 2010).

### Selection of Fast Growing Breeds

The fast growing livestock breeds improve efficiency to convert energy from feed into production, and reduce losses through waste products. Increasing feed efficiency and improving digestibility of feed intake are potential ways to reduce GHG emissions and maximize production. This includes all the livestock practices (such as genetics, nutrition, reproduction, health and dietary supplements and proper feeding management) that result in the improved feed efficiency.

### Improved Feeding Management

The composition of feed has some effect on the enteric fermentation and emission of $CH_4$ from the rumen or the hindgut (Dourmad, *et al.*, 2008). The amount of feed intake is related to the amount of waste product. Replacement of roughage in the cattle diet with concentrates results in a reduction of $CH_4$ emission.

### Improved Waste Management

Improving management of animal waste products through different mechanisms such as covered storage facilities is also important. The amount of GHG emission from manure will depend on the temperature and duration of the storage. Therefore long term storage in high temperature will result higher GHG emissions. In the case of ruminants, pasture grazing is an efficient way to reduce $CH_4$ emission from manure, because no storage is necessary. The use of filters, scrubbers and covered manure pits reduce GHG emission.

### Grazing Management

One of the major GHG emission contributions from livestock production is from forage or feed crop production and land use of feed production. Thus, pasture grazing and proper pasture management through rotational grazing is the most cost effective way to mitigate GHG emissions from feed crop production. Animal grazing on the pasture also helps reduce emission due to animal manure storage. Introduction of grass species and legumes into grazing lands can enhance carbon storage in soils.

## CONCLUSION

Knowledge of how potential environmental stressors (ambient temperature, humidity, thermal radiation, air speed, *etc.*) can directly and adversely affect animal perform-ance, health and well-being is required for a successful animal farming. The indirect consequences of weather include their impact on feed quality and availability. Due to poor availability of good quality of feed and fodders in India, animals are generally maintained on poor quality grasses available in the pastures or are stall-fed, mainly on crop residues. India is already deficit in feed and fodder. These shortages would be further aggravated by the adverse effects of global warming on fodder crop production. Thus, focus should be on both mitigation, to reduce the level of emission of green house gases contributing to global warming, and adaptation, to support local communities deal with the impacts. At the same time, efficient and affordable adaptation practices need to be developed for the rural poor who are unable to afford expensive adaptation technologies.

Methane is generated mainly as a by-product of the fermentation of the digestible organic matter in ruminants; especially those with forage-based diets. The grain-based diets reduce the emission of $CH_4$. Thus, animal diet composition is an important influencing factor to determine the volume of $CH_4$ gas emission. To reduce the emissions of $CH_4$ and $N_2O$ the following strategies should be considered.

1. Replacement of roughage in the cattle diet with concentrates.
2. Development of low-emission production system facilities, including filters, scrubbers, covered manure pits and shallow manure application.
3. Reduction in the concentration of animals in intensive production units to the extent possible, by using more pens and pastures.
4. Use of feed additives to reduce $CH_4$ emissions; lower amounts of nitrogen in manure and urine can reduce $N_2O$ emissions.
5. Increase in feed digestibility and feed conver-sion efficiency.

## REFERENCES

Anderson, K.E. and Carter, T.A. (2007): Hot Weather Management of Poultry. Poultry Science and Technology Guide No. 30, *North Carolina State University*, USA.

Bajagai, Y.S. (2011): Global Climate Change and its Impacts on Dairy Cattle. *Nepalese Veterinary Journal* 30: 2-16.

Calvosa, C., Chuluunbaatar, D. and Fara, K. (2009): Livestock and Climate Change. *International Fund for Agricultural Development*, Rome, Italy. pp. 26.

Dourmad, J., Rigolot, C. and DerWerf, H. (2008): Emission of Greenhouse Gas: Developing Management and Animal Farming Systems to Assist Mitigation. *Livestock and Global Change Conference Proceeding*, May 2008, Tunisia.

EEA. (2001): Total E.U. $CH_4$ Emissions. Environmental Assessment Report No. 8. *European Environment Agency Factsheets.*

FAO. (2007): Adaptation to Climate Change in Agriculture, Forestry, and Fisheries: Perspective, Framework and Priorities. *Food and Agriculture Organisation*, Rome.

FAO. (2008): Climate-related Transboundary Pests and Diseases Including Relevant Aquatic Species. *Food and Agriculture Organisation*, Rome.

Hahn, G.L. (1999): Dynamic Responses of Cattle to Thermal Heat Loads. *Journal of Animal Sciences* **77** (Supplement 2): 10-20.

Hartung, E. and Monteny, G.J. (2000): Methane ($CH_4$) and Nitrous Oxide ($N_2O$) Emissions from Animal Husbandry. *Agrartechn. Forsch.*, 6: E62-E69.

Hartung, J. (2003): Contribution of Animal Husbandry to Climatic Changes. In: Interactions Between Climate and Animal Production. EAAP Technical Series No. 7. *Wageningen Academic Publishers*, the Netherlands.

Hoffmann, I. (2008): Livestock Genetic diversity and Climate Change Adaptation. *Livestock and Global Change Conference Proceeding*, May 2008, Tunisia.

http://en.wikipedia.org

http://www.climatechange.gc.ca

http://www.duckhealth.com/housmngt.html

http://www.eea.europa.eu/publications/signals-2001

http://www.ifad.org

http://www.ipcc.ch/assessment report

http://www.ruralpovertyportal.org

http://www.ruralpovertyportal.org

http://www.wmo.int/pages/themes

Hulzebosch, J. (2006): Effective Heating Systems for Poultry Houses. *World Poultry* 22(2): 18-19.

IPCC. (2007): Climate Change 2007: The Fourth Assessment Report of the Intergovernmental Panel on Climate Change. *Cambridge University Press*, U.K.

Mavi, H.S. and Tupper, G.J. (2004). Agrometeorology: Principles and Applications of Climate Studies in Agriculture. *Food products Press*, Binghamton, New York.

Monteny, G.J. (2003): Strategies for Reducing the Effects of Animal Husbandry on Climate. In: Interactions Between Climate and Animal Production. EAAP Technical Series No. 7. *Wageningen Academic Publishers*, the Netherlands.

Patz, J.A., Campbell-Lendrum, D., Holloway, T. and Foley, J.A. (2005): Impact of Regional Climate Change on Human Health. *Nature* 438: 310-317 (17 November 2005).

Rowlinson, P. (2008): Adapting Livestock Production Systems to Climate Change -Temperate Zones. In: *Livestock and Global Change Conference Proceeding*, May 2008, Tunisia.

Scott, M.L. and Dean, W.F. (1991): Nutrition and Management of Ducks. *Ithaca Publisher*, New York.

Sidahmed, A. (2008): Livestock and Climate Change: Coping and Risk Management Strategies for a Sustainable Future. In: *Livestock and Global Climate Change Conference Proceeding*, May 2008, Tunisia.

Thornton, P., Herrero, M., Freeman, A., Mwai, O., Rege, E., Jones, P. and McDermott, J. (2008): Vulnerability, Climate Change and Livestock - Research Opportunities and Challenges for Poverty Alleviation. *International Livestock Research Institute*, Kenya.

West, J.W. (2003): Effects of Heat Stress on Production in Dairy Cattle. *Journal of Dairy Science* 86: 2131-2144.

WMO. (2010): Agrometeorological Services: Reaching All Farmers with Operational Commitments. *World Meteorological Organisation*, Geneva, Switzerland.

Pages: 108-130

CLIMATE CHANGE, DISASTER MANAGEMENT AND ENVIRONMENT
*Edited by:* Dr. Alka Chauhan; Dr. Pawan Kumar 'Bharti'
ISBN: 978-93-5056-784-5
*Edition:* 2016
*Published by:* Discovery Publishing House Pvt. Ltd., New Delhi (India)

# CHAPTER – 7

# Status of Hydropower Development in India and its Impacts on Environment

Renu Lata*; Madhuri, S.Rishi; and Konchok Dolma

***ABSTRACT***

Hydropower is an important source of renewable energy. In recent years, both at international and national level, policy impetus have been given for increasing hydropower generation through new projects and by encouraging private sector investment. But a renewed focus on hydropower projects may result in a situation of "rapid" hydropower development rather than social and environmentally "responsible" hydropower development. The current chapter argues that, although hydropower will continue to remain an important source for electricity, focus needs to be on "responsible" hydropower development. Responsible hydropower development is also likely to ensure more stable and sustainable investment in the sector over medium-to-long interval of time. Hydropower stations are generally located in hilly

Department of Environment Studies, Punjab University, Chandigarh, (India).

areas where dams can be built easily. Hydropower contributes the major share of power requirement in India. It plays a very important role in development of total energy. Thus this chapter discusses the power development scenario, related issues and its impact on surrounding environment.

**Keywords:** Hydropower, Renewable Energy, Sustainable, Responsible and Environment.

## INTRODUCTION

Power is the prime mover of economic development of a nation and one of the major infrastructure requirements for industrial, rural and agricultural development. It helps in linking rural population with the fast changing technological world. India has faced power shortage since independence but now, it has become critical with huge power cuts in a day. It needs massive additions in capacity to meet the demand of its rapidly growing economy. Considering energy security concerns and commitment for a 'Low Carbon Growth Strategy', Government of India in the Twelfth Five Year Plan (FYP) has made provisions to ensure sustainable development of power sector and is emphasizing in the development of hydropower besides nuclear and other renewable sources. It will help in solving the sustainability problem associated with conventional fuels used for power generation as hydropower are non-exhaustible, free and relatively clean.

Moving water had been used for years to provide mechanical energy, but the first small-scale hydropower scheme was developed in England in 1878 and the first hydropower plant began operation on Fox river in Appleton, Wisconsin in 1882. Growing demand and technological advancements, including the development of the electric generator and improvements to the hydraulic turbine, encouraged the growth of hydropower projects (Anonymous, 2013). Today, share of hydropower in the electricity mix in countries with large resource endowments is as high as 95% in Norway, 80% in Brazil and 68% in Venezuela. China is now the world's largest producer of hydropower, including the largest hydro-power station at Three Gorges Dam, with a generating capacity of 22.5 GW (Ullah, 2015).

India is very rich with hydropower potential and considered as one of the pioneering countries in establishing hydropower plants (Chaurasiya, et.al., 2013). The first hydropower project in India was commissioned in 1897, at Darjeeling (West Bengal). It has a capacity of 130 KW (Kumar and Katoch, 2014). This project was followed by Sivasamudram project of 4.5 MW in Mysore district of Karnataka in 1902, which supplied power to Kolar gold mines (Naidu, 1997). At the time of independence of India i.e. in 1947, installed capacity of hydropower was mere 508 MW (Agarwal and Singh, 2007).

Some of the public sector companies engaged in development of hydropower in India are National Hydroelectric Power Corporation (NHPC), Northeast Electric Power Company (NEEPC), Satluj Jal Vidyut Nigam (SJVNL), Tehri Hydro Development Corporation and National Thermal Power Corporation Limited (NTPC). Now, country is going through a phase of huge gap between demand and supply of power. In order to overcome this shortage, government has opened the hydropower sectors for private sector participation since 1991. The successful completion of Public Private Partnership (PPP) projects in roads, airports and other sectors have given an opportunity to implement in hydropower sector also to fill the gap of power shortage especially in remote and backward regions.

## WORKING OF HYDROPOWER PROJECTS

Hydropower converts the natural flow of water into electricity to light our homes and power our industries. Energy is produced by fall of water turning the blades of a turbine. Turbine is connected to generator that converts energy in to electricity. The amount of electricity a hydropower installation can produce depends on the quantity of water passing through a turbine (volume of water flow) or on the height from which the water falls (the amount of head). Greater the flow and head, more will be the electricity production. Some hydropower facilities include dams to increase the head of a waterfall or to control the flow of water and reservoirs to store water for future energy use (storage dam), while others produce electricity by immediately using a river's water flow (run-of-river) (Lata, *et.al.*, 2013). Some hydropower plants also use pumped storage systems, which stores water for reuse in the production of electricity during periods of high demand. Presently, following forms of hydropower projects exists in India:

## STORAGE PROJECT

Storage project provides storage of poundage and thereby evens out stream flow fluctuations and enhances the water head (Fig. 7.1.). Thus, it increases firm power and total power generation by regulating the flow. However, providing storage is complicated and costly as it involves construction of dam as well as rehabilitation to hydropower projects.

## RUN-OF-RIVER (ROR) PROJECT

As the name implies, project is planned as run-of-the river. Water is diverted from the river, routed through project and finally water after generation of power is thrown back to the river at a lower level on downstream. It takes advantage of the drop in elevation that occurs over a distance in the river and does not involve water storage (Fig. 7.2). Conceptually very simple but it has one big problem that is power generation fluctuates with the river flow and firm power is considerably low, as it depends on the minimum mean discharge. Canal power projects are also considered as run- of-river projects.

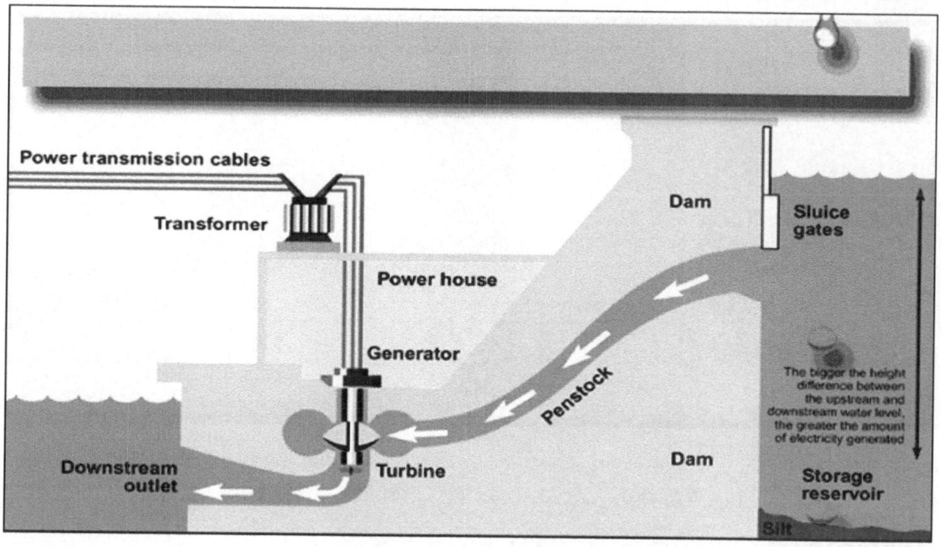


*Fig. 7.1:* **Storage Type Hydropower Project**

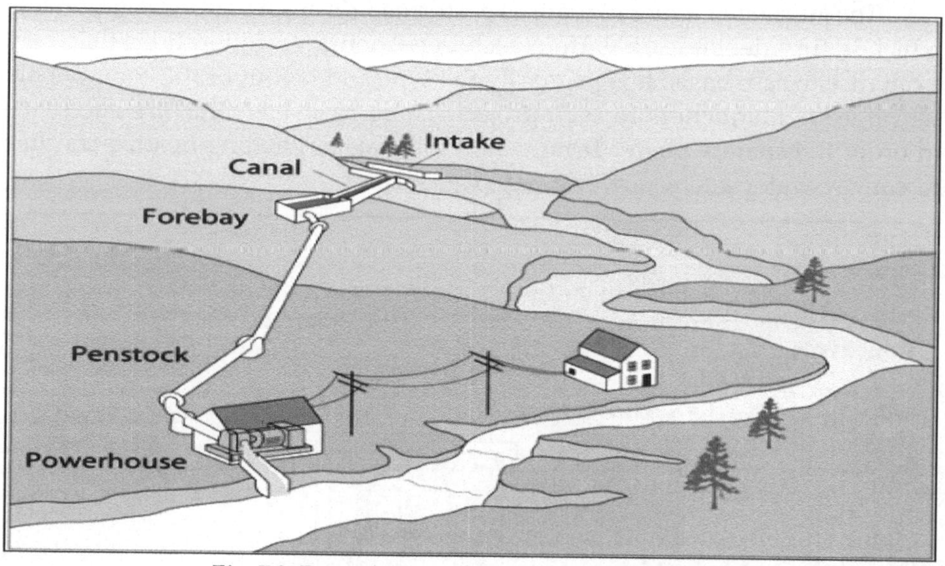


*Fig. 7.2:* **Run-of-River Type Hydropower Project**

## PUMPED STORAGE PROJECTS

Pump storage projects store surplus energy in the power grid system during the off peak hours and utilize the same energy during peak hours. These involve reversible turbines which can generate power from water of upper reservoir during peak hours and pump back water from lower reservoir to upper reservoir during off peak hours (Fig. 7.3). These projects are advantageous in power grid systems of mix type which have thermal and nuclear power houses in addition to hydropower projects.

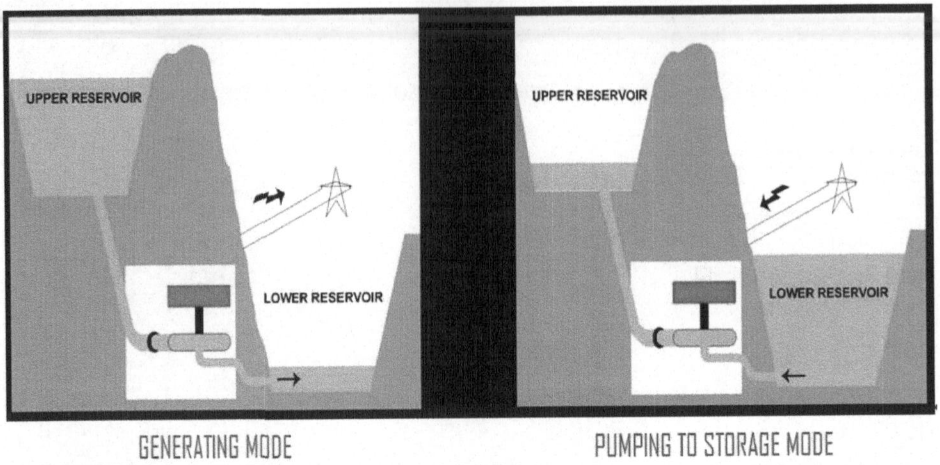


*Fig. 7.3:* **Pumped Storage Type Hydropower Project**

## COMPONENTS OF HYDROPOWER PROJECTS

The journey of water to watts is performed through various components which in turn depends on various techno-economic considerations that vary from case to case basis. It is primarily the type and layout of the components which leads uniqueness to each project. Three basic elements are necessary in order to generate power from water: a means of creating head, a conduit to convey water and a power plant (Fig. 7.4).

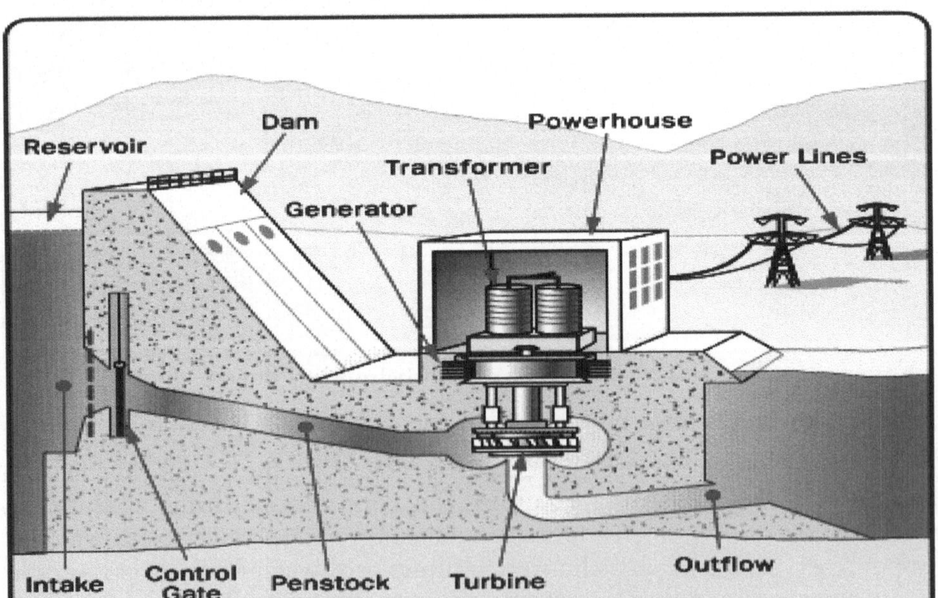


*Fig. 7.4:* **Components of Hydropower Projects**

To provide these functions, following common hydro civil components are used:

1. **Reservoir:** A reservoir is provided to store water during rainy season and supplies the same in dry season. Water from the reservoir is used to run hydraulic turbine.
2. **Dam:** Dam is a structure of considerable height built across the river. Its function is to provide working head of water for power plant and to increase the storage-capacity of reservoir.
3. **Trash Rack:** These are made up of steel bars and trash rack is provided to prevent entry of debris into the intakes from dam or from the forebay. Any debris in the intake water pipe may damage the turbine runners or choke the nozzles of an impulse turbine.
4. **Gate:** Gate controls the flow of water from reservoir to hydraulic turbine through penstock. It is closed when maintenance of system is required.
5. **Waterway and Penstock:** A waterway is used to carry water from the dam to the power house. It includes canal and penstock or a head race tunnel. The penstocks are made up of steel of reinforced concrete which is designed to withstand high pressures. They are supported by anchors and sharp bends in penstock are avoided in order to reduce hydraulic losses.
6. **Surge Tank:** A surge tank is used to absorb water hammer effects due to rapid start or closure of turbine.
7. **Spillway:** A spillway is provided to discharge the flood water and to keep the level of water below designed maximum level in reservoir. Thus a spillway saves the dam from damage during flood.
8. **Power House:** A power house consists of two main parts, a sub-structure to support the hydraulic and electrical equipment and a superstructure to house and protect the equipments. The superstructure of most power plants is buildings that house all the operating equipments. The generating units and exciters are located in ground floor. Turbines which rotate on vertical axis are placed below the floor level while those rotating on a horizontal axis are placed on the ground floor alongside of the generator.
9. **Hydraulic Turbines:** These are used to convert the kinetic energy of water into mechanical energy.
10. **Tail Race Channel:** A tail race canal or tunnel which carries water from the turbine exit back to river.

## REASONS TO INCLUDE HYDROPOWER IN ALL RENEWABLE ENERGY INITIATIVES

### Hydropower is a Renewable Source of Energy

Hydropower uses the power of flowing water without wasting or depleting it in the production of energy; therefore, all hydropower projects – small or large, run-of-river or storage meet the definition of renewable.

### Hydropower Supports the Development of Other Renewables

Hydropower facilities with reservoirs provide a unique operational flexibility that allows them to respond almost immediately to fluctuating demands for electricity. Hydropower's flexibility and storage capacity makes it the best source to support deployment of wind or solar energy.

### Hydropower Contributes to Fresh Water Storage

Hydropower reservoirs harvest rainfall thereby supplying fresh water for drinking and irrigation. This fresh water storage protects aquifers from depletion and reduces our vulnerability to floods and droughts.

### Hydropower helps in Improving the Air

Hydropower projects are considered as clean source of electricity because it produces very few greenhouse gases, no other air pollutants, and it does not generate any toxic waste by-products.

### Hydropower helps in Fighting Climate Change

By offsetting emissions from gas, coal and oil fired power plants, hydropower can contribute to reducing air pollution and to slowing down global warming. Currently, hydropower displaces the consumption of 4.4 million barrels of oil-equivalent each day.

### Hydropower Stimulates Local and Regional Development

Hydropower facilities bring electricity, roads, industry and commerce to communities, developing the economy, improving access to health and education, and enhancing the quality of life.

### Hydropower Optimizes the Performance of Other Energy Technologies

Through flexible, reliable and efficient operation hydropower ensures an effective electricity network where the performances of thermal power plants are optimized and air emissions reduced.

### Hydropower Fosters National Energy Security

Water from rivers is a domestic resource that is not subject to fluctuations in fuel prices therefore hydropower fosters energy independence and security.

### Hydropower means Clean, Affordable Power for Today and Tomorrow

With an average life span of 50 to 100 years hydropower projects are long-term investments that can easily be upgraded to take advantage of the latest technologies. Hydropower is an electricity source with long viability and very low operation and maintenance costs that one generation bestows onto several subsequent ones.

### Hydropower Leads to Sustainable Development

Hydropower projects that are developed and operated in an economically viable, environmentally sound and socially responsible manner represents sustainable development at its best that is "Development that meets the needs of the people today without compromising the ability of future generations to meet their own needs."

### Constraints Affecting Hydropower Development

For several decades, thousands of dams were built all over the world. Their contribution in economic growth is significant but their negative impacts were also realized with time. From the 90's, Environmental Impact Assessment (EIA) is regarded as an effective tool for decision making in many countries. It is a process to assess potential impacts on environment and society before implementing the project and to offer mitigation measures (Brismar and Anna, 2003).

To bring a good lifestyle to people is the purpose of development projects in general. However, in reality to give a better lifestyle for all people is not easy to foresee. It is extremely difficult in most developing countries with weak policies, low awareness, poor knowledge and limited financial resources to support sustainable development. Even if there are global or regional laws on involuntary resettlement, big question for researchers is how to adapt these laws in local context and find a way to apply them in practice.

There are several other constraints that affect the hydropower projects such as:

### Land Acquisition Problems

Land acquisition is done by the State Government and often gets delayed due to litigation, poor maintenance of land records.

### Resettlement and Rehabilitation Problems

Reservoir schemes require large extents of lands to be acquired resulting in displacement of families. For example –Sardar Sarovar, Tehri and Indirasagar projects. The national resettlement & rehabilitation policy addresses some of these issues.

### Law and Order Problems

Most hydropower projects are located along the Himalayas. Projects in J&K and North East face problems on account of insurgency and terrorists. Projects like Dulhasti (J&K) and Tuirial have faced several problems.

### Difficult/Inaccessible Sites

Most of the untapped hydropower potential is in remote areas of the Himalayas for which access roads running into over 100 km at a time have to be first constructed before work can commence. Further, power needs to be transmitted over long distances to load centers from these remote areas requiring construction of long transmission lines.

**Geological Surprises**

In the Himalayan Mountains in particular, geological surprises while tunneling cause large time and cost overruns.

**Delays in Environment and Forest Clearances**

The process for getting clearance is cumbersome and involves inputs from both State and Central Agencies. Delays occur particularly at the State level.

**Inter-State Aspects**

Inter-State water disputes have come in the way of taking up of many projects.

**Funding of Hydropower Projects**

Till recently, hydropower projects were funded only by Government agencies and hence only limited number could be taken up. The scenario has changed considerably in recent years with introduction of different private sector participation.

**Status of Hydropower Projects in India**

India is having a total installed power capacity of 2,28,721.73 MW from all energy resources (including renewable) (Ministry of power, 2014). Out of this share of hydropower (excluding small hydro power projects) is 39,788.40 MW that is only 17.39%. Total economically exploitable and viable hydropower potential in India is assessed to be about 84,000 MW at 60% load factor (Singh, 2008). In addition 6780 MW in terms of installed capacity from small, mini and micro hydropower schemes have been assessed. Also, 56 sites for pumped storage schemes with an aggregate installed capacity of 94,000 MW have been identified. However only 19.9% of the total potential has been harnessed so far (NHPC, 2014).

India is blessed with enormous amount of hydropower potential and ranks 5$^{th}$ in terms of exploitable hydropower potential on global scenario. As per assessment made by Central Electricity Authority, India is endowed with economically exploitable hydropower potential to the tune of 1,48,700 MW of installed capacity. India's hydropower system is divided into five major provinces namely, Northern region, Western region, Southern region, Eastern region and North-Eastern region, with each region facing separate issues. While the Eastern and North-Eastern regions are power abundant, Northern and Western regions have greater power demands. Hydropower potential is largest in NE region with 98% of it still untapped. Northern, Eastern, Western and Southern regions have 79%, 77%, 23% and 33%

unexploited hydropower potential respectively (Subrahmanyam, 2013). A large part of the hydropower projects are concentrated in North-eastern states by virtue of the availability of water and required topography but the demand for power in these areas is not significant.

Four states out of 29 states and 7 union territories carry the lion's share (about 80%) of hydropower potential in India. These states are Arunachal Pradesh, Himachal Pradesh, Uttarakhand and Jammu &Kashmir. These states may be called 'Power Banks' of India. Figure 7.5 shows the location of these states on political map of India (in rectangular boxes). Percentage share of hydropower potential in these hydro rich states has been shown in table 7.1 & figure 7.6. All these states are situated in young and fragile Himalayan region. Hence development of hydropower projects in these regions poses harsh sustainability challenges.

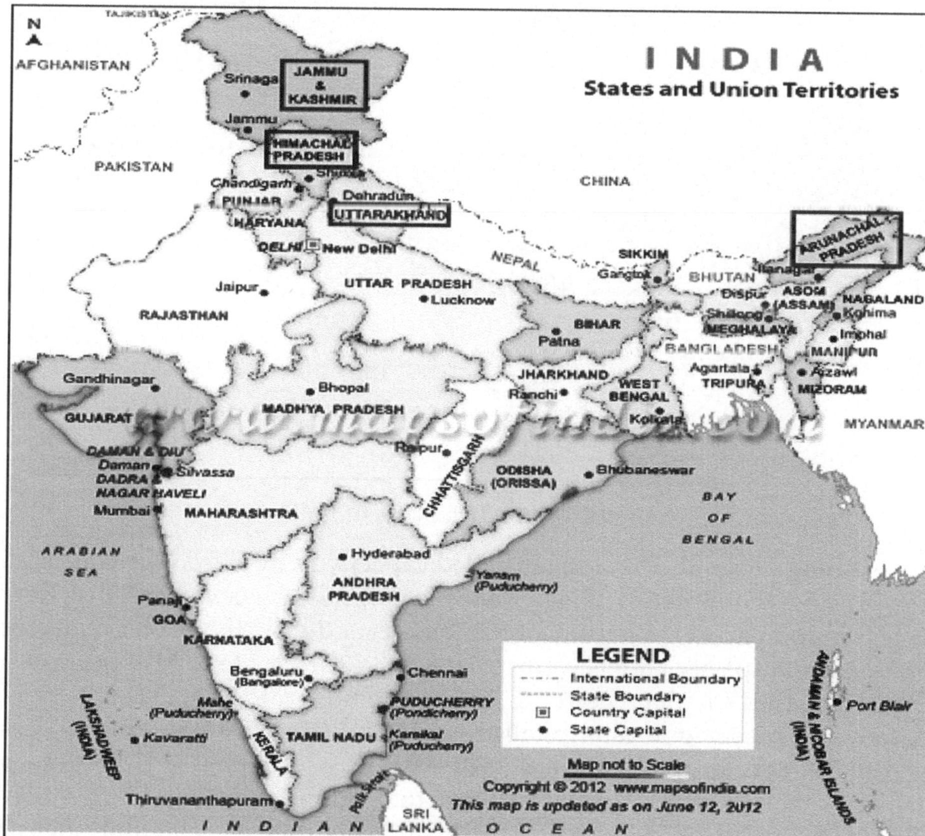


*Fig. 7.5:* **Location of the Hydro Rich States in India**

*Source:* Political Map of India, 2014

**Table 7.1: Share of Hydropower Potential in Hydro Rich States of India**

| Sl. No. | Name of the State | Estimated Hydropower Potential (MW) | Percentage of Total Hydropower Potential in India (out of 148701 MW) |
|---|---|---|---|
| 1. | Arunachal Pradesh | 50328 (MDoNER, 2014) | 33.8 |
| 2. | Uttarakhand | 26215 (UJVN, 2014) | 17.6 |
| 3. | Himachal Pradesh | 23000 (DoE, 2014) | 15.5 |
| 4. | Jammu & Kashmir | 20000 (JKSPDC, 2014) | 13.4 |
| | **Total percentage** | | **80.3** |

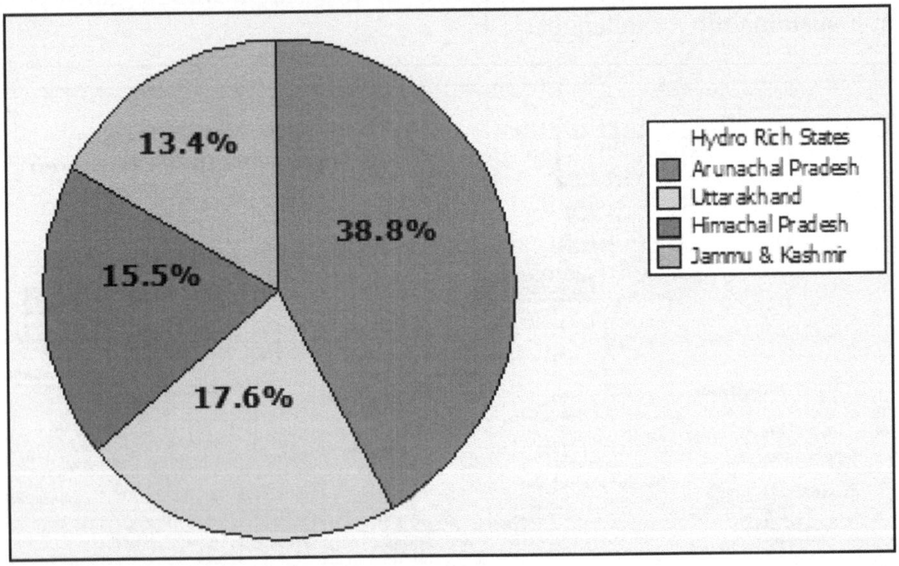


*Fig. 7.6:* **Hydro Rich States of India**

During Eleventh FYP, total installed capacity in hydro-power was 5,544 MW against the target of 15,627 MW. State sectors achieved most of their targets in comparison to central targets. However during the midterm review, hydropower capacity targets were revised to 8,237 MW (2,922 MW in Central Sector, 2,854 MW in State Sector & 2,561 MW in Private Sector) (Ministry of Power, 2014). The aggregate installed capacity during this period was 5,544 MW (1,550 MW in central Sector, 2,702 MW in state Sector & 1,292 MW in private sector). During Eleventh FYP, actual achievement was 54,964 MW against the target of 78,700 MW that includes hydro, thermal and nuclear sectors. The private sectors contribution was more than the central and state shares. Table 7.2 shows the detail list of current status of hydropower projects under various stages of implementation with region wise as well as state-wise in terms of installed capacity above 25 MW.

**Table 7.2: Status of Hydro Electric Potential Development in India**

| Region/State | Identified Capacity as per Reassessment Study | | Capacity Under Operation | | Capacity Under Construction | | Capacity Under Operation + Under Construction | | Capacity yet to be taken up Under Construction | |
|---|---|---|---|---|---|---|---|---|---|---|
| | Total (MW) | Above 25 MW <MW) | (MW) | (%) | (MW) | (%) | (MW) | (%) | (MW) | (%) |
| 1 | 2 | 3 | 4 | 5 | 6 | 7 | 8 | 9 | 10 | 11 |
| **NORTHERN** | | | | | | | | | | |
| Jainrnu & Kashmir | 14146 | 13543 | 2609.0 | 19.26 | 1690.0 | 12.48 | 4299.0 | 31.74 | 9244.0 | 68.26 |
| Himachal Pradesh | 18820 | 18540 | 7594.0 | 40.96 | 3948.0 | 21.29 | 11542.0 | 62.25 | 6998.0 | 37.75 |
| Punjab | 971 | 971 | 1206.3 | 100 | 206.0 | 21.22 | 1412.3 | 100.00 | 0.0 | 0.00 |
| Haryana | 64 | 64 | 0.0 | 0 | 0.0 | 0.00 | 0.0 | 0.00 | 64.0 | 100.00 |
| Rajasthan | 496 | 483 | 411.0 | 85.09 | 0.0 | 0.00 | 411.0 | 85.09 | 72.0 | 14.91 |
| Uttarakhand | 18175 | 17998 | 3426.4 | 19.04 | 1196.0 | 6.65 | 4622.4 | 25.68 | 13375.7 | 74.32 |
| Uttar Pradesh | 723 | 664 | 501.6 | 75.54 | 0.0 | 0.00 | 501.6 | 75.54 | 162.4 | 24.46 |
| Sub Total (NR) | 53395 | 52263 | 15748.3 | 30.13 | 7040.0 | 13.47 | 22788.3 | 43.60 | 29474.8 | 56.40 |
| **WESTERN** | | | | | | | | | | |
| Madhya Pradesh | 2243 | 1970 | 2395.0 | 100 | 400.0 | 20.30 | 2795.0 | 100.00 | 0.0 | 0.00 |
| Chhattisgarh | 2242 | 2202 | 120.0 | 5.45 | 0.0 | 0.00 | 120.0 | 5.45 | 2082.0 | 94.55 |
| Gujarat | 619 | 590 | 550.0 | 93.22 | 0.0 | 0.00 | 550.0 | 93.22 | 40.0 | 6.78 |
| Maharashtra | 3769 | 3314 | 2487.0 | 75.05 | 0.0 | 0.00 | 2487.0 | 75.05 | 827.0 | 24.95 |
| Goa | 55 | 55 | 0.0 | 0.00 | 0.0 | 0.00 | 0.0 | 0.00 | 55.0 | 100.00 |
| Sub Total (WR) | 8928 | 8131 | 5552.0 | 58.28 | 400.0 | 4.92 | 5952.0 | 73.20 | 2179.0 | 26.80 |

(Table Contd...)

| 1 | 2 | 3 | 4 | 5 | 6 | 7 | 8 | 9 | 10 | 11 |
|---|---|---|---|---|---|---|---|---|---|---|
| **SOUTHERN** | | | | | | | | | | |
| Andhra Pradesh | 4424 | 4360 | 2177.8 | 49.95 | 410.0 | 9.40 | 2587.8 | 59.35 | 1772.3 | 40.65 |
| Karnataka | 6602 | 6459 | 3585.4 | 55.51 | 0.0 | 0.00 | 3585.4 | 55.51 | 2873.6 | 44.49 |
| Kerala | 3514 | 3378 | 1881.5 | 55.70 | 100.0 | 2.96 | 1981.5 | 58.66 | 1396.5 | 41.34 |
| Tamil Nadu | 1918 | 1693 | 1782.2 | 100 | 0.0 | 0.00 | 1782.2 | 100.00 | 0.0 | 0.00 |
| Sub Total (SR) | 16458 | 15890 | 9426.9 | 59.33 | 510.0 | 3.21 | 9936.9 | 62.54 | 5953.2 | 37.46 |
| **EASTERN** | | | | | | | | | | |
| Jharkhand | 753 | 582 | 170.0 | 29.21 | 0.0 | 0.00 | 170.0 | 29.21 | 412.0 | 70.79 |
| Bihar | 70 | 40 | 0.0 | | 0.0 | 0.00 | 0.0 | | 40.0 | 100.00 |
| Odisha | 2999 | 2981 | 2027.5 | 68.01 | 0.0 | 0.00 | 2027.5 | 68.01 | 953.5 | 31.99 |
| West Bengal | 2841 | 2829 | 272.2 | 9.62 | 160.0 | 5.66 | 432.2 | 15.28 | 2396.8 | 84.72 |
| Sikkim | 4286 | 4248 | 669.0 | 15.75 | 2322.0 | 54.66 | 2991.0 | 70.41 | 1257.0 | 29.59 |
| Sub Total (ER) | 10949 | 10680 | 3138.7 | 29.39 | 2482.0 | 23.24 | 5620.7 | 52.63 | 5059.3 | 47.37 |
| **NORTH EASTERN** | | | | | | | | | | |
| Meghalaya | 2394 | 2298 | 282.0 | 12.27 | 40.0 | 1.74 | 322.0 | 14.01 | 1976.0 | 85.99 |
| Tripura | 15 | 0 | 0.0 | | 0.0 | | 0.0 | | 0.0 | |
| Manipur | 1784 | 1761 | 105.0 | 5.96 | 0.0 | 0.00 | 105.0 | 5.96 | 1656.0 | 94.04 |
| Assam | 680 | 650 | 375.0 | 57.69 | 0.0 | 0.00 | 375.0 | 57.69 | 275.0 | 42.31 |
| Nagaland | 1574 | 1452 | 75.0 | 5.17 | 0.0 | 0.00 | 75.0 | 5.17 | 1377.0 | 94.83 |
| Arunachal Pradesh | 50328 | 50064 | 405.0 | 0.81 | 2710.0 | 5.41 | 3115.0 | 6.22 | 46949.0 | 93.78 |
| Mizoram | 2196 | 2131 | 0.0 | 0.00 | 60.0 | 2.82 | 60.0 | 2.82 | 2071.0 | 97.18 |
| Sub Total (NER) | 58971 | 58356 | 1242.0 | 2.13 | 2810.0 | 4.82 | 4052.0 | 6.94 | 54304.0 | 93.06 |
| **ALL INDIA** | **148701** | **145320** | **35107.8** | **24.16** | **13242.0** | **9.11** | **48349.8** | **33.27** | **96970.2** | **66.73** |

*Source:* Ullah, 2015.

## ENVIRONMENTAL AND SOCIAL IMPACTS OF HYDROPOWER

The impact of hydropower plant on environment is varied and depends upon the size and type of the project. Although hydropower generation does not burn any fuel to produce power and hence does not emit greenhouse gases, there are definite negative effects that arise from the creation of reservoir and alteration of natural water flow. It is a fact that dams, inter-basin transfers and diversion of water for irrigation purposes have resulted in the fragmentation of 60% of the world's rivers.

Over the past decade, Hydropower projects around the world have attracted much attention concerning environmental and social impacts that have arisen from such developments. Construction and operation of dams have always been associated with changes in the physical and biological environment. Impacts arising as a result of manipulation and utilization of water resources are complex as they tend to affect terrestrial and aquatic ecosystems alike. Several authors have reviewed the impacts of hydro-projects and their related activities on different environmental resources (Petts, 1984, Brooks, 1988, Gregory and Walling, 1987, Goudie, 1990, Box and Forbes, 1992) but these do not address issues like impacts on habitat loss, degradation and fragmentation.

Hydropower Projects involving construction of big dams, tunnels and powerhouses are causing several environmental problems. Though these projects bring economic advantages in terms of electricity, employment, economy and water for industrialization and agriculture but there are other adverse effects which have been overlooked. These include environmental pollution, disturbance of aesthetics and ecology (both terrestrial and aquatic) and the submergence of forests in the reservoir also towns and villages. The extensive felling of trees for rehabilitation of displaced population from submerged areas, the constructions of new roads, neglect and tardy implementation of afforestation work in the catchment areas have contributed to rapid siltation of reservoirs and diminishing benefits. Such a situation calls for extreme vigilance. Fig. 7.7 summarizes the environmental impacts of HEPs.

## ENVIRONMENTAL IMPACT

Physical environment is affected rather significantly by the construction of a hydropower power station. The river and ecosystem of the surrounding land area will be altered as soon as dam construction begins.

### Impact of Size and type of Hydropower Plant

It is difficult to correlate the damage caused by dams to their size or type, as the impacts depend on local conditions. Generally plants with smaller dams are considered less environmentally damaging than those with larger dams.

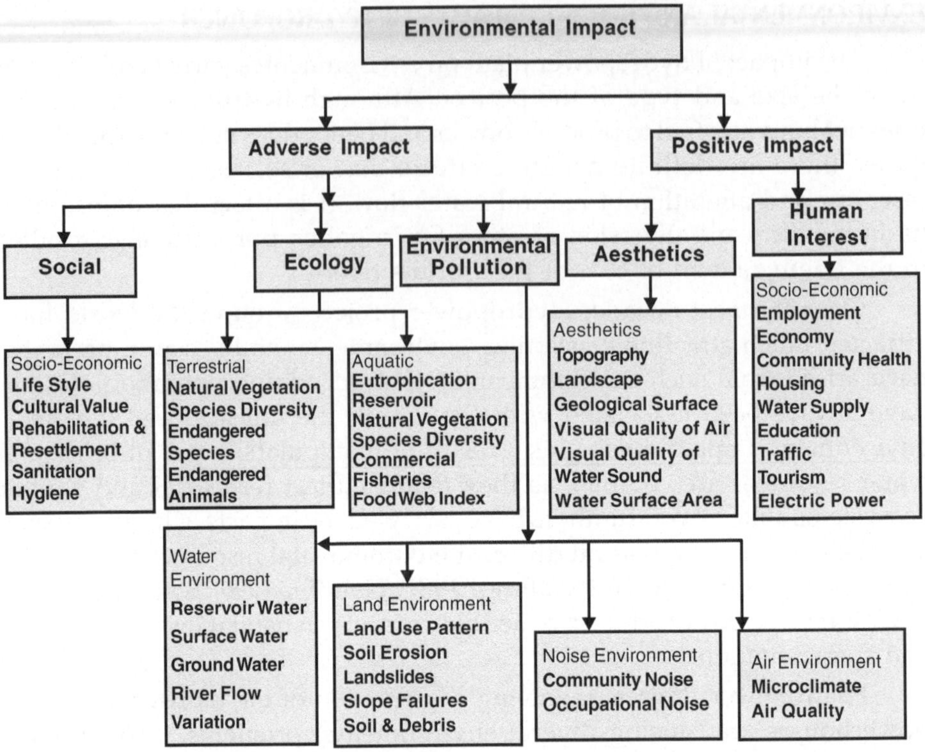


*Fig. 7.7:* **Environmental Impacts of Hydroelectric Power Projects**

Also run-of-river (RoR) hydropower plants are generally less damaging than reservoir power plants because it is not necessary to flood large areas upstream of the project for storage. Yet in some cases run-of-river impacts can also be severe due to river diversion over long stretches of the river.

## Impact of River Diversion

While both RoR and reservoir types of hydropower dams may divert water, this is always the case with RoR plants, since they seek to increase kinetic energy with an increased head. The length of diversion can range from a few meters or less to kilometers (km). Often downstream flows are reduced considerably or even completely stopped during certain periods of time with sudden intervals of high flows. Such drastic variability in water flow impacts the structure of aquatic ecosystems often leading to a loss of biodiversity. Also under normal conditions increased sediment transport from low to intermediate flows provides a warning to aquatic organisms that high flows may follow. Abrupt changes from low to high flows obliterate this cue, making it difficult for organisms to respond to impending environmental changes. A decrease in fish population had been observed in dewatered reaches below diversions. After long periods of little to no flow some species may not be able to recover and go extinct.

## Impact of the Reservoir

Dams have major impacts on the physical, chemical and geo-morphological properties of a river. Environmental impacts of dams have largely been negative. Worldwide, at least 400,000 square kilometers have been flooded by reservoirs. Once the barrier is put in place, free flow of water stops and water will begin to accumulate behind the dam in the new reservoir. This land may have been used for other things such as agriculture, forestry, and even as residences but it is now unusable. The loss of habitat may not seem severe but if this area was home to a threatened or endangered species, the dam construction could further threaten that species risk of extinction.

### *Sedimentation*

Large dams with reservoirs significantly alter the timing, amount and pattern of river flow. This changes erosion patterns and the quantity and type of sediments transported by the river. Sedimentation rate is primarily related to the ratio of size of the river to flux of sediments. The reservoir that has been rapidly filling up with water immediately begins filling up with sediments as well. The trapping of sediments behind the dam is a major problem. Every year it is estimated that 0.5 to 1% of reservoir storage capacity is lost due to sedimentation. The engineering problem with sedimentation is that less power is generated as the reservoir's capacity shrinks.

### *Downstream Erosion*

Trapping of sediments at the dam also has downstream impacts by reducing the flux of sediments downstream which can lead to gradual loss of soil fertility in floodplain soils. Clean water stripped of its sediment load is now flowing downstream of the dam. This clean water has more force and velocity then water carrying a high sediment load and thus erosion of the riverbed and banks becomes problematic. Since this is unnatural and a form of "forced erosion" it occurs at a much faster rate than natural river process erosion to which the local ecosystem would be able to adapt.

### *Impact on Local Climate*

Another often-ignored environmental effect of the reservoir is impact on the microclimate level. Studies indicate that man-made lakes in tropical climates tend to reduce convection and thus limit cloud cover. Temperate regions are also impacted with "steamfog" in the time period before freezing. Since water cools and warms slower than land, coastal regions tend to be much more moderate than land-locked regions in terms of temperature. Therefore large dams have a slight moderating effect on the local climate.

### *Greenhouse Gas Emission from Dams/Reservoirs*

Freshwater reservoirs can emit substantial amounts of greenhouse gases like methane and carbon dioxide as organic matter submerged in a reservoir decays under anaerobic and aerobic conditions respectively. Studies indicate that GHGs emissions from hydropower reservoirs in boreal and temperate regions are low relative to the emissions from fossil fuel power plants but higher relative to lifecycle emissions from wind and solar power. Tropical reservoirs with high levels of organic matter and shallow reservoirs have higher emission levels. A recent compilation of greenhouse gas emissions from reservoirs found a correlation between age of the reservoir and latitude. Younger reservoirs and those in low latitudes are the highest emitters. For example, of four Brazilian dams in the Amazon, showed that GHG emissions factor of electricity produced by hydropower dams exceed those from a coal-fired power plant (Dale,et.al., 2013).

### *Dams Inducing Earthquakes*

A least studied and most disputed physical impact of reservoirs is the possibility of inducing earthquakes. Many scientists believe that seismic activity can be attributed in the creation of dams and their adjacent storage reservoirs. They postulate that added forces of the dam along inactive faults seem to free much stronger orogenic tensions. Early research indicates that depth of the water column may be more important in inducing earthquakes rather than total volume of water in the reservoir. While more research is needed on this subject several disasters such as the Koyna Dam in India seem to provide some truth to this theory. While these impacts can be quite severe often they do not receive the attention of the biological impacts that people tend to associate more with animals like fish.

### *Impact on Fisheries*

Dams and river diversion can impact freshwater, as well as marine fisheries. Estuarine and marine fisheries are dependent on estuaries and rivers as spawning grounds and the transport of nutrients from river to the sea. Migratory fish are especially vulnerable to impacts of dam construction. Dams can prevent migrating fish such as salmon and eel to reach their spawning grounds. A survey of 125 dams by the World Commission on Dams (WCD) reported that blocking the passage of migratory fish species has been identified as a major reason for freshwater species extinction in North America. Lower catch is a common side effect of dams and has been reported worldwide.

## Biological Impact

Animal and plant life are impacted significantly by dam construction. As mentioned earlier large scale flooding destroys a large area of habitat for animals and destroys an equally large number of plants. If the region was forested prior to construction of the dam, timber is harvested before the flooding begins. Reservoirs that in the future will be used for recreation such as boating or fishing tend to be completely cleared of trees.

### *Impact on Flora*

Another negative biological impact of dams is the growth of aquatic weeds. Tropical and semi-tropical regions seem to have the largest problem with weed growth. Impacts of weeds can be significant to water loss. Weeds growing in the reservoir results in high rates of evapo-transpiration. The weeds compete with fish for space and nutrients that are already under stress living in an unnatural setting. Some insects such as malaria and schistosomasis tend to increase as weeds provide a very favorable habitat for mosquitoes and other diseases spreading agents. How do we contain these problems? The weeds can be controlled, although the task is often very difficult and expensive. In shallow water mechanical or manual clearing is by far most effective. However, in deeper waters this is not an option and either chemical or biological means must be used to remove the weeds. Chemical herbicides work well but bring whole new set of environmental hazards to organisms, humans and ecosystem in general. The scariest part about using chemical herbicides is that their overall effect is generally not known until they have caused a problem.

### *Impact on Fauna*

For some kinds of fish building of a dam makes completion of their life cycle nearly impossible. Anadromous fish, such as salmon are hatched upstream in a freshwater environment but spends their adult lives at sea in salt water. The eel, a kind of fish classified as catadromous is hatched at sea but spends much of its adult life in freshwater streams. Since these fish rely on streams and rivers to get to and from different environments, creating a dam makes a large roadblock for these animals to overcome. Without features such as fish ladders these fish would die off. However, even the fish ladders do not work perfectly and many fish die due to dams. There are a number of measures that can be taken to help minimize fish mortality at hydropower plants. The most obvious step is to lower the number of fish that pass through the turbine. This can be accomplished by using better screens to capture the fish or establishing diversion passageways. A more complicated and emerging technology involves in making "fish-friendly" turbines. Pelton turbines which are small turbines designed for high head installations cause nearly complete mortality of fish passing through it. Kaplan, Francis, and Bulb turbines tend to be safer for small fish with mortality rates of only about 30%. These types of turbines have much larger areas of water passage. Kaplan turbines are thought to be most fish-friendly of the conventional turbines and they have low mortality rates of just 10-15 percent.

## Social Impact

Similar to other large infrastructure projects, dams have both negative and positive social impacts. The benefits of hydropower include having a renewable source of electricity with little GHG emissions, delivery of peak power and avoidance of health and environmental impacts associated with fossil fuels especially coal. Multipurpose dams can also reliably deliver water and flood control as well as other ancillary services. Negative impacts on the other hand include displacement, loss of livelihood, poorer health and loss of cultural heritage. Often groups that bear social and environmental costs of dams are not the ones who reap the benefits. Poor, vulnerable groups such as rural populations, subsistence farmers, indigenous communities and ethnic minorities often bear a disproportionate share of negative impacts while the main beneficiaries are urban dwellers, commercial farmers and industries. For example, although indigenous people are just 8% of India's population they comprise 60% of those displaced by dams from their native regions.

### Displacement

Often the most discussed topic when a new hydropower plant is planned is dislocation of a large number of people. The prospect of displacement often comes as a brutal shock because the affected people come from small villages where different cultural values and beliefs are held and now suddenly people have to embrace a new and uncertain lifestyle altogether in a new setting. It is painful when people are forced to leave behind all their ancestral roots – ancestral homes, shrines and graves of their ancestors. Suddenly all local cultural heritage is gone. Displacement often results in loss of sacred land and common property resources. Alienation and marginalization are major risks for displaced communities. It is estimated that 40-80 million people have been physically displaced by dams worldwide. In India and China alone, 26-58 million people have been displaced during 1950 – 1990 due to dam projects. In-depth case studies of eight large dams on four continents by the WCD found that in each case expected numbers of displaced people were initially highly underestimated by 2,000 - 40,000 people. Among dams funded by the World Bank, 47% more people were displaced than initially estimated. Impacts for down-stream communities are often only clear after the dam comes into operation and often impacts worsen over the period of time. Resettlement has mostly been involuntary and there has been little meaningful participation of those affected in the resettlement and rehabilitation processes. Compensation usually only occurs once as a cash payment or in the form of an asset such as housing and/or land. Lands provided for resettlement are often resource-depleted and in environmentally degraded areas. The focus of resettlement programmes is on physical relocation rather than economic and social development. In China, almost half (46%) of those displaced are living in extreme poverty. In India, 75% of people displaced by dams have not been rehabilitated.

## Health Impacts

The edge of tropical reservoirs and irrigation canals provide ideal conditions for disease vectors such as insects and snails. There are numerous documented examples of the spread of schistosomiasis after the construction of dams. Increase in transmission of malaria due to construction of reservoirs and irrigation canals in malaria-prone areas have also been reported by World Bank (World Bank, 2004). Other health impacts include release of toxins by cyanobacteria due to rapid eutrophication in new dams and bioaccumulation of mercury in fish which is released from soil by bacteria decomposing organic matter in the reservoir. The prime reason why large projects are given go-ahead is likely due to the benefits for those living downstream and the overall economy. The ecological footprint of hydropower projects appear to be far smaller compared with other power sources but the issues are certainly important enough to be debated.

## Cultural Heritage

Cultural heritage is present manifestation of human past and refers to sites, structures and remains of archaeological, historical, religious, cultural and aesthetic value. Exceptional natural landscapes or physical features of the environment are also an important part of human heritage as landscapes are endowed with a variety of meanings. The creation of a reservoir might lead to the disappearance of valued exceptional landscapes such as spectacular waterfalls and canyons (World Bank, 1994). Long-term landscape modifications can also occur through soil erosion, sedimentation and low water levels in reservoirs as well as through associated infrastructure impacts (e.g., new roads, transmission lines). It is therefore important that appropriate measures be taken to preserve natural beauty in the project area and to protect cultural properties with high historic value. Possible measures to minimize negative impacts, for example: ensuring on- site protection; conserving and restoring, relocating and/or re-creating important physical and cultural resources; creating a museum in partnership with local communities to make archaeological findings, documentation and record keeping accessible; including landscape architecture competences into the project design to optimize harmonious integration of infrastructure into the landscape; using borrow pits and quarries for construction material that will later disappear through impoundment; re-vegetating dumping sites for soil and excavation material with indigenous species; putting transmission lines and power stations underground in areas of exceptional natural beauty; incorporating residual flows to preserve important waterfalls at least during the tourism high season; keeping as much as possible the natural appearance of river landscapes by constructing weirs to adjust the water level using local rocks instead of concrete; and by constructing small islands in impounded areas which might be of ecological interest for waterfowl and migrating birds.

## CONCLUSION

Environmental challenges of developmental activities especially for hydropower projects have been a regular phenomenon. Overall, evidence suggests that relatively high levels of deployment in the next 20 years are feasible. It is suggested that developing countries construct well-performing hydraulic infrastructures to be used for hydropower generation and water management that also meet environmental and social standards (World Bank, 2004).

While hydropower dams can produce power with low GHG emissions and can in some cases also deliver flood and irrigation control, the adverse social and environmental costs can be substantial as we have described earlier. Such negative impacts are not compatible with promotion of sustainable development. Growing awareness among people about global warming and climate change issues, combined with centralized manner of project planning with little input from the common people, is making implementation of projects increasingly difficult. Inter-state dispute is another source of trouble. All major power projects are facing determined opposition; that becomes worse when political parties begin to exploit people's unrest. In order to meet the ever growing demand for energy and rocketing fossil fuels prices, development of hydropower projects are need of the hour particularly in developing countries. It is equally important to fulfill this need in a sustainable way. So, constructing technically feasible, economically viable, environmentally sound, socially and culturally acceptable projects has been the present thrust of the nation. Thus, it is concluded that framing of policies favoring sustainable development and their effective implementation at grass-root levels involving all stakeholders can only set the ball rolling for desired pace of hydropower development in India.

## THE WAY FORWARD

Government of India is vigorously promoting large scale development of hydro power in India through changes in policies, all driven to involve greater private entrepreneurs. Major issues plaguing the hydropower sector have been identified and policy changes to mend these barriers are now required. These issues have been discussed earlier in the paper. The way forward to meet energy demand is as follows:

- Recommendations made by the Standing Committee for hydropower development are crucial and should be enforced for maximum benefit to the Indian hydropower sector.
- Consistent policies and regulations should be made through the States. Any variation in policies and benefits offered by different states will cause problems in development of many project sites in different states.
- Large scale hydropower projects which involve greater risks due to geological uncertainties should be implemented by the state nodal

agencies while the relatively safer projects with reduced risks and smaller capital investments should be offered to the private entrepreneurs.

- ❖ A single window clearance setup for hydropower projects will solve most problems related to the clearances.
- ❖ Renovation and Modernization of existing/old hydro power plants should be promoted and planned for instead of complete focus on setting up of green field power projects.
- ❖ Financial issues like long term debt financing/long tenure loans, differential tariff for peak and off-peak hours need serious thinking and early implementation.
- ❖ Private sector participation in large scale development of hydropower should be promoted. This can be achieved either through public-private partnerships or through independent private projects (IPP). The Government of India has already recognized the need to increased private involvement and has referred to it in the national policy document.

The hydropower sector needs to develop a set of competent civil engineers/contracting agencies that have technical and management expertise to conceptualize and develop a project of the required scale. Contract management practices with a transparent system of selection of contractors and resolve any disputes that may arise needs to be reviewed.

## REFERENCES


1. Agarwal, P.K. and Singh, V.P. (2007): Hydrology and Water Resources of India, Major uses of Water in India, The Netherlands: Springer, 849p.
2. Anonymous (2013): Energy Vision Report-Energy Transitions: Past and Future, World Economic Forum, January 2013, 17p.
3. Box, J.D. and Forbes, J.E. (1992): Ecological Considerations in the Environmental Assessment of Road Proposals, Highway Transport, April 1992: 16-22.
4. Brismar and Anna (2003): Environmental Consideration in the Planning of Large Dam Projects, Thesis Submitted to Linkoping University, Sweden, for Doctor of Philosophy.
5. Brooks, B.L. (1988): The Breeding Distribution, Population Dynamics and Habitat Availability and Suitability of an Upper Midwest Loggerhead Shrike Population, Thesis Submitted to the University of Wisconsin-Madison.
6. Chaurasiya, P.K., Prasad,V. and Khare, R. (2013): Scenario And Risk Of Hydro Power Projects In India, International Journal of ChemTech Research CODEN( USA): IJCRGG, Vol. 5 (2), 1068-1075.
7. Dale, A.T., Lucena, A.F.P.D., Marriott, J., Borba, B.S.M.C., Schaeffer, R. and Bilec, M.M. (2013): Modeling Future Life-Cycle Greenhouse Gas Emissions and Environmental Impacts of Electricity Supplies in Brazil, Energies, Vol. 6, 3182-3208.
8. DoE (2014): Status of Hydropotential in Himachal Pradesh, Directorate of Energy (DoE),Government of Himachal Pradesh (GoHP), )#http:/admis.hp.nic.in/doe/DOEAuth/ welcome.aspx*#.
9. Goudie, A. (1990): The Human Impact on the Natural Environment, The MIT Press, Cambridge, Massachusetts, 388 p.

10. Gregory, K.J. and Walling, D.E. (1987): Human Activity and Environmental Processes, John Wiley and Sons, New York, XV + 466.
11. http://www.walkthroughindia.com/attraction/the-5-biggest-dams-in-india/
12. JKSPDC (2014): Jammu & Kashmir State Power Development Corporation (JKSPDC) Ltd. )#http:/www. jkspdc.nic.in/*#.
13. Kumar, D. and Katoch, K.K. (2014): Harnessing 'Water Tower' into 'Power Tower': A Small Hydropower Development Study from an Indian Prefecture in Western Himalayas, Renewable and Sustainable Energy Reviews, Vol. 39, 87-101.
14. Lata, R., Rishi, M.S., Kochhar, N. and Sharma, R. (2013): Impact Analysis of Run-off –The River Type Hydropower Power Plants in Himachal Pradesh, India, International Journal of Civil, Structural, Environmental and Infrastructure Engineering Research and Development (IJCSEIERD) Vol. 3 (2), 77-82.
15. MDoNER (2014): Hydro Electric Potential Development in NER & Sikkim, Ministry of Development of North Eastern Region (MDoNER), )#http:/www.mdoner.gov. in/content/ development-hydro-power*#.
16. Ministry of Power (2014): Forty Third Report, Standing Committee on Energy (2013-14), Lok Sabha Secretariat, Ministry of Power, New Delhi, 7p.
17. Ministry of Power (2014): Power Sector at a Glance "All India" Ministry of Power (MoP), Government of India. )#http:/powermin.nic.in/JSP_SERVLETS/internal. jsp*#.
18. Naidu, B. S. K. (1997): Small Hydro in India: Environmental Friendly Alternative Energy source, TERI (The Energy and Resource Institute), Inf Monit Environ Sci, Vol. 1 (2), 81-93.
19. NHPC (2014): Hydro Potential in India, National Hydropower Power Corporation Ltd., Government of India (GoI) enterprise, )#http:/www.nhpcindia.com/potential.htm*#.
20. Political Map of India (2014): )#http:/www.mapsofindia.com/maps/india/india-politi cal-map.htm*#.
21. Singh, N.P.(2008): Hydro Power: An Indian Experience and Future Trends, Ministry of New and Renewable Energy, G.O.I., Global Renewable energy Forum, 1-30.
22. Subrahmanyam, D.S. (2013): Status of Electric Power Generation in India with Special Emphasis on Hydropower Expansion, International Journal of Renewable Energy and Environmental Engineering, Vol. 1(1), 31-33.
23. UJVN (2014): Importance of Small Hydro Projects, Uttarakhand Jal Vidyut Nigam (UJVN) Ltd., )#http:/uttarakhandjalvidyut.com*#.
24. Ullah, A. (2015): Public Private Partnership in Hydro-Power Development of India: Prospects and Challenges, Journal of Business Management and Social Sciences Research (JBM &SSR), Vol. 4 (2), 190-201.
25. World Bank (1994): Culture Heritage and Environmental Assessment. Environmental Assessment Sourcebook Update, No. 8, World Bank, Washington, DC, USA, 8 p.
26. World Bank (2004): Water Resources Sector Strategy: Strategic Directions for World Bank Engagement. International Bank for Reconstruction and Development/ World Bank, Washington, DC, USA.

Pages: 131-150

CLIMATE CHANGE, DISASTER MANAGEMENT AND ENVIRONMENT

*Edited by:* Dr. Alka Chauhan; Dr. Pawan Kumar 'Bharti'

ISBN: 978-93-5056-784-5

*Edition:* 2016

*Published by:* Discovery Publishing House Pvt. Ltd., New Delhi (India)

# CHAPTER – 8

# Agrometeorology *A Supportive Tool for Agricultural Research and Development*

**Alok Kumar Patra**[1] and **Ranjan Kumar Patra**[2]

***ABSTRACT***

Climate and weather is a basic input or resource considered the most vital in agricultural production system since it affects the agricultural planning and activities directly or indirectly in a big way starting from land preparation to harvesting, processing and transportation. Thus, climate may be considered as the most critical factor determining the sustainability of agricultural systems. However, among all the resources that are essential for agricultural production, climate receives the least attention.

Agrometeorology is primarily concerned with the interactions among meteorological, hydrological and pedological factors that influence

1 Associate Professor (Agronomy), All India Coordinated Research Project on Integrated Farming Systems, Orissa University of Agriculture and Technology, Bhubaneswar - 751 003, Odisha, (India).

2 Professor (Soil Science & Agricultural Chemistry), College of Agriculture, Orissa University of Agriculture and Technology, Bhubaneswar - 751 003, Odisha, (India).

production systems in agriculture and allied sectors like horticulture, animal husbandry, fishery, forestry, *etc.* Since agrometeorology is multidisciplinary in nature, a good understanding of the interrelationships that exist among all the concerned disciplines is required. An agrometeorologist defines all these interactions and correlates physical environments to biological responses and applies the acquired and relevant meteorological skills to help farmers for exploiting weather conditions to improve agricultural production both in quality and quantity. In this paper, an attempt has been made to enumerate the scope, importance and applications of agrometeorology to increase agricultural productivity through research with well defined objectivity. The challenges that an agrometeorologist would face in future is also discussed in the chapter.

## INTRODUCTION

Meteorology is derived from the Greek word *meteoro* which means above the earth's surface; *i.e.* the atmosphere. The state of the atmosphere experienced at a given time, in any location on the surface of the earth is known as weather. Thus meteorology is the scientific study of the atmosphere or the weather. It is a branch of physics dealing with atmosphere and it is often quoted as the 'physics of the lower atmosphere'. The main focus of meteorology is to understand the weather processes and forecast the weather. Solar radiation, the air mass and moisture are the three key ingredients that make up weather. The exchange of heat, moisture and momentum between the earth's surface and the atmosphere determines the characteristic of weather.

The observable weather events are known as meteorological phenomena and are defined by a set of variables called weather elements. Atmospheric temperature, atmospheric pressure, humidity, precipitation, cloudiness, wind and visibility, *etc.* are examples of such weather elements. The weather elements are not separate entities. They are closely related with each other and are highly variable in nature. Meteorology explains and analyses the changes of these weather elements.

## METEOROLOGY

The major subdivisions of meteorology are dynamic meteorology (or atmospheric dynamics) and physical meteorology (or atmospheric physics). The dynamic meteorology is concerned with the analysis and interpretation of the three-dimensional, time-varying, macro scale motions and energy transformations in the atmosphere. The science of dynamic meteorology is meant to develop models based on the hydrodynamic and thermodynamic equations. The physical meteorology is concerned with the processes that alter the physical properties and the chemical composition of air parcels as they move through the atmosphere.

Depending on the temporal and spatial scope of interest, meteorology can be divided into distinct areas of emphasis such as micro, meso, synoptic and planetary scale meteorology. These scales are related to the size of the atmospheric motion and the spatial size of each of them corresponds to appropriate timescale. Micro-scale meteorology pertains to short-lived atmospheric phenomena which last for minutes or hours rather than days and cover a distance of about one km or less. It controls the most important mixing and dilution processes in the atmosphere. Important topics in micro-scale meteorology include heat transfer and gaseous exchange between soil, vegetation and/or surface water and the atmosphere caused by near-ground turbulence. Most of the micro-scale phenomena occur within the planetary boundary layer, where the frictional force of ground topography can influence the air motion. Individual cloud systems at higher levels also come under the purview of micro-scale meteorology. Meso-scale meteorology ranges in horizontal dimensions from 5 to 500 kilometres and typically possesses lifetimes of a day or less.

Vertical velocity often equals or exceeds horizontal velocities in meso-scale meteorological systems. Examples of meso-scale weather systems are tornadoes, thunderstorms, cloud bursts, land and sea breeze, *etc*. Synoptic (or cyclonic) scale meteorology has a horizontal length scale of the order of 500-3000 km and lasts for several days. Synoptic scale meteorology is best studied through the air mass concept. Synoptic scale weather systems are the major features shown on the weather maps such as mean sea level surface charts and the daily forecast charts. They are characterised by mainly horizontal motion. Tropical and extra tropical cyclones are the best examples of synoptic scale systems. Planetary (or global) scale meteorology studies weather patterns related to the transport of heat from the tropics to the poles and other very large scale oscillations. The atmosphere acts like a gigantic heat engine and the temperature difference between the poles and the equator provides the energy supply needed to drive planetary atmosphere and ocean circulation. Planetary scale systems last from several days to weeks, and extend over several thousand kilometres.

## CLIMATOLOGY

Climatology is derived from the Greek word *klima* which means slope of the earth. Climatology is the scientific study of climate, which is usually defined as the average weather. It seeks to describe and explain the nature of the climate and how it differs from place to place. Climate can be defined as the state of the atmosphere expressed over a longer period of time (generally 30 years) and includes a statistical description in terms of the mean and variability of relevant weather elements. It really represents a kind of frequency distribution of weather types in a given region and over a period of time. Until mid-twentieth century, climate was considered to be sufficiently constant and the average weather of 30 years at any location usually represented the climate of that location. However, the variation of climate averaged over time is now widely acknowledged.

The distinction between weather and climate can be appreciated with the popular quotations '*Climate lasts all the time, weather only for few days*' (Mark Twain) or '*Climate is what you expect, weather is what you get*' (Robert Heinlein). Weather refers to the state of atmosphere at any given time denoting the short-term variations of atmosphere in terms of temperature, pressure, wind, moisture, cloudiness, precipitation, *etc*. It is highly variable, constantly changing, sometimes from hour to hour and at other times from day to day. These weather elements are closely related with each other. Climate on the other hand, is the sum total of the varieties of weather conditions of a place or an area. It may be defined as the sum of all statistical weather information of a particular area during a specified interval of time, usually several decades. The World Meteorological Organisation has suggested a standard period of 31 years for calculating the climatic averages of different weather elements.

Meteorology and climatology are two closely related fields of study. Both of these study the elements of atmosphere and the causes of atmospheric behaviour. Meteorology focuses on short term weather systems lasting up to a few weeks. On the other hand climatology studies the frequency and trends of those systems. It studies the periodicity of weather events over years to millennia, as well as changes in long-term average weather patterns, in relation to atmospheric conditions. Meteorology draws its fundamental principles from physics and applies them to the behaviour of the atmosphere, which follows certain basic rules. Changes in the pattern of heat, moisture and motion in three dimensional spaces can be described and accounted for by the laws of physics. Meteorology treats weather processes as a set of physical changes and can be considered as a branch of physics, whereas climatology is concerned with the weather process as the expression of regional and seasonal influences and often is considered as a part of geography. Due to the present concern about global warming related climate change, the areas of research in both meteorology and climatology are rapidly growing and many overlapping areas of multidisciplinary nature are being developed. Thus, the distinction between the two subjects is getting blurred and it is advantageous to treat meteorology and climatology together.

The three basic sub divisions of climatology are physical climatology, regional or descriptive climatology and applied climatology. Physical climatology seeks to explain the factors responsible for bringing out the temporal and spatial variations in heat exchange, moisture exchange and air movement. It is closely related to meteorology and includes not only the physics, chemistry and dynamics of the atmosphere, but also many of its direct effects upon the earth's surface, the oceans and life in general. Regional climatology is concerned with the description of various types of climates and spatial distribution of climatic elements. Applied climatology is concerned with the application of climatic knowledge to specific practical problems. The ultimate aim of climatology is to discuss various climatic elements as well as factors that control the distribution of climate over earth.

Climate can be considered under micro, meso and macro levels. Climatic conditions in a relatively small area, within a few feet above and below the earth's surface and within canopies of vegetation is called microclimate. Microclimates are affected by not only the weather elements such as temperature, humidity, wind and turbulence, dew, frost, heat balance, evaporation, but also by the nature of soil and vegetation, the local topography, elevation and season. The climate of small areas of the earth's surface which may not be representative of the general climate of the district is known as meso-climate. It is controlled by local factors. The large-scale climate of a large area or country, as distinguished from meso-climate and microclimate is known as macro climate. Any portion of the earth's surface over which the broad climatic characteristics are similar is called a climatic region. It can be further grouped into climate types and climate groups.

## AGROMETEOROLOGY

Agrometeorology, abbreviated from agricultural meteorology is a branch of applied meteorology, which investigates the physical conditions of the environment for growing plants, animals or other organisms. It is an applied science, which deals with the relationship between weather/climatic conditions and agricultural production or it is a science concerned with the application of meteorology to the measurement and analysis of the physical environment in agricultural systems.

Agrometeorology is defined as the science investigating the meteorological, climatological, and hydrological conditions that are significant to agriculture owing to their interaction with the objects and processes of agriculture production (Molga, 1962). Agrometeorology puts the science of meteorology to the service of agriculture in its various forms and facets to help with the sensible use of land, to accelerate the production of food, and to avoid the irreversible abuse of land resources (Smith, 1970). Agrometeorology is concerned with meteorological, hydrological and pedological factors affecting agricultural production and also with agriculture's interaction with the environment. Its objectives are to elucidate such effects, and then to assist farmers to apply this supportive knowledge and information in agrometeorological practices and services.

Agrometeorology is an interdisciplinary science in which the main scientific disciplines involved are atmosphere sciences and soil sciences, which are concerned with the physical environment, and plant sciences and animal sciences (including their pathology, entomology, and parasitology, *etc.*), which deal with the contents of the biosphere (Mavi and Tupper, 2004). Though interdisciplinary in nature, agrometeorology is a well-defined science. Its subject matter links together the physical environment and biological responses under natural conditions. An agrometeorologist applies every relevant meteorological skill to help farmers make the most efficient use of their physical environment in order to improve agricultural production both in quality and quantity and to maintain the sustainability of their land and resources (Bourke, 1968). Using a four-stage approach, an agrometeorologist first formulates an accurate description of the physical environment and biological responses. At the second stage, he or she interprets biological responses in terms of the physical environment. Third, he or she makes agrometeorological forecasts. The final goal is to develop agrometeorological services, strategies, and support systems for on-farm strategic and tactical decisions and to implement them in collaboration with specialists in agriculture, livestock, and forestry (Mavi and Tupper, 2004).

## SCOPE AND IMPORTANCE OF AGROMETEOROLOGY

Among all the human activities, agriculture is possibly the most dependent on the weather. Weather and climate are natural resources and are considered as basic inputs in agricultural planning. Climate influences the distribution of crops over different regions of the world, while weather influences crop production and productivity. All the farm operations from land preparation to harvesting, threshing, storage and transport of farm produce are affected by weather. The field of interest of an agrometeorologist extends from the depth down to which tree roots penetrate to the highest levels in the atmosphere through which the transport of seeds, spores, pollen, and insects may take place. Agrometeorology is concerned with the interactions among meteorological, hydrological and pedological factors on the one hand and agriculture, in the broader sense including horticulture, animal husbandry, fishery, and forestry, on the other. Thus, the role of an agrometeorologist is to find out and define these interactions, and then apply this acquired knowledge in the operational field of agriculture and allied sectors to increase the productivity. All the agricultural activities are affected directly or indirectly by weather and climate. Agrometeorology has therefore, the greatest scope on agriculture and other allied enterprises as summerised below.

1. **Characterization of agroclimate:** The growth, development and yield of a crop depend on the climatic parameters such as solar radiation, air temperature, precipitation, wind, humidity, *etc*. Agrometeorology

considers and assesses the suitability of these parameters in a given region for maximum crop production and economical benefits. The meteorological data supplemented with soil and topographic information help to develop a suitable land use planning.

2. **Crop planning for stability in production:** To get stabilized yields even under weather adversity, suitable cropping patterns/ contingent cropping planning can be adopted by considering water requirements of crops, effective rainfall and available soil moisture. This may reduce the risk of crop failure due to abiotic stresses.
3. **Crop management:** Farm operations such as sowing, fertilizer application, plant protection, irrigation scheduling, harvesting, drying and processing, *etc.* are carried out more effectively and scientifically if the prevailing or forecasted weather conditions are available to the farmers. Weeding, harrowing, mulching, *etc.* are undertaken during dry spells forecasted. Similarly, fertilizer application is advisable when rainfall is not heavy and soil moisture is between 30 and 80%. Spraying/ dusting is undertaken when there is no rainfall, soil moisture is 90% and wind speed is < 25km/hr.
4. **Crop monitoring:** Meteorological tools such as crop growth models, water balance technique or remote sensing are used to evaluate the crop growth performance and recommend suitable remedial measures.
5. **Crop modelling and yield-climate relationship:** Suitable crop models can be developed by using the current and past weather data and these models can predict the growth and yield of a crop before its harvest.
6. **Research on crop-climate relationship:** Agrometeorology can help to understand crop-climate relationship so as to resolve complexities of a plant process in relation to its microclimate. Thus, the microclimatic conditions can be modified by appropriate agronomic practices for increasing agricultural productivity.
7. **Climate extremities:** Climatic hazards like frost, floods, droughts, hail storms, high wind velocity, *etc.* can be forecasted and the crops at various stages in the field may be saved by taking appropriate protective measures against these climatic extremities.
8. **Climate as a tool to diagnose soil moisture stress:** Soil moisture can be determined through water balance technique, which is used to diagnose the soil moisture stress and necessary protective measures such as irrigation, mulching, application of antitranspirant, defoliation, thinning, *etc.* can be undertaken to supply water to or reduce the moisture loss from the system through evapotranspiration.
9. **Livestock production:** Meteorological parameters can be related to the growth, development and production of livestock. Favourable and unfavorable weather conditions for livestock are studied in the

agrometeorology and the climatic normal is worked out for optimization of milk, meat and egg production. Animal growth simulation models may be developed for prediction of productivity in advance and also obtaining potential yield in different agroecological zones.

10. **Fisheries:** Fishermen need information on atmospheric and oceanic changes before they proceed on sea for fishing and this is possible from meteorological knowledge.
11. **Weather-crop pest and disease relationships:** The weather-crop pest and disease relationships are studied in agrometeorology. It helps in taking preventive and curative measures to avoid or check the outbreak and spread of biotic stress in crops and livestock.
12. **Delineation of agroecological zones:** Study of agrometeorology of a region helps to delineate agroecological zones for efficient use of resources and faster transfer of technology.
13. **Crop weather calendars:** Study of agrometeorology helps in preparing crop weather diagrams and crop weather calendars for timely agricultural operations by farmers.
14. **Agroadvisory:** Value added weather based agroadvisory can be developed for different agroclimatic zones and by its real time dissemination to farmers, the input cost can be reduced and productivity can be increased.
15. **Soil formation:** Soil formation process depends on climatic factors like temperature, precipitation, humidity, wind, *etc.*, thus climate is a major factor in soil formation and development.
16. **Climate change:** Study of agrometeorology helps to understand the impact of climatic variability or climate change on agricultural production systems. It also helps in devising suitable approaches to climate change adaptation and mitigation in agriculture.
17. **Environmental pollutions:** Modern intensive agriculture affects the environment through the generation of air pollutants, greenhouse gases ($CO_2$, methane and nitrous oxide), ammonia and tropospheric ozone. Other modes of production cause soil erosion by wind and water. Agrometeorology has a major role to play in the understanding of emissions and pollutions from various unsustainable production systems.

## APPLICATIONS OF AGROMETEOROLOGY

Despite impressive advances in agricultural technology, agricultural production is still dependent on weather and climate. The need for agrometeorological services have increased in recent years because of the increasing climate variability and associated extreme events. The fields of interest of agrometeorology include agricultural and horticultural production, forestry, animal husbandry, fisheries, agricultural planning, processing, transport and storage of food, poverty reduction and sustainable development aspects of the livelihood of farmers. Other important subjects are agroclimatic characterisation of pests and diseases and their safe control, quality of agricultural products, animal comfort aspects, plant production for other than food purposes, including biomass as a renewable energy resource and ecological considerations. Agrometeorological services are useful for the following activities:

- climate monitoring and analysis leading to planning and early warnings of climate anomalies
- real time monitoring leading to the provision of operational advices, for example, in determining irrigation efficiency
- microclimate manipulation and prediction, within crops, soils and managed environments (glass houses, stores, *etc.*)
- preparedness for agricultural hazards (including pests and diseases)

The agrometeorological services are mainly applied in two areas, *viz.*, for planning purposes and for operational management purposes. The long term climatic data sets and seasonal global applications are mainly used together with the crop or livestock requirements for crop/livestock-climate matching. This planning level is of vital importance when introducing new varieties and breeds into an area or evaluating the effects of global warming on agricultural production in a specific area. Meteorological information are important for tactical agrometeorological decisions in short term planning of agricultural operations at different growth stages such as ploughing, sowing/planting, mulching, manuring, weeding, thinning, pruning and harvesting. At an operational level, the data analysis and application is usually at a more local, district or on-farm level during the growing season. Therefore, meteorological data are analysed for decision making with regard to irrigation scheduling, spaying of herbicides, crop/livestock disease and pest control and other daily/weekly farm operations. Operational agricultural meteorology also concerns itself with small scale climate modifications as brought about by agronomic or engineering approaches.

Rational use of climate information in agricultural production requires knowledge on climatic requirements of crops and climatic characteristics specific to a given farming area expressed in basic statistical terms. The crop-weather relationship could be better understood if the various aspects of environmental stress on crops are taken into account. Crop simulation modelling highlights the yield potential constraints analysis under different crop growing environments of a given crop. Rainfall, air and soil temperature, photosynthetically active radiation, soil moisture, wind, humidity and evapotranspiration are the atmospheric variables that play dominant roles in crop production. In developed countries mathematical models are increasingly used in operational agrometeorology, in conjunction with

Geographic Information Systems to provide inputs to Decision Support Systems. These models have utilized meteorological observations. These forecasts may be exploited to increase the utility of models to decision makers. The possible utilities of agrometeorological information in agriculture are discussed below.

**Monitoring and Early Warning**

The availability of adequate and quantitative agrometeorological data is an absolute prerequisite for analyzing and managing production processes in agriculture, including livestock and forestry. Decision making in agricultural operations for well grown crops or crops endangered by pests, diseases and/or other environmental disasters needs weather forecasting and climate prediction to the required accuracies. A number of crop monitoring systems and yield forecasts are now being implemented worldwide and upscaling to regional scales are being attempted. In these, commercial crops like soybean, maize, wheat, sorghum, *etc*. are continuously monitored and forecasted.

**Crop, Forest and Livestock Protection**

Weather effects on plant, tree and animal discomfort and injury, as well as crop, forest and livestock losses are highly complex. Protection can take the preparative form of either planning crops, varieties and sites to avoid or mitigate the effects of the relevant meteorological extremes detrimental to plants or improving sites to reduce and/or avoid the impact of these extremes. Response farming is the best example of the former (Stewart, 1991). Microclimate management and manipulation is the best example of the latter (Stigter, 1994). Meteorologists play key roles in crop, forest and livestock protection by offering better preparedness strategies by environmental avoidance or mitigation through improved understanding of the processes and phenomena involved. Agrometeorology can play a significant role in reducing the negative impacts caused by pests and diseases. The use of climate in land-use planning, scheduling agricultural activities and preparing crop calendars as well as in crop, forest and livestock protection have benefited the agricultural communities of many regions. Information like return periods, frequencies of occurrences and intensities of extreme events and assured rainfall in different growing periods are valuable in choices for preparedness strategies. An appropriate, preferably integrated pest management system using meteorological and microclimatological information can reduce pre- and post-harvest losses appreciably. The tactical use of weather information in the prediction of pest and disease development allows for near optimum use and timing of pesticides and/or release of predators. Major applications of meteorology and climatology to forest operations include pest and disease control, frost protection and fire prevention. Monitoring fire-weather parameters such as moisture conditions of the soil and ground litter, wind speed and direction, temperature, humidity and lightning strikes are crucial for preparedness of forest fire and for early action before it gets out of control.

### Water Resources Assessment

Because of the scarcity of water in many places of the world, prudent water management and increasing water use efficiency are essential, especially in arid and semiarid regions. Global and national policies and strategies are now being developed to increase awareness of water shortage, promote water conservation and water harvesting, redress mismanagement of ground water, increase water use efficiencies, promote the use of additional sources of water and promote recycling of water. Even in humid areas increasing climate variability and climate change are forcing water use planners to adopt and promote more efficient water use and water management techniques (Stigter *et. al.*, 2004). In many countries, substantial resources have been used to monitor floods and droughts and to design appropriate irrigation and drainage systems for agriculture. Water budget/ balance calculations, including elaborate evapotranspiration calculations based on physics and plant factors, and soil moisture determinations are widely applied tools in water waste determinations and water use planning in agriculture. Water management to ensure adequate supplies while maintaining the quality of surface and groundwater is a key topic. Meteorological services are required in designs of irrigation and drainage schemes, decisions related to land-use and farming patterns, and within these choices selections of crops and animals, varieties and breeds, and farm machinery.

### Soil and Biomass Resources Assessment

Climate and weather affect the chemical, physical and mechanical properties of soil, the organisms it contains and its capacity for retaining and releasing heat and moisture. Rainfall adds chemical constituents to the soil but also washes out soil nutrients. Weathering is an important factor in determining the nature of soil. Topsoil composition, vegetation cover with surface contact and local weather factors largely determine the existence and extent of the problems of wind and water erosion. The state of the soil affecting cultivation, pest control and harvesting is also much influenced by weather conditions. Both chemical and physical components of soil degradation are of importance in soil resources assessments. Exposed agricultural land losing topsoil by wind and/or water actions needs to be stabilized and covered. It is important to keep the soil covered in economically useful ways. Demographic pressure on natural resources like forests has caused weather and climate to change locally, regionally and even globally. Forest fires are also a serious source of local and transboundary air pollution and atmospheric degradation. Correct application of meteorological and climatological information can be of considerable benefit to the protection, sustainable development and conservation of forest resources, greening of degraded areas through forest rehabilitation, afforestation and reforestation.

## HISTORICAL DEVELOPMENT OF METEOROLOGY AND AGROMETEOROLOGY

Greek philosopher Aristotle is considered the founder of meteorology and his *Meteorologica* (340 B.C.) is the oldest comprehensive treatise on meteorological subjects. The most impressive achievements of *Meteorologica* are the description of the hydrologic cycle, weather phenomena and earthquakes. Aristotle's work remained as the authority in meteorology for some 2,000 years. In addition to further commentary on the *Meteorologica*, this period also saw attempts to forecast the weather according to astrological events using techniques introduced by Claudius Ptolemy (90-168 A.D.), a Greco-Egyptian geographer. Folklores and indigenous knowledge were also used to weather forecasting. Following the scientific revolution in 16$^{th}$ century onwards, speculation gave way to experimentation. The invention of instruments for measuring atmospheric conditions contributed to the advancement of meteorology. Leonardo da Vinci's wind vane (1500 A.D.), Galileo Galilei's thermometer (1593 A.D.), Evangelista Torricelli's mercury barometer (1643 A.D.) and Horace Benedict de Saussure's hair hygrograph (1783 A.D.) helped meteorological observation through measurement of wind, temperature, pressure and relative humidity, respectively. Recording of rainfall started in the late seventeenth century in England though its measurements are described in India in the fourth century.

The first prolonged instrumental meteorological observation was initiated by Dr. John Lining in Charleston, USA in 1738. Thomas Jefferson and James Madison made the first simultaneous meteorological measurements in America in 1778. The invention of the telegraph in 1843, made possible the rapid collection of nearly simultaneous weather observations for large continental and marine regions. It provided a view of the large-scale pressure and circulation patterns that determine the weather. In 1849 Joseph Henry of Smithsonian meteorological project began compiling weather reports collected from telegraph operators and displayed the results on a large map. The Smithsonian project provided a uniform set of procedures and some standardized instruments to observers. Following it, network of observing stations was established in Europe and North America in 1850s. James Coffin mapped the winds of the globe using data collected through Smithsonian exchanges. A cloud classification scheme was devised by Luke Howard in 1803. In 1817 Alexander von Humboldt produced a treatise on global temperature containing a map of mean annual isotherms for the northern hemisphere. Heinrich Wilhelm Dove, a Prussian meteorologist published the first world map of monthly mean temperature in 1848. Precipitation map was produced by Heinrich Berghaus, a German geographer in 1845. First mean global pressure map showing the cyclonic and anticyclonic centres of action was prepared by Teisserenc de Bort in 1883. In 1886 de Bort published the first world map of annual and monthly cloudiness. Beginning in 1875, the weather service of USA issued *Bulletin of International Simultaneous Observations*, which contained worldwide synoptic charts and weather observations. American astronomer and meteorologist Elias Loomis improved weather-plotting methods and developed synoptic charts depicting winds, precipitation, isotherms, and lines of minimum pressure in 1841.

The meteorological observations were used by many workers to understand the underlying processes and develop theories. English astronomer and meteorologist Edmond Halley accounted of the trade winds and monsoons through thermal convection theory in 1686. Schmidt (1830) was the first to calculate the amount of solar energy being received and reradiated from the earth's surface theoretically. Major advances in understanding the large scale motions of the atmosphere took place in early part of the 20$^{th}$ century. In 1917 the Norwegian physicist Vilhelm Bjerknes introduced his theory for the formation of wave cyclones. In 1922, L. F. Richardson perceived the basis for the mathematical prediction of the atmospheric circulation. In 1924, Sir Gilbert Walker identified the 'southern oscillation', an east-west seesaw of atmospheric pressure and the resulting rainfall. In the 1930s a number of visiting scientists from Scandinavia to the USA, including Vilhelm Bjerknes, Jacob Bjerknes, C. G. Rossby, and Sverre Petterssen developed the new method of air mass and frontal analysis (known as Bergen School). This became the basis of weather forecasting till the development of computers and numerical weather prediction in 1960s. Serbian geophysicist and astronomer Milutin Milanokovitch in 1930 contributed to the understanding astronomical controls of climate. Wladimir Koppen (1918) produced the first detailed classification of world climate based on plant geography. Thornthwaite (1931-33) classified climates employing evaporation and precipitation amounts.

The comprehensive development and use of plant and animal dynamic simulation models started with the availability of computers in the early 1970s. By the close of the twentieth century, several thousand computer-based plant and animal dynamic simulation models had been developed to expand scientific insights into complex biological and environmental systems, and their use has resulted in huge economic benefits (Mavi and Tupper, 2004). The application of crop simulation models and simulation based decision support systems became more acceptable to the agricultural community during the 1990s (Hoogenboom, 2000). The development and deployment of earth satellites in the 1970s brought a revolution in remote sensing. Remote sensing now provides a sequence of reliable and irreplaceable information for agriculture planning and management (Maracchi, *et. al.*, 2000).

International Meteorological Organisation (IMO) was created in 1873 to co-ordinate the collection and international exchange of meteorological data and information. In 1950, it was transformed into an intergovernmental World Meteorological Organisation (WMO) with its headquarters at Geneva. Over the past 60 years, WMO has assisted the National Meteorological and Hydrological Services (NMHS) of its member countries to provide weather, climate and water services to various socio-economic sectors of their countries. It initiated the study of global climate in 1970s through co-ordinated intensive programme of observation. Global meteorological observation became a major concern and a series of observation programmes such as GARP (Global Atmospheric Research Programme) and WCRP (World Climate Research Programme) were launched. The World Weather Watch (WWW), organized by the WMO, collects and disseminates information on a global basis. A number of private companies are also engaged in operational and research meteorological activities. The World Meteorological Day is celebrated on 23rd March every year all over world, focussing annual themes related to the science and its impact on society. The Commission for Agricultural Meteorology (CAgM) is one of the eight technical commissions of WMO, which provides technical assistance to the member countries in improving agrometeorological services. The WMO also organises and patronises international conferences on the issues related to meteorology and agrometeorology to create awareness and disseminate the latest technological developments among the member countries. India became a member of the WMO on April 27, 1949.

## DEVELOPMENT OF METEOROLOGY AND AGROMETEOROLOGY IN INDIA

The beginnings of meteorology in India can be traced to ancient times, the 3000 B.C. era. Early literatures, such as the Upanishadas, contain serious discussion about the processes of cloud formation and rain and the seasonal cycles caused by the movement of the earth round the sun. Varahamihira's classical work, the *Brihatsamhita*, written around 500 A.D., provides a clear evidence that a deep knowledge of atmospheric processes existed even in those times. It was understood that rains come from the sun and that good rainfall in the rainy season was the key to bountiful agriculture and food for the people. Kautilya's *Arthashastra* contains records of scientific measurements of rainfall and its application to the country's revenue and relief work. Kalidasa in his epic, *Meghdoot*, written around the seventh century, mentions the date of onset of the monsoon over central India and traces the path of the monsoon clouds.

In 1636, Halley, a British scientist, published his treatise on the Indian summer monsoon, which he attributed to a seasonal reversal of winds due to the differential heating of the Asian land mass and the Indian Ocean. The British East India Company established several meteorological observatories in India. Meteorological stations were established at Calcutta in 1785 and Madras in 1796 for studying the weather and climate. The Asiatic Society of Bengal founded in 1784 at Calcutta, and in 1804 at Bombay, promoted scientific studies in meteorology. Captain Harry Piddington at Calcutta published 40 papers during 1835-1855 in the Journal of the Asiatic Society dealing with tropical storms and coined the word 'cyclone', meaning the coil of a snake. In 1842 he published his monumental work on the 'Laws of the Storms'. In the first half of the $19^{th}$ century, several observatories began functioning in India under the provincial governments.

A disastrous tropical cyclone struck Calcutta in 1864 and this was followed by failures of the monsoon rains in 1866 and 1871. The Government of India established the India Meteorological Department (IMD) in 1875. Mr. H. F. Blanford was appointed Meteorological Reporter to the Government of India. The first Director General of Observatories (DGO) was Sir John Eliot who was appointed in May 1889 at Calcutta headquarters. Dr. S.K. Banerji was the first Indian DGO in 1944. The headquarters of IMD were later shifted to Shimla in 1905, then to Pune in 1928 and finally to New Delhi in 1944. The IMD headquarters are known as *Mausam Bhavan*. The National Data Centre was created at IMD, Pune in 1977, where climatological data from 1875 are stored in computerized form. The Indian Institute of Tropical Meteorology, Pune is another premier institute in the country to carry our research on tropical meteorology.

Blanford initiated the system of Long Range Forecasting. IMD has always used contemporary technology for meteorological observations, communications, forecasting and weather services. In the telegraph age, it made extensive use of weather telegrams for collecting observational data and sending warnings. Later IMD became the first organisation in India to have a message switching computer for supporting its global data exchange. One of the first few electronic computers introduced in the country was provided to IMD for scientific applications in meteorology. India was the first developing country in the world to have its own geostationary satellite, INSAT, for continuous weather monitoring and cyclone warning. Over the years the IMD has brought out several useful publications, including rainfall atlas of India for the benefits of farming community.

A separate division of Agricultural Meteorology was started in 1932 as one of the division of the IMD to deal with meteorological applications in agriculture. It got the status of permanent division of the IMD in 1943 under the auspice of Indian council of Agricultural Research (ICAR). The Division supports and participates in multi-disciplinary activities in the field of agrometeorology. Forecasts and advisories for farmers are issued by IMD's Forecasting Offices located at different State capitals. The Agricultural Meteorology division of IMD was initially led by Dr. L.A. Ramdas, who is known as the father of Agricultural Meteorology in India.

The National Centre for Medium Range Weather Forecasting is a Centre of Excellence in Weather and Climate Modelling under the Ministry of Earth Sciences. The mission of the Centre is to continuously develop advanced numerical weather prediction systems, with increased reliability and accuracy through research, development and demonstration of new and novel applications, maintaining the highest level of knowledge, skills and technical bases. All the 127 agroclimatic zones across the country are covered for dissemination of agroadvisories based on the medium range weather forecasts.

The National Commission on Agriculture (1976) had recommended the establishment of separate departments of Agricultural Meteorology in all the State Agricultural Universities (SAU) and ICAR research institutes to strengthen teaching, research and extension in the field of Agricultural Meteorology and train the human resources. Anand Agricultural University, Anand, Punjab Agricultural University, Ludhiana, Kerala Agricultural University, Vellanikkera, Mahatma Phule Krishi Vidyapeeth, Pune are among the first few SAUs in the country to offer post graduate degrees in agrometeorology. At present many SAUs have started the post graduate programmes on agrometeorology. The Division of Agricultural Physics at Indian Agricultural Research Institute, New Delhi offers courses on Agricultural Meteorology at Masters and Ph. D. levels.

The ICAR in its earliest attempts, in collaboration with IMD, had launched a crop-weather scheme in 1948 for compilation of phenological data and weather. The ICAR has started a separate 'All India Coordinated Research Project on Agrometeorology' (AICRPAM) in 1983 under dry land agriculture and attached to the Central Research Institute on Dry and Agriculture (CRIDA), Hyderabad with 12 centres. At present there are 25 AICRPAM operating from different SAUs and ICAR research institutes.

## AGROMETEOROLOGY AND FUTURE NEEDS AND CHALLENGES

The welfare, safety and quality of human society are subject to profound effects of the vagaries of weather and climate. Meteorological hazards such as drought, flood, tropical storms, heat and cold waves may endanger lives and property and disrupt even the most sophisticated system. Climatic conditions have a complex bearing on soil, crops, plant disease and the factors, both biotic and abiotic that is related to agricultural and animal production systems. The greenhouse effect and global warming, destruction of ozone layer, protection of land and water resources and renewable energy are few areas where climate will be increasingly important.

### Agroclimatological Database and Research

The availability of a proper meteorological and agrometeorological database is a major prerequisite for studying and managing the processes of agricultural production. A major and inevitable priority is to build a database of meteorological, phenological, soil related and agronomic information (Mavi and Tupper, 2004). The acquisition of pertinent climate and agrometeorological data, their processing, quality control, and archiving, and timely access and database management are important components that will make the information valuable to agrometeorological research and operational programmes (Stigter *et. al.*, 2000). Agrometeorological models have many potential uses for answering questions in research, crop management, and policy. As society becomes more computerized and technology oriented, there will be a greater possibility for the application of crop simulation models and decision support systems to help provide guidance in solving real-world problems related to agricultural sustainability, food security, the use of natural resources, and protection of the environment (Mavi and Tupper, 2004).

Crop-weather models for a large number of crops have been generated. But many of these models need to be further refined and tested before their practical application. Current research is being focused on detailed soil-water-crop relationships, determining the adjusted crop genetic coefficients, bridging simulation model outputs with user needs for applications, and developing practical decision support systems. The results of these findings may be of immense utility and form an important component of the decision support system which when coupled with the crop status on a regional scale would go a long way to alleviate the farmers' problems to a great extent.

### Early Warning System and Weather Based Agroadvisories

Agriculture plays a significant role in the overall socio-economic fabric of India. Weather becomes more significant in crop management. The farmers are adversely affected by climate risks in their farming, which include increase in temperature, decrease in rainy days, increase in precipitation intensity and amount, shorter winter periods, decreased ground water availability, increased occurrence of drought and floods, increased duration of water logging, *etc.* which in turn result in yield losses. Agrometeorology has advanced over decades from a descriptive to a quantitative science using physical and biological principles. Much of the developed world is less vulnerable to climate now-a-days than in the past. They have applied climate knowledge and early warning systems to allow adaption to mitigate the impacts of extreme events. Though India has acquired the relevant sophisticated technologies but these are yet to be fully translated to the benefits of the farming community

### Use of Satellite Remote Sensing Technology

Despite the technological advances, Indian farmers are mostly dependent on seasonal rains which are highly variable in time and space. Thus, weather forecasts are of great importance to agricultural activities.

Much research has gone into characterization of various crop environments, quantification of crop-weather interactions in relation to crop yield, crop weather modelling and crop-pest-weather dynamics. Now it is time to consolidate these findings in different locations, make use of this information and reach the farmers through agroadvisories on a larger scale in a more realistic way. These advisories are to be more farmer-friendly. A more accurate forecast along with actionable agroadvisories is required at block level. Remote sensing aided weather based agroadvisories may be a promising way which would enable the farmers to take the most appropriate actions on real time basis. Satellite remote sensing technology is increasingly gaining recognition as an important source of many agricultural applications as it is superior to the traditional methods in terms of accuracy and saving of time. Geographic Information Systems technology is becoming an essential tool for combining various maps and satellite information sources in models that simulate the interactions of complex natural systems.

### Assessment of Climate Change

Agrometeorology has to play a leading role in the assessment of climate change, its impact on agriculture, and adaptation strategies to increasing climate variability. Increasing environmental, population, and economic pressures are creating difficulties in solving agricultural pest and disease management problems (Mavi and Tupper, 2004). Future climate change and increased variability will further complicate pest and disease management problems. This will require improved analyses of the weather to develop new pest management techniques and strategies (Strand, 2000). In addition to weather predictions, the agrometeorologists should be able to estimate the likelihood of unusual weather events and their potential impact on crops and animals through quantitative analysis, which will be a great challenge.

## CONCLUSION

Agrometeorology deals with the application of meteorology to the measurement and analysis of the physical environment in agricultural systems. It is primarily concerned with the interactions among meteorological, hydrological and pedological factors that influence production systems in agriculture and allied sectors like horticulture, animal husbandry, fishery, forestry, *etc*. All the agricultural activities are affected directly or indirectly by weather and climate. Agrometeorology has therefore, the greatest scope on agriculture and other allied enterprises.

The need for agrometeorological services have increased in recent years because of the increasing climate variability and associated extreme events. The fields of interest of agrometeorology include agricultural and horticultural production, forestry, animal husbandry, fisheries, agricultural planning, processing, transport and storage of food, poverty reduction and sustainable development aspects of the livelihood of farmers. Agrometeorological services are useful for climate monitoring and analysis leading to planning and early warnings of climate anomalies, real time monitoring leading to the provision of operational advices, microclimate manipulation and prediction, within crops, soils and managed environments and preparedness for agricultural hazards. Climatic conditions have a complex bearing on soil, crops, plant disease and the factors, both biotic and abiotic that is related to agricultural and animal production systems. The greenhouse effect and global warming, destruction of ozone layer, protection of land and water resources and renewable energy are few areas where climate will be increasingly important. Lot of research has been done in various aspects of agrometeorology and now it is time to consolidate the results and translate them to actionable weather based agroadvisories.

## REFERENCES


Bourke, P.M.A. (1968). The Aims of Agrometeorology. *In*: Agroclimatological Methods. Proceedings of the Reading Symposium, UNESCO, Paris, pp. 11-15.

Hoogenboom, G. (2000). Contribution of Agrometeorology to the Simulation of Crop Production and its Applications. *Agricultural and Forest Meteorology* 103: 137-157.

http://en.wikipedia.org

http://nidm.gov.in

http://remote-sensing-agriculture.blogspot.in/agrometeorology

http://science-edu.larc.nasa.gov

http://www.academia.edu/Documents/in/Agrometeorology

http://www.bom.gov.au

http://www.climatechange.gc.ca

http://www.ifad.org

http://www.imd.gov.in

http://www.imdagrimet.gov.in

http://www.indiaweather.gov.in

http://www.ipcc.ch/assessment report

http://www.krishiworld.com/html/crop_pat

http://www.noaa.gov

http://www.theweatherprediction.com/habyhints

http://www.wmo

http://www.worldwatch.org

Maracchi, G., Perarnaud, V., and Kleschenko, A.D. (2000). Applications of Geographical Information Systems and Remote Sensing in Agrometeorology. *Agricultural and Forest Meteorology* 103: 119-136.

Mavi, H.S. and Tupper, G.J. (2004). Agrometeorology: Principles and Applications of Climate Studies in Agriculture. Food products Press, Binghamton, New York.

Molga, M. (1962). Agricultural Meteorology. Part II—Outline of Agrometeorological Problems. Polish Academy of Sciences, Warsaw.

NCA. 1976. Report of the National Commission on Agriculture: Part V, IX and Abridged. Ministry of Agriculture and Irrigation, Government of India, New Delhi.

Patra, P.K. (2012). A Text Book on Climatology. Kalyani Publishers, Ludiana. 255 pp.

Smith, L.P. (1970). Aims and Extent of Agricultural Meteorology. *Agricultural Meteorology* 7: 193-196.

Stewart, J.I. (1991). Principles and Performances of Response Farming. *In*: Muchow, R.C. and Bellamy, J.A. (eds.), *Climatic Risk in Crop Production: Models and Management in Semiarid Tropics and Subtropics*. CAB International, Wallington. pp. 361-382.

Stigter, C.J. (1994). Management and Manipulation of Microclimate. *In*: J.F. Griffiths (ed.), *Handbook of Agricultural Meteorology*. Oxford University Press, Oxford, UK. pp. 273-284.

Stigter, C.J., Dawei, Z., Onyewotu, L.O.Z. and Xurong, M. (2005). Using Traditional Methods and Indigenous Technologies for Coping with Climate Variability. *Climatic Change* 70: 255-271.

Stigter, C.J., Sivakumar, M.V.K. and Rijks, D.A. (2000). Agrometeorology in the 21st Century: Workshop Summary and Recommendations on Needs and Perspectives. *Agricultural and Forest Meteorology* 103: 209-227.

Strand, J.F. (2000). Some Agrometeorological Aspects of Pest and Disease Management for the 21st Century. *Agricultural and Forest Meteorology* 103: 73-82.

Pages: 151-173

**CLIMATE CHANGE, DISASTER MANAGEMENT AND ENVIRONMENT**
*Edited by:* **Dr. Alka Chauhan; Dr. Pawan Kumar 'Bharti'**
**ISBN: 978-93-5056-784-5**
*Edition:* **2016**
*Published by:* **Discovery Publishing House Pvt. Ltd., New Delhi (India)**

# CHAPTER – 9

# Leh District Disaster Management Plan
## *A Feasibility Check in Current Times of Environmental Challenges and Crisis in Leh Town*

**Konchok Dolma*; Madhuri, S.Rishi** and **Renu Lata**

***ABSTRACT***

As the debate over human induced global warming and climate change still goes on mounting, environmental concerns in many fragile areas and other regions facing rapid urbanization cannot be unfounded wholeheartedly even though we have no concrete proof of the anthropogenic induced global warming. Still significant skepticism looms over natural rate of warming and human induced rate of warming which is stated to be higher than the normal rate. One conclusive fact definitely is that environmental challenges if not met at right time are bound to rise into hazards and will finally develop into disasters later on causing massive loss of life and property. Formulation of an effective disaster management plan and its implementation is need of the fragile Himalayan ecosystems in current climate changing times of $21^{st}$ century.

**Department of Environment Studies, Punjab University, Chandigarh - 160 014, (India).**

Even though if rising temperatures and climate change are a natural phenomenon in this region but the scale of lives effected in these environmentally sensitive areas are massive. Leh Town is the main centre of Leh District which is located in Himalayan region of Ladakh in the state of Jammu and Kashmir, India which was most affected in recent times by cloudbursts. After 2010 August flashfloods, the district formulated Leh District Disaster Management plan in order to manage any future disaster situations. Henceforth, ex-ante phase which is the preparedness phase in any disaster management cycle was evaluated and it was found that there is still room for increasing awareness among masses to make this plan inclusive in true sense.

***Keywords:*** Disaster Management, Ecosystem, Leh town, Ladakh, Preparedness.

## INTRODUTION

Ladakh is a cold desert where precipitation averages around 61mm/ annum and occurs in the form of snow and rain both in winter and summer months respectively. It comprises of two districts Leh and Kargil located in the state of Jammu and Kashmir which is the northern most state of India (Figure 9.1). *Leh Town* which is situated in District Leh is divided into 21 administrative wards and the relief ranges from 3250m (amsl) to 4500m (amsl). It is about 434 kilometers from Srinagar (NH 1D) and 474 kilometers from Manali (NH 21) and is a NAC (Notified Area Council) encompassing an area of 1893 hectares/18.93 km$^2$ (Gondhalker et al., 2013). The population as per 2011 census is 30,870 which had risen from 28,639 according to 2001 census thus recording a growth rate of 7.8% which is quite a significant change which indicates a steady rising trend of increase in population.

Leh Town is vulnerable to various disasters like flash floods, cloud bursts, snow avalanches, agricultural droughts and also being a mountainous region; roads in such altitudes are prone to landslides, especially road blockades which are a major cause of worry. The region is connected by air routes only during long winters which make it even more vulnerable in the harsh winter months as essential supplies are scarce in that time as air transportation is not cheap for ferrying logistics and not profitable for intermediaries. During winter months when weather is cloudy and snowing, visibility is a major hindrance for various flights thus making the area totally isolated from rest of world on such cloudy days as no airplanes could land on such days. Even communication networks like internet, works dismally during winter months when road passes like Zojila becomes inaccessible for repair of optic cables due to heavy snowfall as this pass which carry out digital signals underneath is inaccessible in harsh winters. In India the seismic zones ranges from II to V that is, from lowest to highest as per their magnitude.

This clearly shows that in India there is no place where seismic intensity is absent or less than II and the maximum highest intensity is limited within V intensity magnitude. So, according to Indian standards this state is located in the highest seismic zone area and parts of Leh District lies both in V and penultimate to the highest intensity earthquake prone areas in India that is at IV magnitude. This place needs special emphasis in the nation's disaster management plan especially in earthquakes and related disasters management plan.

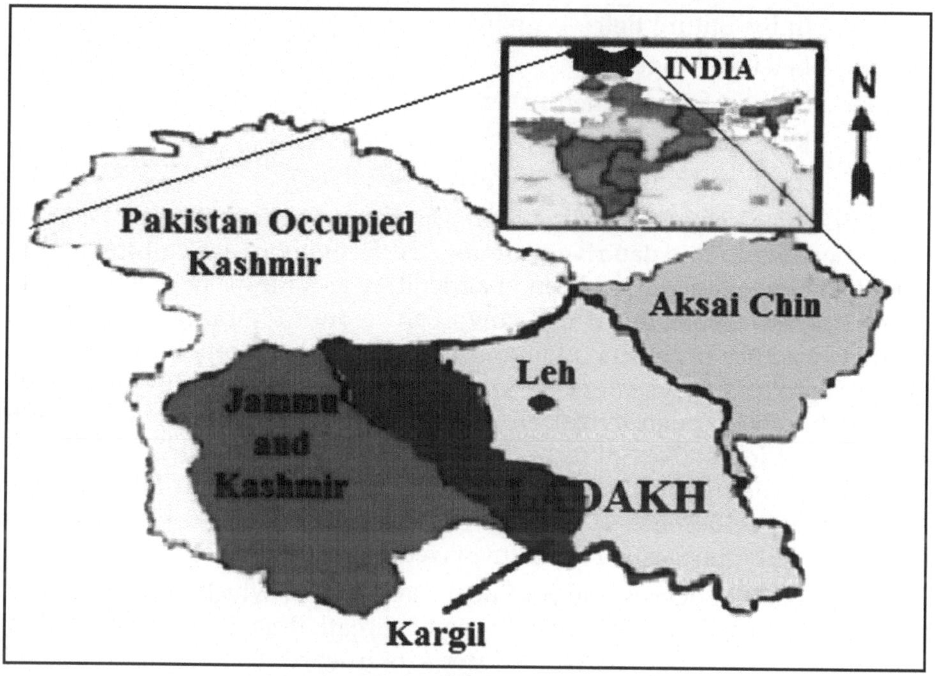


*Fig. 9.1:* **Location Map of the Study Area**
*Source:* **Dolma et al., 2015**

## Leh District Geological Profile and Climate

Leh district which lies in the northernmost state of Jammu and Kashmir is situated between 32° N to 36°N latitude and 75°E to 80°E longitude with an altitude ranging from 2300 meters to 5000 meters above sea level. District Leh with an area of 45110 km$^2$ makes it 2$^{nd}$ largest district in the country after Kutch (Gujarat) with an area of 45652 km$^2$. In terms of area the district is bounded by Pakistan Occupied Kashmir (POK) in West and China in North and Eastern part while Lahul-Spiti of Himachal Pradesh in South-east. Many major mountain systems commence from northwest are Kunlun, Aghil, Karakorum, Kailash, Ladakh, Zanskar and Great Himalayan range. These ranges show distinct parallelism in northwest and south west direction and many of the beautiful valleys can be found in between these ranges most famous like Zanskar, Indus, Shyok, Nubra. Geologically Ladakh region is formed due to collision of two continental masses which was Indian (southern) and Tibetan (northern) plates bringing in a juxta-position of dissimilar rock assemblages with volcanic and ultrabasic rocks. The geological sequence running SE–NW are:

1. Rocks of Kashmir-Warzwan sedimentary basin
2. Great Himalayan Range
3. Zanskar Structural Belt
4. Indus Suture Belt
5. Ladakh Range
6. Shyok-Nubra Structure Belt
7. Karakoram Range
8. Karakoram Tethyen Basin (Gansser, 1964).

Since time immemorial agriculture was the main occupation for people of this region and to this day rivers are revered throughout agricultural regions of Ladakh. Eventhough the sheen of agriculture as a means of sustenance has been reduced especially in Leh town centre and adjoining areas due to alternative source of livelihood and availability of cheap ration food through Public Distribution System (PDS) of Indian government. Indus river is the lifeline due to its huge irrigation potential in this cold desert along with tributaries of Indus like Shyok and Hanle rivers. As the region lies in Trans-Himalayas where monsoon clouds from Indian subcontinent fails to reach, irrigation per se becomes necessary for crop cultivation and thus irrigation since very early times is very well managed in this particular area.

The area experiences cold continental arid climate which can be described as semi-arid to arid or even desert type of climate thus the area generally is referred as 'Cold Arid Desert'. Winter sets in early October and lasts till ending April eventually noting a short summer season and particularly long winters. During winter months day temperature touches sub-zero mark whereas night temperature goes down as much as -35° C to -40° C. Area receives snowfall during winter months and days in summers are quite warm and pleasant. Area experiences strong dusty winds almost every day in evenings because the region falls in rain shadow regions of Himalayas. Annual precipitation in form of rainfall is of order 80-120 mm whereas snowfall is 140 mm/year. Unlike major parts of India which has a usual tropical type of climate Ladakh has a European type of climate in which winters are long and cold whereas summers are short and moderate (Figure 9.2).

### Historical Significance of Leh Town in Silk Route Trade

The name of this region Ladakh is derived from Tibetan word La-tags which means mountain land but other names are also synonymous with this region known as 'Mar-Yul' given by Cosmo-de-Kores. Here *mar* in local dialect means red and *yul* means land or in more concrete terms means red-land

and also Huen-Tsang, the Chinese pilgrim in 604 A.D called this land Ma-Lo-pho or Mar-Po which stands for red land but still there are doubts regarding this whole notification in exact terms (Lone, 2013). Buddhism entered Ladakh during the reign of emperor Ashoka in 204 B.C and since then this religion flourished by leaps and bounds in the region, evolving by accommodating some of the peculiarities of already existing bon religion indigenous to this area.

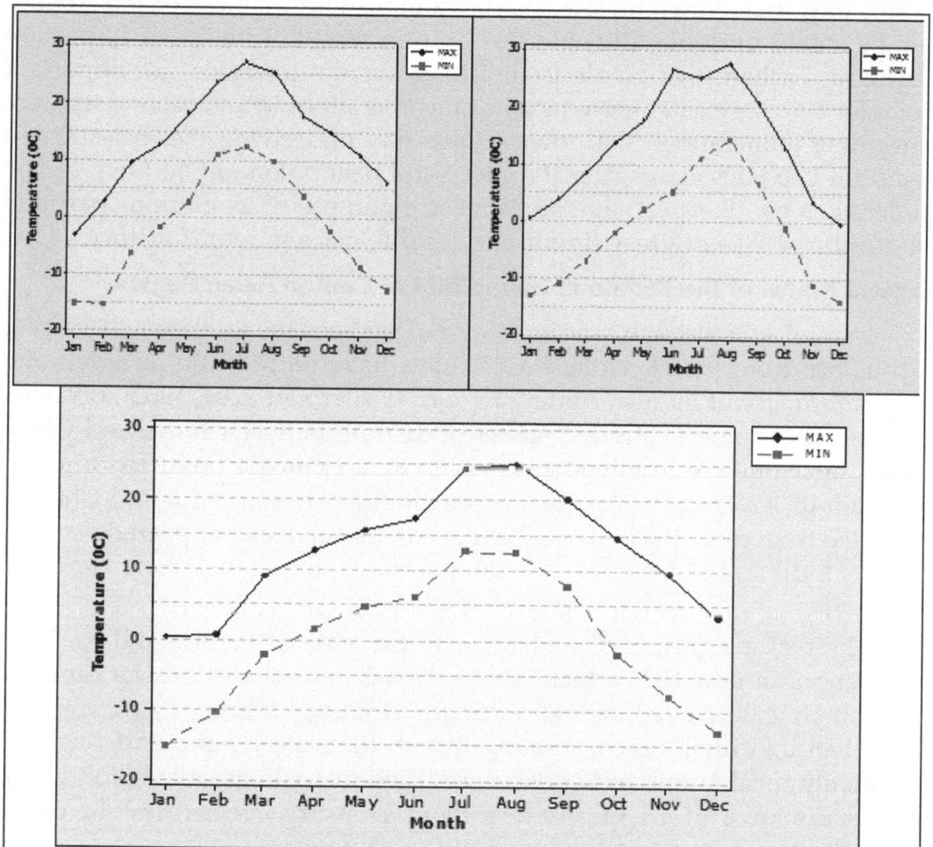


*Fig. 9.2:* **Temperature Variation in Year 2008, 2009, 2010**

Even before the advent of British rule in this region Leh, especially the centre of Leh town was a key trading point for traders from Central Asia, Tibet and mainland traders from Kashmir and India, eventually this region served as a focal resting place for all traders who came from far off places. Leh as a region was already cosmopolitan even before British ruled in the area and Leh town which was located in Ladakh near key mountain passes was a trading network hub. The Ladakhi traders who chose to distribute or transport Japanese cotton cloth over British cloth inspite of higher prices, participated in South Asian movement against colonialism (Fewkes, 2012). Historical significance of Leh town cannot be refuted easily and even to this day the main bazaar of Leh town has its own significance with traces of different cultural mélange in form of old dilapidated buildings having minor central asian architectural influences and inspirations from Tibetan architectural structures. Along with the main buddhist population also a significant array of muslims and hindu population having their ancestral shops, who were mostly traders and businessmen since early times are found to this day, thus enriching the societal composition richness of this area. It can be stated undoubtedly that not only in terms of being an important centre for exchange of goods from all regions the town was an important point for cultural exchanges which has reverberations in and around its areas since time immemorial. Leh town to this day underlying the majestic and beautiful Leh palace and after the successful restoration of Old town of Leh undertaken by Tibet Heritage Fund gives a glimpse of its glorious past and eloquently speaks of great significance of this place in world history.

**Present Status of the Region in Geopolitics of Central Asian Region**

Central Asia through time immemorial has been the focal point of chronic turbulence from which violent explosions have periodically erupted and spread throughout its surrounding regions (Fisher and Rose, 1962). Likewise Ladakh lies in one of the key areas of dispute between India and China which later on in current times evolved as a strategic point for India to maintain its sovereignty. The main contentions between India and China is indicated from early 1950s after which major discrepancies appeared between maps of India and China both showing some areas under their own respective territories.

The real integration of Ladakh with the state of Jammu and Kashmir commenced in year 1834 which is the year when General Zorawar Singh of Dogra regiment invaded Ladakh through marching his army by crossing the Suru river and finally incorporating it with the state Jammu and Kashmir. Eventually royal family of Ladakh was exiled in a village called Stok which is at a distance of 13 kilometers from Leh city centre devoid of all administrative powers with a king only in namesake.

From a very long time Leh situated in Ladakh region was an important resting centre for traders from Central Asia, Tibet and India which was of utmost importance for the British administration having an independent identity of its own. Leh town from early trading era, crossed the major trade route that is east-west central asian trade route and later on progressed into not only as an important place for trade but evolved as a listening post. According to the initial policies of Government of India after Independence, Leh was not considered important enough from security point of view as China was not looked from a point of suspicion which completely changed in current times of ever advancing Chinese might in the Asian subcontinent. With an ever evolving advancement and improvement in technology, Ladakh region is connected throughout the year via air routes and in summers by road connectivity also. India has no alternative but to maintain status quo in this region by integrating it more and more with mainland India and from a national security point of view, to keep vigil by deployment of more army men in the area. This is evident from the fact that Indian air force is extending the existing defence airport situated in Leh town which is partly leased for civilian use. Another striking change which can be noted is that in recent times Indian army is building permanent houses for the defence establishments while in earlier times only temporary houses were built as the long term strategic significance of Ladakh was still not fully realized then and long term border dispute problems with Pakistan and China has not been pictured yet. This stance has been reverted in recent times and this is the very reason why Ladakh is in utmost focus in defence policy making processes of this nation.

## RESEARCH SIGNIFICANCE

Seismically Ladakh lies in Zone IV of Damage Risk Zone as strike slip fault is running along Zanskar and Ladakh Ranges (Sharma *et al.*, 2013). While the state of Jammu and Kashmir as a whole lies in high hazard Zones IV and V and historically, parts of the state have experienced seismic activity in magnitude between 6.0-7.0 ranges. This region further lies in two main faults zone of Indus Suture Zone (ISZ) and Karakoram Fault (KKF) which makes it highly vulnerable to seismic activity. On top of it due to closing of two passes in harsh winter months (Dec-March), rescue and recovery would be a major impediment in times of any disaster. Town of Leh is a broad U shaped glacial valley of Indus River situated between high ranges of Ladakh in north and Zanskar in south (CGWB, 2008).

Due to presence of varied, unconsolidated Quaternary drift deposits perched over gentle to fairly steep slopes which are prone to mass movement under conditions of heavy saturation like heavy rainfall, as the vegetation on mountains is very sparse or completely absent which makes this area highly prone to erosion activities. This was the reason when rainfall of 240mm within 24hrs due to cloud bursts in Leh region on 4-6 August 2010 caused excessive mass movement in the area due to gooey mud which ran off from mountain tops due to lack of vegetation and this mud suffocated people, causing major deaths and injuries to the victims caught in that disaster. A school of thought believes that recent cloud bursts, high intensity of rainfall and increase in average humidity of the area during peak summers is due to climate change. While others blame the increase in afforestation rate, generally caused by increase in man-made planting of trees in region which increased evapo-transpiration rate and hence increased intensity of rainfall in recent years.

This school of thought believes that weather of the area is changing due to anthropogenic plantation drive and is causing recent environmental changes and crises in the area. They want original cold desert environment to be left untouched and unaltered, as the original topography is suitable enough to sustain the delicate balance of this fragile ecosystem. There is a mounting need, especially now to undertake scientific studies in such remote ecosystems which are facing the twin pressures of climate change and urbanization problems all at the same time. Only conclusive scientific data generated for such areas can be helpful in chalking out solid ex-ante plan formulation for meeting the so called environmental challenges and crisis evolving in recent times. Earlier these areas were not facing many challenges and climate change was not hyped that much especially in Himalayan remote areas and so not much emphasis was needed to have a management plan ready for contingencies of future times. With the unanimous endorsement of climate change and looming environmental challenges highlighted in recent times, need to have a solid plan to cope with evolving environmental challenges were felt in these fragile Himalayan regions now bearing the brunt of changing global climatic conditions.

**Basics of a Disaster Cycle**

Disaster Management Cycle consists of three main aspects *prevention, mitigation* and *preparedness* for capacity building which should be carried out before disaster strikes and after the disaster most immediately, *response, rehabilitation* and *reconstruction* activities should be carried out during the recovery phase. Pre and post phases are attributed as *ex-ante* and *ex-post* respectively which is interconnected through developmental phase where capacity building occurs during which the area undergoes massive transformation in infrastructure and also value addition in human resource through trainings. The *ex-ante* phase is most important one because in this phase prevention and mitigation measures are generally undertaken to prevent any disaster or make it less severe and still if prevention not possible.

Disaster management is a gender and economic based issue as vulnerability of the said area or population increases manifold if weak or lacks sufficient economic resources. This is the reason why women and children are most vulnerable also poor developing countries of the world which lacks optimum resources for prevention or mitigation of said disasters. Connectivity is another major factor in effective disaster management and mitigation so the most remote and backward areas lying in harsh inaccessible conditions are more prone to disasters because relief and rehabilitation measures are not effectively and instantly carried out like in far-flung hilly areas like during the recent Nepal earthquake in 2015. These areas suffered most because response and relief was not easy to reach within the critical timeframe which is first few hours after disaster strikes due to harsh weather conditions and severe road connectivity problems.

**Stages of Disaster** (Figure 9.3)

- **Warning Stage:** This stage lasts from few minutes to hours and involves warning activities before any disaster strikes like meteorological, seismological or anthropological. Warning activities can be carried out through the medium of print and visual media in form of news, warning announcements and doing further predictions.
- **Impact Stage:** It is a stage which lasts for few minutes when disasters like earthquakes, flash floods and cyclones actually strikes and causes massive destruction. So, this is the stage when in few time all major loss to life and property takes place during any disaster scenario.
- **Rescue Stage:** This is a very crucial stage of any disaster situation which lasts for 2-3 days and if effective implementation of this programme is achieved than it can be successful in saving enormous lives. In this stage actual rescue of victims takes place but real rescue operations even for worst disasters lasts for 2-3 days and after that if delay in such operations occurs than it becomes very difficult to save the affected people.
- **Rehabilitation Stage:** Rehabilitation goes on for years and years as this is also a humane and structural issue. If rehabilitation is not carried out properly then problems like refugees, slums, unemployment and deprivation occurs which creates social problems and unrest in the society as a whole. It is very much needed for effective rehabilitation to be conducted, taking many aspects in consideration for rehabilitation.

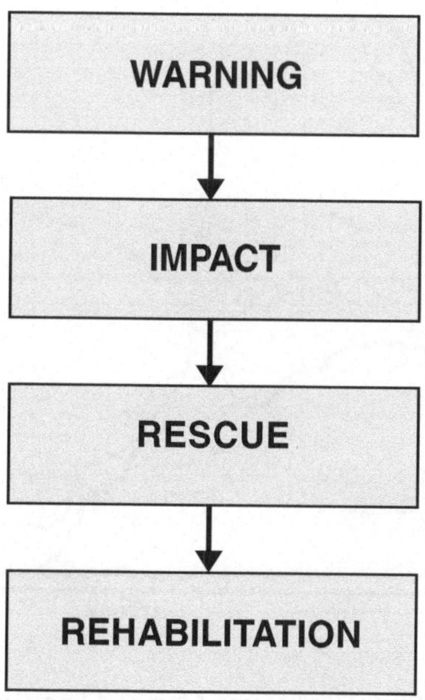


*Fig. 9.3:* **Flow Chart of Stages of Disaster**

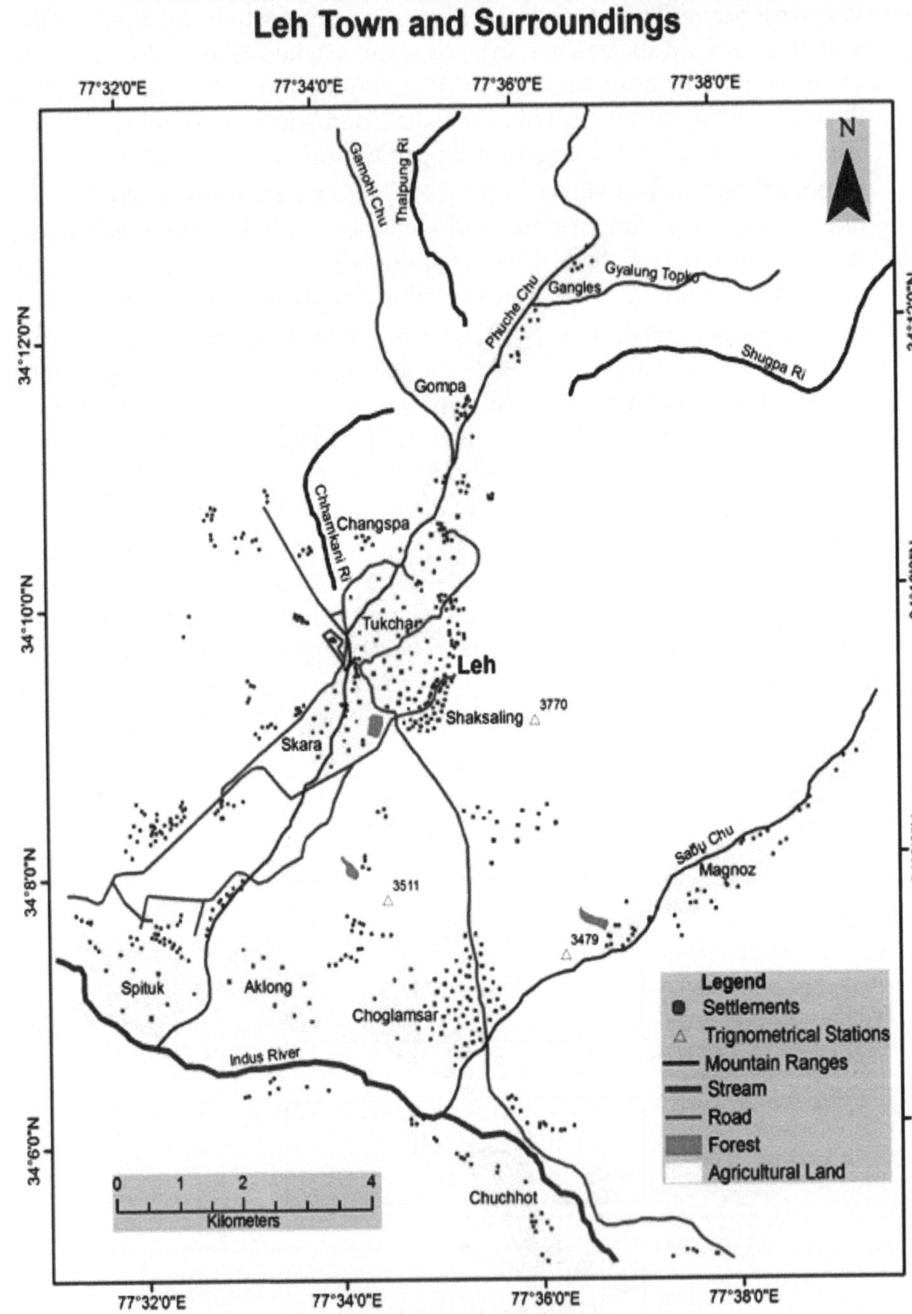


*Fig 9.4:* **Leh Town Map and Location**

### Leh District Disaster Management Plan Overview

Disaster management plan of Leh district was formulated after the 2010 flash floods which occurred in month of august. Leh town was completely paralyzed during that disaster which affected the district hospital, BSNL (Bharat Sanchar Nigam Limited) telephone exchange which is the focal centre for all telecommunication links for the whole district and various other important services like ATMs (Automatic Teller Machine) and internet connectivity depended on it. In current digital age when our reliance on internet connectivity has increased manifold, particularly in Leh town (Figure 9.4) and it was brought to a standstill during august flash floods of 2010 so, a comprehensive plan was drafted eventually for future effective disaster management of the district.

Plan gives a gist of management measures before, after and during disaster situations in the district like earthquakes, floods, snow avalanche, drought, locust menace and cloud bursts. The plan is formulated keeping various attributes in concern and even designated the disaster management committee involving all necessary stakeholders at district, zonal and village level. Here committee at district level is depicted with deputy commissioner at the apex who along with the respective members coordinate any disaster management related activities in the whole district (Table 9.1). Along with district committee, zonal and village committees were also formulated with their respective members for effective decentralization in disaster management and have an all encompassing outlook from various stakeholders.

**Table 9.1: District Disaster Management Committee Members**

| Sl.No. | Designation |
|---|---|
| 1. | Deputy Commissioner, *Chairperson* |
| 2. | Additional Deputy Commissioner, *Chief Executive Officer* |
| 3. | Senior Superintendent of Police, *Member* |
| 4. | Divisional Forest Officer, *Member* |
| 5. | Superintending Engineer (PWD), *Member* |
| 6. | Superintending Engineer (PDD), *Member* |
| 7. | Superintending Engineer (PDC), *Member* |
| 8. | Telephone District Manager, *Member* |
| 9. | Chief Medical Officer, *Member* |
| 10. | Administrator Municipal Committee, *Member* |
| 11. | Chief Animal Husbandry Officer, *Member* |
| 12. | District Sheep Husbandry Officer, *Member* |
| 13. | Executive Engineer Irrigation and Flood Control, *Member* |

(Table Contd...)

| Sl.No. | Designation |
|---|---|
| 14. | Executive Engineer Public Health Engineering, *Member* |
| 15. | Executive Engineer Roads and Building, *Member* |
| 16. | Assistant Director Consumer Affairs and Public Distribution, *Member* |
| 17. | Deputy Superintendent of Police Civil Defence, *Member* |
| 18. | Deputy Director Motor Garages, *Member* |
| 19. | Chief Officer Fire Services, *Member* |
| 20. | District Youth Services and Sports, *Member* |
| 21. | Incharge National Service Scheme EJ Memorial College, Leh, *Member* |
| 22. | Assistant Commissioner Revenue, *Member* |
| **ARMY AND PARAMILITARY FORCES** | |
| 23. | Nodal Office, Air Force, *Member* |
| 24. | Nodal Officer, Army (14 Core), *Member* |
| 25. | Nodal Officer, ITBP, *Member* |
| 26. | Nodal Officer representing Chief Engineer Himank, *Member* |
| 27. | Deputy Commanding Officer, CRPF, *Member* |

No doubt the basics of any disaster management plan is same but formulating detail plan for different disasters individually should be the aim of concerned authorities as one size fits all approach is redundant in current dynamic times especially in Leh district.

## Disaster Management Plan for District Hospital (SNM)

Leh district has one district level hospital along with respective hospitals at zonal and village levels. Thus evolving a disaster management plan especially for the district hospital is required but disaster committee for hospital is still in proposal phase and needs emphasis for application on ground. There is a tentative list of committee members already mentioned for district hospital in the existing district disaster management plan (Table. 9.2).

**Table 9.2: Hospital Disaster Management Committee Members**

| Sl.No. | Designation |
|---|---|
| 1. | Medical Superintendent |
| 2. | Deputy Medical Superintendent |
| 3. | General Surgeon |
| 4. | Orthopedician |
| 5. | Casuality Medical Officer |
| 6. | Matron |
| 7. | Station House Officer of Hospital Area |

In the formulated plan a detailed layout plan of disaster management is mentioned for Sonam Norbu Memorial (SNM) hospital which is the largest and only district level hospital of Leh district. Various colour coded information is described in the plan for saving time and lives especially during the crucial first time of few hours when disaster strikes. An overview of general colour codes which is described theroritically in the actual text have been depicted (Table 9.2). So, it is needed in actual plan to incorporate an appendage booklet focussing solely on the hospital sector or the actual plan needs to be written in a more easy to comprehend manner not just for hospital staff but general public also.

**Contribution of Media and Communication in Disaster Management**

For any effective disaster management, role of media and communiction of relevant knowledge to the end user is very crucial. Right now, know how of tackling any disaster situation and disaster related issues proves beneficial immensely for general public and thus preventing any chaotic situation. In the existing plan there is a brief mention of agencies and their medium of information dissemenation, for instance agencies like offices of Chief Medical Officer (CMO), Block Development Officer (BDO) and district offices of Non Governmental Organisations stationed in Leh district. Wall paintings, street plays and volunteer trainings are some of the few mentioned activities through which required disaster related knowledge can be dissipated among the general masses. Along with it media and press releases by the concerned Information Officer of the Disaster Control Room (DCR) and hand bills along with advertisements published in leading dailies having wide readership in the area which are some of other significant modes of information dessimination. Media is an important mode of disaster manageement and eventually equipping the public with an effective tool in the war against disaster menace.

## MATERIALS USED FOR THE STUDY

A closed-ended questionnaire (dichotomous type) survey was conducted among the literate residents of Leh town to evaluate various aspects of disaster management. A random sampling method was used in this study. Out of total, 30 per cent of local gazetted officers, college students, lecturers and hospital staff (Statistical Handbook, 2012-13) were surveyed in field of seismic and ecological fragility of the region; disaster management plan knowhow; mock drill participation and knowledge of community hall in nearby locality during. Simultaneously Microsoft Excel (2007) software was used for data analysis and representation while for map making of Leh town, survey of India toposheet 52F/12 was used for digitization and a sketching application running on Android 4.1.2 was used.

## RESULTS AND DISCUSSION

### Population

Demography of the region gives a lucid idea about the area in concern and forms the basis for any policy formulation by policy makers. Leh district population along with the male female ratio shows a rising trend as depicted in (Figure. 9.5). This table shows the population of Leh district as per 2011 census as 1,47,104 while in 2001 it was 1,17,232 thus recording a growth rate of 25.48 % (Dolma et al., 2013).

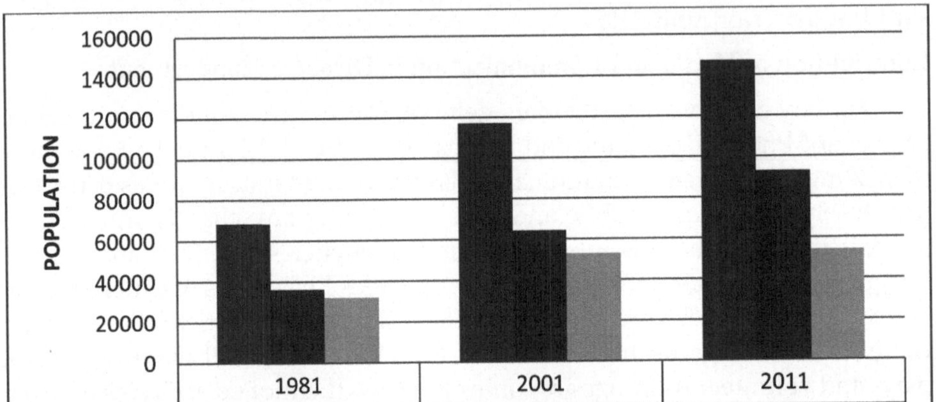


| | 1981 | 2001 | 2011 |
|---|---|---|---|
| ■ TOTAL | 68380 | 117232 | 147104 |
| ■ M | 36248 | 64306 | 92907 |
| ■ F | 32132 | 52926 | 54197 |

*Fig. 9.5:* **Male-female Ratio for Three Decades**

*Source:* **Handbook (2011-2012)**

Above data gives a skewed data on sex ratio according to 2011 census which puts difference between male and female at 38,710 while in year 2001 difference was 11,380. Also, previous census sex ratio puts difference below 5000 and this spiked gender difference as per 2011 census which is a sharp increase in male numbers was refuted by the public and state tourism minister Nawang Rigzin Jora (Thaindian News, 2011) inspite of state census department stating that this sex ratio is correct. The people in Leh also have doubts regarding this low sex ratio which is low in comparison to average national numbers and ground workers accept the fact that they were instructed to enumerate people living for a while in Leh including army personnel. While state census office says, it is because so many girls are studying outside the district thus the gender difference is skewed as compared to the previous decade. Thus, this situation definitely creates doubts among locals, regarding the data collection methodology being followed by state agencies which can also hamper people's participation aspect of the district disaster management plan. As it is a known fact of knowledge that the data on which policies are formulated should be of best quality and authentic which means proper precautions should be undertaken while data procurement or generation following standard procedures and measures.

**Leh District Disaster Management Plan and Intricacies: Breakdown of Major Areas**

Disaster management plan of Leh district (D.C Office, Leh., 2011) like any standard plan speaks volumes of various attributes and measures to be taken before, during and after any disaster. It has described various colour codes for various disaster scenarios but the draft is more theoretical and descriptive in nature which was encoded by the author in an earlier article (Table 9.3). This simple colour encoding enlisted in an easy to comprehend manner even for layman will help in speedy communication among various stakeholders for effective task completion in any given disaster situation.

**Table 9.3: Various Codes and Their Interpretation**

| Codes | Emergency Codes | Available Intensity Code | Hospital Code (Victims) |
|---|---|---|---|
| 10 | Disaster | | |
| Red | Fire | Most Frequent and Impact Pressure of >3 Tonnes/$M^2$ | Emergency Department |
| Blue | Cardiac Arrest | Avalanche Force is <3 Tonnes/$M^2$ | – |
| Black | Bomb Threat | – | Morgue |
| White | Security Emergency | – | – |
| Yellow | – | Snow Avalanche Occurs only Occasionally | Post Anesthesia Recovery Unit |
| Green | All Clear | – | Clinic |

*Source:* Dolma et al., 2015

The plan encompasses management practices during various natural disasters as a whole but more emphasis is required during anthropogenic and other non natural disaster predicaments as well like terrorism, insurgencies or war situations. Leh district lies in one of the most strategic zones for India as it lies in areas which are bounded by China and Pakistan in its north eastern and north western sectors respectively. World's highest battlefield Siachen glacier also lies in this area which is a vantage point for India and it spends lots of monetary resources and manpower in maintaining this position. No doubt the army has been involved in capacity building to overcome any war like situation in the area but civilian knowhow in dealing with any war situation is limited in the fringes. So, training modules involving local communities through civil administration needs to be incorporated in the existing disaster management plan. Overall plan is drafted in a reasonable fashion which roughly meets all requirements of an adequate disaster management plan on paper but implementation part is still a long way to go as this management plan of the region itself is drafted for the very first time in 2010 and needs lot of time and effort to make it a truly functional plan which meets its original objective of causing minimal loss of life and property in any disaster situation.

**District Control Room**

During any disaster management cycle a focal point is always mentioned in theoretical literature which becomes the centre point for coordinating all disaster management related functions before, during and after any disaster. This focal area is generally termed as the control room which mainly in districts becomes the office of deputy commissioner of that district. According to the drafted plan, specifications which are mentioned to be needed in DCR are:

- District Disaster Management Plan
- District maps showing identified school buildings/shelters.
- School buildings and high elevated places identified as shelters.
- List of resource persons with contact addresses.
- Database on resource and inventory
- First aid and other basic medical assistance.
- One retiring room with adequate facilities.
- Generator sets/emergency lights/candles, etc.
- Telephone, fax, satellite phones, telephone linkages with army, paramilitary like ITBP, CRPF, etc.
- Functioning computers with printers and modems.
- Thermometers and fire extinguishers.

Above statement shows the ironic situations which persists in theory and practice in actual application of disaster management plan in the district. In initial stages after 2010, flash floods at least management plan was formulated but mention of maps showing critical points is a long road ahead. Firstly, Leh district lies in one of the most strategic Indian locations from security point of view and falls in one of the restricted areas which are debarred by Indian government for dissemination of their locations. Even the maps which are already made by Survey of India are restricted and not available for general public except for use by certain government department officials. So, generation of further maps showing school buildings/shelter points is a far cry from real situations and even a well equipped GIS cell with knowledgeable people is lacking in the district. Eventually a disaster control room with all necessary requirements is still a pipe dream and even the basic equipments of such a room are still in dearth. There is an alternative aspect in developing maps of the region due to this area evolving as a major tourist's destination since partial opening of the area for tourists in year 1974. Now, due to increased adventure tourism activities in the region many self generated maps which area usually not to scale have been flooded in the market especially made by the travel companies and due to advanced technologies like google earth and ready availability of aerial pictures map-making of the area, even though not as accurate has become a piece of cake.

**Lack of Public, Private, Partnership (PPP) model in plan formulation**

Another striking aspect, deficient in final disaster plan is definitely no detail description of participation of Non Government Organisations (NGOs) which are exclusively based in Ladakh and the plan encompasses only a list of all major NGOs of this region which assisted in post relief operations after 2010 flash floods and no further mention of any collaborative work among them so far in the existing plan (Table 9.4). Mobilization of these agencies is required in such a way that collective work and effective partnership becomes a reality making optimum use of available talents and expertise. Also in order to make judicious use of resources, it is required that repeated work is not carried out by different agencies, rather cohesive, innovative assignments should be carried out in partnership for best work results. Due to the region lying in Trans-Himalayas and having one of the most hostile conditions for human survival, there is an optimum presence of NGOs, especially which generate funding from international agencies for developmental work and are improving lives in such harsh regions. Many of these organisations are experimenting and carrying out new innovative methods which are very successful like *mixing of certain percent of cement in the mud bricks* which was the traditional material for building construction but this improved version is more useful than the earlier mud bricks in protection of buildings especially now in the changing climatic scenario which is recording high rainfall pattern in recent times. Long term scientific data of this region is still deficient scientifically but weather pattern has definitely become erratic in recent times, noting a higher intensity of humidity levels for past few years than average and there is a wide belief in the climate changing theory of the region. As regional climate variability, within the broader dynamics of global climate change is affecting natural and human systems in Ladakh (Daultery and Gergan, 2011).

**Table 9.4: List of NGOs Participated in Post 2010, Flash-floods**

| Sl.No. | Non-Governmental Organisations |
|---|---|
| 1. | Indian Red Cross |
| 2. | CII (Confederation of Indian Industries) |
| 3. | LEDeG (Ladakh Ecological Development Group) |
| 4. | LEHO (Ladakh Environment and Health Organisation) |
| 5. | Save the Children India |
| 6. | AIDMI (All India Disaster Mitigation Institute) |
| 7. | WWF India (World Wide Fund) |
| 8. | Bond |
| 9. | CASA Mountain Forum Himalayas |
| 10. | Oxfam India and Rural Development and You |
| 11. | Medecins Sans Frontieres |
| 12. | Care Today |
| 13. | CENSFOOD |
| 14. | Centre for Environment and Education |
| 15. | EFICOR (Evangelic Fellowship of India Commission on Relief) |
| 16. | Gaden Relief |
| 17. | GERES (Groupe Energies Renouvelables, Environment Et Solidarites) |
| 18. | Handicap International |
| 19. | Himalayan Cultural Heritage Foundation |
| 20. | INTACH (Indian National Trust for Art and Cultural Heritage) |
| 21. | Ladakh Arts and Media Organisation (LAMO) |
| 22. | Ladakh Relief |
| 23. | Lutheran World Relief Service |
| 24. | PAGIR (People's Action Group for Inclusion and Rights) |
| 25. | People's Action Group for Inclusion and Rights |
| 26. | Pragya |
| 27. | SAMARPAN Foundation |
| 28. | School Educational and Cultural Movement of Ladakh (SECMOL) |
| 29. | SEEDs (Social Empowerment & Economic Development Society ) |
| 30. | Snow Leopard Conservancy India Trust |
| 31. | Tibet Heritage Fund |
| 32. | Welthungerhilfe-Mahabodhi International Meditation Centre |

Interesting innovative solutions and methods are being carried out in the field of solar renewable energy, in which use of passive solar technology like *thrombe wall* definitely stands out. This very technology is making ample improvement in the lives of locals as the region is deficient in general fuelwood, being a cold desert but abundant in maximum solar days out of total 365 days in a whole year thus tapping this resource will compensate the burden on already scarce resources like wood and cattle dung. On top of it, these not for profit organisations have expert guidance and ample funding from many parts of the world and they impart training to locals through their workshops and seminars frequently. Volunteers are from all over the world and this provides lots of opportunities for locals in getting exposure and cultural exchanges. Even the state administration is adapting with evolving times which can be seen in the form of building up centralized sewerage treatment facility for meeting the needs of a growing town (Dolma et al., 2015).

### Disaster Management Quotient Among Masses in the Region

Therefore in order to assess practical application of disaster management plan and to assess the knowhow of disaster management knowledge among masses, a closed-ended, dichotomous type questionnaire survey was conducted among literate Leh town people in July 2013. Decoding of this data shows the feasibility aspect and basic know how of the plan among residents thus focusing on areas which needs improvement to make it user friendly and also to increase overall awareness among masses (Fig. 9.6). The sample size was derived from Statistical Handbook (2012-13) for the town and breakdown of sample composition is given:

**Gazetted Officers (Numbers)**
Local - 30% (252) = 76
Non Locals - 90

**College (Numbers)**
Students – 30% (388) = 117
Lecturers - 15

**Hospital Staff (Numbers)**
Compounders – 30% (21) = 7
Doctors -37
Nurses - 32

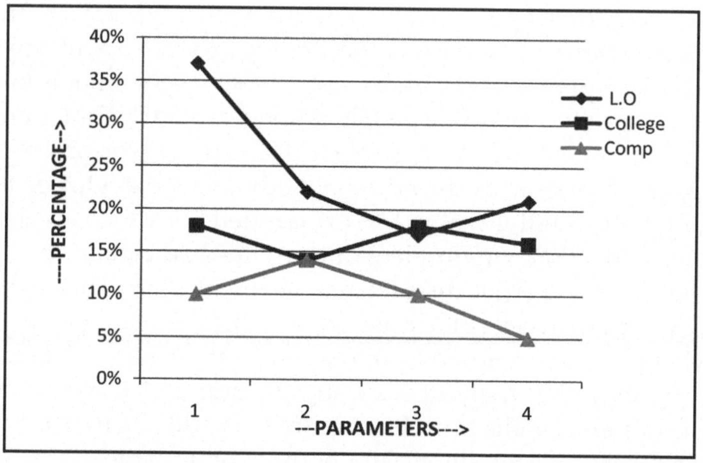


*Fig. 9.6:* **Disaster Awareness Among Masses on Scale of Four Parameters**

1. **Seismicity and ecological fragility of Ladakh:** Due to the well known fact that Ladakh lies in zone IV of earthquake risk zone which is the second highest risk prone zone, so any disaster management plan formulation is incomplete without taking this aspect under consideration. The know how about *seismicity and ecological fragility of Ladakh* region was enumerated through a dichotomous close ended questionnaire survey among the 30% of Gazetted Local Officers, College students and compounders out of total population in the individual sections in Leh district. Here 37 per cent Local Officers, 18% college students and 10%t compounders out had knowledge about it out of the 30% total. Aforementioned parameters are bed rock which promulgates the need for any disaster management plan due to high intensity of seismic risk of the region and assessing level of awareness of such parameters among general masses is sure to improve feasibility of existing disaster management plan on ground.

   Here we can conclude that among three, Local Officer's percentage is highest and hospital compounders are least through which we can derive that region's basic geological knowledge is a factor dependent on education class and status. Thus, there is a need for generating awareness among the lower strata of workers of the district hospital as these are first line of contact people during emergency aid in relief and first aid situations. Also, knowledge should be dissipated among general population and not limited among the higher educated sections of any society. Ground level workers needs maximum training and exposure about basics of disaster management plan and existing know how of region, in order to have maximum application of the plan.

2. **Existence of the District Disaster Management Plan:** Next knowledge about *existence of District Disaster Management plan* was evaluated among the aforementioned population class as any disaster management plan's feasibility starts with knowledge among masses about any disaster management plan already in existence. Awareness among masses that too some specific classes of people among general population gives an idea about feasibility and practical applicability of any disaster management plan with resources already available. Out of the 30 per cent population individually, 22% of Gazetted Local Officers, 14% college students and 14% compounders of hospitals had certain idea about the prevalence of a district disaster management plan. This output again indicates the direct relationship of education level and disaster knowledge among common population in the region. This knowledge again needs to be dissipated among general and common masses so that maximum benefits to society becomes a reality by increasing disaster management quotient among the population at large.

3. **Participation in mock drills:** Finally comes hands on practical training in situation of exact disaster scenario which is *participation in mock drills for disaster preparedness*. This part of disaster management plan requires maximum input and unfortunately as per the survey conducted this point gives most dismal results in the region. While any mock drill if ever conducted should encompass people from a wide variety of sections of the society to ensure maximum outreach but still if we assess awareness quotient of mock drills performed among certain sections of society and found dismal results. Now again taking 30% of population of local officers, college students and hospital compounders individually out of their respective totals and were evaluated for participation in mock drills. Here we get 17% of Local Officers, 18% of college students and 10% of hospital compounders who had participated in such drills and ultimately we conclude that the lower hospital staff which should have a higher participation rate is lacking and also among college students the participation rate needs to be boosted.
4. **Knowledge about location of a community hall in their respective locality:** Community halls are the places where people congregate during common meetings but also are the points which can be used as centers for first aid and relief materials during disaster times. So, awareness among general masses about whereabouts of community halls in their livelihood gives an idea about tackling disaster scenarios especially emergencies of disaster times. As first few hours are most crucial when any disaster strikes and immediate response and relief material needed which is usually carried out of the community halls in small regions, thus knowledge among locals about their neighbourhood community halls is very important. The community hall becomes the focal point for food, first-aid and shelter during disaster period thus knowhow of its existence was evaluated among the sample people which were surveyed. The questionnaire survey about awareness of community hall in their local neighbourhood was enumerated among said 30% population individually out of their respective totals for the same set of section beforehand. It was further found that 21% of local officers,16% of college students and 5% of compounders had knowledge about it out of their respective 30% total numbers.

## CONCLUSION

District disaster management has all the elements of any standard disaster management plan but is short on essential innovative ideas which are the requirement of this fragile ecosystem. Even the respondents who were surveyed, only a fraction had any knowledge of this particular plan and among the people who had any idea, it is restricted among educated people especially those who are employed as high government officials in this area. While among lower class government employees, need for more awareness was felt as they form a bulk of the population and are required during preparedness phase. Mock drills which are very important for increasing capacity building and to increase practical knowledge are more important than any theoretical one in disaster management. As the participation rate among masses in mock drills is low, it shows gaps which need to be bridged among people in improving feasibility of existing disaster management plan of the region. Ultimately need of the hour is to popularize intricacies of existing disaster management plan among masses for a feasible, innovative and cost-effective disaster management plan particularly catering to needs of this region which will be sustainable in true sense.

## REFERENCES

Deputy Commissioner Office, Leh. (2011): Disaster Management Plan Leh District, pp: 17, 19, 61-62.

Dolma, K., Rishi, M.S. and Sharma, A.D. (2013): Ecological Sanitation (Ecosan) in Cold Arid Ladakh: An Ecofriendly Traditional Approach for Water Conservation and Waste Utilization. in Integrated Water, Wastewater and Isotope Hydrology 2013 Proceedings of the International Conference in Banglore 2013, *Himalayan Publishing House Pvt. Ltd, Mumbai*, pp: 49-54.

Dolma, K., Rishi, M.S...(2015): Leh District Disaster Management Plan: A Road Map for Sustainable and Effective Development. *International Journal of Physical and Social Sciences,* 5(7), pp: 296-304.

Daultery, S. and Gergan, R. (2011): Living with Change: Adaptation and Innovation in Ladakh. Ladakh Renewable Energy Development Agency (LREDA) available at: http://www.ourplanet.com/climate-adaptation/Daultrey_Gergan.pdf (accessed on 10 July 2015).

Fewkes, J.H. (2012): Living in the Material World: Cosmopolitanism and Trade in Early Twentieth Century *Ladakh. Modern Asian Studies,*46(2), pp: 259-281.

Fisher, M.W. and Rose, L.E. (1962): Ladakh and the Sino-Indian Border Crisis. *Asian Survey*, 2(8), pp: 27-37.

Gansser, A. (1964). Geology of Himalayas. *John Wiley and Sons Ltd, New York*, pp: 289.

Geneletti, D. and Dawa, D. (2009): Environmental Impact Assessment of Mountain Tourism in Developing Regions: A Study in Ladakh, Indian Himalaya. *Environmental Impact Assessment Review*, 29, pp: 229-242.

Gondhalekar *et al.*, (2013): Water-related Health Risks in Rapidly Developing Towns: The Potential of Integrated GIS-based Urban Planning. *Water International*, 38(7), pp: 902-920.

Lone, M.A. (2013): Ladakh: Society, People and Place: A Sociological Outlook. *Acme International Journal of Multidisciplinary Research,* 1(5), pp: 112-119.

Madegowda C. and C. Usha Rao. (2014): The Traditional Ecological Knowledge of Soliga Tribe on Eradication of Lantana Camara and Their Livelihood Through Mahatama Gandhi National Rural Employment Guarantee Act at Biligiri Rangaswamy Termple Wildlife Sanctuary, South India. *Antrocom Online Journal of Anthropology*, 10(2), pp: 165.

Mohiddin, S.K. (2008): Ground Water Information Booklet of Leh District Jammu and Kashmir State. Central Ground Water Board available at: http://cgwb.gov.in/District_Profile/JandK/Leh.pdf/ (accessed on 5 December 2014).

Raksha, A. and Aswathanarayana, L.G. (2013): Selection of Sustainable Sources for Reliable Water Supply Schemes, In the Localities of Abnormal Climatic Conditions, Research and Reviews. *Journal of Engineering and Technology*, 2(3), pp: 256-264.

Sharma,S., Kumar, A. and Gangas, V. (2013): Seismicity in Jammu and Kashmir Region with Special Reference to Kishtwar. *International Journal of Scientific and Research Publications*, 3(9), pp: 1-5.

Statistical Hand Book (2012-13): Area and Population available at: http://leh.nic.in/pages/handbook.pdf/ (accessed on 5 December 2014).

Thaindian News (2011): Ladakh Indeed has Worst Sex Ratio, Says Census Office available at: http://www.thaindian.com/newsportal/business/ladakh-indeed-has-worst-sex-ratio-says-census-office_100530842.html/ (accessed 5 December 2014).

# Index

**Z**



◆ ◆ ◆ ◆ ◆ ◆